ROOKMANGUD KATAWAL

MY STORY

Published by

Publication nepa~laya
Kalikasthan, Kathmandu, Nepal
Phone: +977-1-4439786
email: publication@nepalaya.com.np
www.nepalaya.com.np
Originally written in Nepali in association with Kiran Bhandari.
First published in Nepali by Publication nepa~laya in 2014.

© **Author**

Translated by Bhrikuti Rai

Cover Design : INCS

Digital Partner: Awecode

ISBN - 978-9937-9058-9-3 (Paper back)
ISBN - 978-9937-9090-0-6 (Hard bound)

Rookmangud Katawal- My Story an autobiography

Thank you.

Myanmar's democratic leader, Aung San Suu Kyi, once said to me, "Thank you, General. Please tell the Burmese Army to do what the Nepalese Army has done."

I had the opportunity to lead Nepal's army at a time when it steadfastly supported democracy. We fought against the Maoists in their attempt to establish a one-party dictatorship and were major players in the dramatic transition from monarchy to republic. Although I was just a soldier, this struggle to defend democracy made me known outside my immediate military circle, so my friends encouraged me to write about my life story and how it was interwoven inextricably with Nepal's recent history.

When I retired as Chief of Army Staff in 2009, friends from Nepa~laya offered to publish my autobiography. I told my life story to writer, Kiran Bhandari, and, as I spoke to him, things I thought I had forgotten came back vividly. Kiran Bhandari didn't just discuss my life with me, however. He spoke with more than a hundred people, including all ranks of Nepal's armed forces, to piece together a more objective version of the story of my life and career. I am grateful to each and every one of them. As well as Kiran, I would also like to thank Sudeep Shrestha for editing the original Nepali edition of this book. I thank Bhrikuti Rai for translating and Kunda Dixit for his helpful suggestions. Mikel Dunham and Linda Trigg's editing has brought the book to this shape. I am grateful to Mikel for his foreword to the book.

President Ram Baran Yadav, the political parties and their affiliated organisations, the judiciary, legal professionals, journalists, formation commanders, my Principal Staff Officers (PSOs) and my own staff stood by the Army through a turbulent time, and created an environment conducive to the Army continuing its professional dharma. I value their contribution to protecting democracy and thank each and every one of them. I also respect those Maoist leaders who chose to support and stand by the truth. And this list would not be complete without remembering my parents and everyone in the rank and file of the Nepalese Army who helped me throughout my career.

I drew strength throughout my tenure in the army from my wife, Uma, who also encouraged and motivated me during my work on this book. I am grateful to everyone in my family, including my ever-helpful daughter-in-law, my son, my daughter and my grandchildren who are inspirations to me.

Rookmangud Katawal

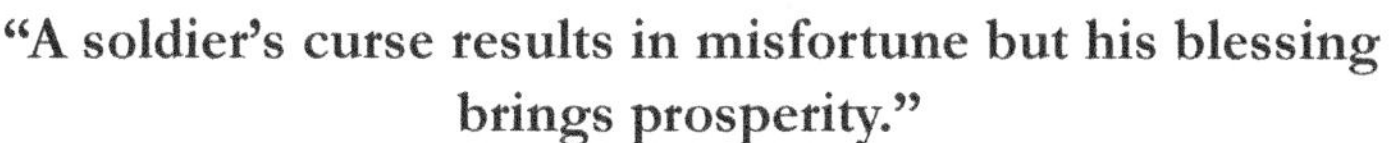

"A soldier's curse results in misfortune but his blessing brings prosperity."

This is the guiding philosophy of my life. I owe it to the blessings of soldiers for helping me reach the heights I have and for everything I have gained in my life so far.

Dedicated to the soldiers of the Nepalese Army who are the source of its faith and courage and the pillars of the nation.

Contents

Timeline Incarnate

When I first met General Rookmangud Katawal, he was at the height of his career. It was during a pivotal moment in Nepal's history. Only a few days before, on 10 April, the historic 2008 Constituent Assembly Elections had been held. Prior to the elections, the country thrummed with trepidation over regional outbreaks, mob threats and the probability of widespread violence in and around the polling stations. As it turned out, the day came and went with less hostility than predicted. The unexpected victory of the Maoists sparked self-congratulatory dancing in the streets. The defeated parties hung back in shell-shocked silence. The King had not yet made a public statement. Whatever one's party affiliation may have been, there was palpable relief that – if nothing else – the long-postponed event was finally over. The day I drove to Army Headquarters, there was still celebration in the air, but also emerging sobriety – a kind of election-day hangover. The country had undeniably reached a turning point. But now what? The rollercoaster ride wasn't over. The opportunities and challenges were multifold; both required ethics and transparency, attributes in short supply among the political parties.

I interviewed General Katawal on the top floor of the sprawling Army Headquarters. Brigadier General Rajendra Chhetri, (now promoted to the Chief of Army Staff), invited me to ink my signature in HQ's oversized visitor's book. I signed directly below the two previous visitors: Jimmy Carter and American Ambassador to Nepal Nancy Powell. I then followed Chhetri further down the hallway, windowed on the right side, the panes streaked with late afternoon rain. The view was looking down over Kathmandu. I couldn't decide if HQ's vantage point was above the fray or at the very heart of it.

Chhetri stopped at a door on the left, knocked, paused, then ushered me into a dimly lit, expansive, but sparsely appointed conference room. Stretching away in the background was an impressive table that might seat a score of brass. There were two non-military oil paintings – mountainscapes – on the panelled walls and that was about it in terms of visual diversion. Closer to the entrance was a heavy desk and a seating arrangement of crimson stuffed armchairs with matching sofa.

The Chief of Army Staff was alone. Chhetri left us, closing the door behind him.

The ironclad handshake of General Katawal is something one doesn't forget. Coupled with direct eye contact and upturned anvil jaw, his grip conveys a message that here is a man who once topped the 61-day United States Army Ranger School, and who probably could still carry, without flinching, 40 kilos of weaponry and equipment on his back.

General Katawal asked me to take a seat on the sofa. Cameras and recorders were forbidden so I pulled out a notebook and pen. Before I could ask my first question, Katawal cut to the chase: "What do you want?"

It was meant as a challenge and I appreciated it. It was like pitching a movie to a producer. You had five minutes to either sell your story or get booted. He didn't care if I liked him or not, which I found refreshing after having interviewed numerous politicians, including Maoists, who seemed to be taking a civilised break in front of the camera before resuming their dogfights. The main political actors in the continually changing governments of Nepal – supporting each other one day, betraying each other the next – offered me pre-scripted answers, with attendants nearby to cut short interviews should their bosses tread thin ice or should I become too annoying. In stark contrast was General Katawal. He was perfectly comfortable being alone with me. He didn't need backup. Who he was today, he would be tomorrow.

I put my questions aside. Instead, I briefed him on what my recent activities in Nepal had entailed. The Election Commission of Nepal had chosen me to be one of their international observers. On Election Day, I canvassed three districts – Morang, Sunsari and Dhankuta – pinpointing various polling stations that had experienced tampering in the past. I saw plenty of irregularities. I photographed a twelve-year-old boy stuffing "his" ballot into the box with a policeman standing three feet away. I saw entrances to polling stations flanked by scores of sullen but intimidating Young Communist League (YCL) members, sitting in the shade and monitoring the locals who dared to vote. I took a side-trip to a hospital in Dharan, where a man was said to be in critical condition from a beating at the Bhutaha polling station. When I arrived, he had already died. At twilight, on the return trip to Biratnagar, my car was stopped and surrounded in Itahari by a large group of young drunk thugs. No security in sight. After some fairly aggressive haggling, my international observer vehicle was reluctantly waved through. As I approached Biratnager around 8:45 pm, I videoed a squad of armed police retrieving an unexploded bomb. As I entered the small hotel where I was spending the night, I heard Jimmy Carter's voice blaring from the television mounted on the wall of the dining room next to the entrance. A group of reporters were gathered there, looking up at the screen. The former US President – who was in Nepal, but never left the Kathmandu Valley – was proclaiming that the elections had been peaceful, free and fair. The reporters laughed at his naïve appraisal. It was only then that the general smiled and took over the conversation.

The whole problem in Nepal was misinformation, General Katawal told me. His frustration was evident in his tightened lips. Everyone dismissed him as the "adopted son of King Mahendra" and therefore jumped to the conclusion that he was against democracy. Nothing could have been further from the truth, he told me. He supplied me with a thumbnail sketch of his hardscrabble childhood in the eastern part of Nepal, far away from the Kathmandu-centric elite. He told me, in no uncertain terms, that his supposed close connection to the royal family was a fairytale. He believed in the constitution and rule of law. More important, he believed that one of the main duties of the Nepalese Army was to protect the constitution and rule of law.

The man spoke from his chest and from his heart. I could take it or leave it. I left Army HQ aware that there had been no interview, *per se*. I never published a word from that 40-minute meeting. But I came away with something far more valuable: someone to respect.

Although I don't live in Nepal, I return here frequently and, if possible, touch base with General Katawal. After his retirement in 2009, and the klieg lights moved elsewhere, the general and I became trusted friends.

I was in Nepal during the horrific 2015 earthquakes. Although it was difficult to reach anyone in Kathmandu by phone, I was in contact with Katawal every day. Finally, five days after the first quake, I had dinner with the general and his family at his home. There was a large tent set up in his garden where his wife, daughter-in-law and her children slept. He preferred bunking in his office on the ground floor, with quick exit to the outside when the never-ending aftershocks became too threatening. It was during that typical Nepali dinner – one of the best I've ever had – that he asked me if I would be interested in editing the English translation of his autobiography. I pounced on the opportunity.

What man had experienced a more intimate relationship with the broad spectrum of Nepali culture and society – from powerless peasants to the aristocracy of old Nepal? Katawal was like a Nepali timeline incarnate.

He was born in 1948, just when the stage was being set for the demise of the 100-year-old reign of the Ranas. He was a toddler when King Tribhuvan returned to Nepal from Indian exile and re-established Shah rule. The pampered existence of the royal family was as distant from his goat-herding childhood as was Kathmandu from Okhaldhunga, the isolated district where he was born. But local holy men said he was destined for great things and his mother took the prophesy to heart, instilling in him a relentless drive to get a proper education and rise to the top.

It was King Mahendra, assuming the throne in 1955, who gave young Rookmangud his chance to break away from a rural existence. On a royal tour of eastern Nepal, Mahendra heard the young lad recite poetry, was impressed by the boy's intellect (and perhaps amused by his bravado), and selected him to be taken to one of the preeminent schools in the Kathmandu Valley, Pharping Boarding School. This was one year before a new constitution was written wherein the king accepted the establishment of a parliamentary government.

Rookmangud found himself in classrooms with boys who came from some of the most privileged families in Nepal. It was a challenge to fit in, but he made a name for himself by taking first in most of his classes. Meanwhile, in 1960, Mahendra launched a royal coup, jailed political party leaders and established absolute rule, thus putting an end to the nascent development of democracy in Nepal. In its place, the king established the Panchayat system, basically a one-party system grafted to bolster Mahendra's rule.

In 1969, Katawal began his career in the then *Royal* Nepal Army, eventually graduating from the Indian National Defence Academy, receiving a Bachelor of Arts from Tribhuvan University, a Master's Degree in National Defence from Pakistan's Qaeda Azam University, the Distinguished International Honor Graduate of the US Special Forces Course, the Gideon Award in the US Ranger Course, and a graduate of UK's Army Command and Staff College. He had come a long way from his rural years, when, in order to be able to practice writing the alphabet, he had had to make his own ink from soot.

In 1972, King Birendra assumed the throne, continuing his deceased father's absolute rule in Nepal.

While Katawal was given increasingly key Army staff appointments, Birendra was faced with growing hostility from his subjects. In 1979, a nationwide pro-democracy movement erupted in protest of the Panchayat system. The following year a national referendum was held that resulted in unqualified support for the Panchayat system, although many thought the process had been rigged. Minor amendments to the constitution were announced to mollify the public. But in 1981, when elections to the National Panchayat were held, the political parties boycotted the elections, a process repeated in 1983 and with the same dubious results.

That same year, Katawal left Nepal along with his family. He had been selected for the plum assignment of becoming Nepal's Government's Liaison Officer to the Brigade of Gurkhas of the British Army and Government of Hong Kong. The position was for three years and, during that stint, he had numerous opportunities to host the royal family en route to and from their various international tours. Katawal was nothing, if not a careerist, and he made the most of the opportunity by developing relationships with people who, otherwise, would have been beyond his station in life.

In 1988, he was appointed the Chief Military Personnel Officer of the United Nations Interim Force in Lebanon.

While Katawal's career constantly moved upward, King Birendra's Panchayat system – ever more dysfunctional and despised – was on the verge of collapsing. In 1989, India imposed an economic embargo on Nepal. It struck a devastating blow to the nation's economy and, in turn, enraged the people, who put the blame squarely on Birendra's shoulders. This led to the 1990 People's Movement (*Jana Andolan*), which resulted in the promulgation of a new constitution that significantly compromised the Crown's power and legitimised a multiparty democratic system.

Meanwhile, after serving in the Research and Development Wing at Army HQ, Katawal became Commandant of the Royal Nepal Military Academy in 1993.

In 1996, Katawal was promoted to Brigadier General. Some of his superiors – all hailing from the rarified background of the ruling class – were fond of telling Katawal that, no matter how well he performed, a poor eastern boy with no pedigree would "never become Chief of Army Staff." And they weren't joking. An Army Chief's last name was either "Rana", "Shah", "Basnyat" or "Thapa". One of the most interesting things about Katawal's life story is that, the higher he rose in the Army hierarchy, the more he encountered the pushback, the rigidity of the upper class. The discrimination wasn't universal, but the undercurrent was always there. Likewise, as he rose through the ranks, his direct access to the palace became increasingly restricted. The king's inner circle, all from the old aristocracy, distrusted this "upstart", this "easterner" and further stigmatised him – quite erroneously – as an avid supporter of the pro-democratic Nepali Congress political party.

The same year that Katawal became a Brigadier General, a Maoist faction of the Communist Party of Nepal went underground and declared a "People's War". At first, most of the politicians in Kathmandu labelled the Maoists as "terrorists", but otherwise paid insufficient attention to them, tucked away as they were in the western hilly districts of Rolpa, Rukum, Pyuthan and Salyan. Out of sight, out of mind. Besides, the political parties were too preoccupied with their interminable internecine war with one another. Corruption, coercion, lust for ministerial offices and jealousy of each other's power was the political culture of Nepal. Between 1991 and 2000, there were ten different governments – the perfect storm for political instability – and the crafty Maoists took full advantage of it.

In 1999, Katawal became Director of Military Intelligence. No one in Nepal was in a better position to see the Maoist threat and yet there was little that he or the Army could do, since the palace had refused to mobilize the Army in order to crush the insurgents. That job was left to the police and later, in 2001, the newly created Armed Police Force.

On June 1, 2001, an unspeakable tragedy occurred that rocked the nation: the Palace Massacre. At a private family dinner party, Crown Prince Dipendra apparently gunned down his father, his mother, his brother, his sister and numerous other royal family members before turning the gun on himself. Soon after, without knowing what had actually taken place, General Katawal was ordered to rush to the HQ and stay there. As the hours passed, information slowly trickled in. Prince Dipendra was still alive, in a coma, intensive care. Against strict orders, Katawal jumped on a motorcycle and raced to the hospital:

Chhauni Hospital was heavily guarded. Members of the extended royal family were going in with stunned looks on their faces. Despite so many people milling about, the hospital was eerily quiet.

After sunrise, he managed to get into Dipendra's room:

"Can I see His Royal Highness?" I asked. I was led in and saw Dipendra with his head completely covered in bandages. His motionless body lay on the bed and I gave up hope of him coming out alive. …

Katawal's account of the aftermath of the Palace Massacre is one of his autobiography's most poignant narrations. By the next morning, although the palace was ridiculously slow to admit what had happened, the basic facts of the tragedy leaked out to the public and the nation was overcome by grief, suspicion and, above all, anger. Katawal remembers:

...I couldn't shed tears and grieve for the loss like other Nepalis.

I was assigned to take charge of the arrangements for the funeral procession. In the evening, I took my position and walked beside King Birendra's body in the procession. Some hooligans near Swayambhu threw stones at Prime Minister Girija Prasad Koirala's car. Their anger was directed at the Prime Minister and Prince Gyanendra.

Dipendra finally succumbed to his head wound, and his uncle, Gyanendra, was crowned king. Thirteen days later, Katawal was promoted to Major General. It was a ceremony filled with mixed emotions. Birendra had supported Katawal's career – from the beginning of his reign until his ghastly death.

It wasn't long after the Palace Massacre that Katawal took over as Adjutant General of the Nepalese Army. In November 2001, following a breakdown of peace talks with the government, the Maoists ended a four-month-old ceasefire with a wave of attacks on police posts and army barracks. King Gyanendra declared a state of emergency, erasing a decade of civil liberties including freedom of press and freedom of assembly. The following year, in October 2002, the king sacked the entire cabinet, assumed executive powers and indefinitely postponed parliamentary polls. The "People's War" intensified.

By May 2003, nearly 7,200 Nepalis had been killed in the Maoist revolt, with no end in sight. Five of the six political parties with seats in the dismissed parliament had had their fill of King Gyanendra's direct rule and launched the Joint People's Movement. A new slogan gained momentum: Abolish the monarchy and establish Nepal as a republic. The increased political chaos, coupled with the rising number of dead from the guerrilla conflict was reaching the boiling point. And it was at this juncture, at the end of the year, that General Katawal was selected to command the army's Western Division – ground zero – the very area where the "People's War" had begun seven years before. According to the Maoists, it was completely under their control.

The national and international media parroted *ad nauseam* the Maoists' claim. Katawal capitalised on his transfer to Western Nepal by revealing a different picture in the hinterlands. For example, he foiled the Maoists' attempt to block King Gyanendra's scheduled tour of Western Nepal. The Army cleared the path; Gyanendra made his scheduled stops and Katawal made sure the media was there to cover it. "Where are the Maoists?" Katawal asked the cameras. In addition, Katawal focused on ramping up development projects that increased interaction and trust with the local villages. The Army and Police presence was so great in places that numerous Maoist leaders were driven across the Indian border. Not surprisingly, Katawal was in the crosshairs of Maoist leadership. But since they were powerless to actually kill him, they resorted to a cowardly alternative: Katawal's wife began getting anonymous phone calls, advising her to buy a white sari – the customary garb for a widow.

In September 2004, Katawal was promoted to Lieutenant General and took over as Chief of General Staff. Being back in Kathmandu was perhaps more contentious than his direct skirmishes with rebels in the West. The king was getting into the habit of dismissing prime ministers on an almost yearly basis. He blamed them for failing to hold elections on time and not being able to bring Maoists leaders to a roundtable negotiation. Finally, on 1 February 2005, Gyanendra declared himself absolute ruler, promising the country that he would return Nepal to normalcy within three years. His announcement was unapologetically heavy handed and he repressed any form of dissent, restricting civil liberties, including freedom of speech. By the time the royal address was over, all of Nepal's mobile phone networks and landlines went dead. The king had ordered a nationwide communication blackout.

The diplomatic community publicly denounced the move as a "setback to democracy." But off the record, ambassadors told Katawal:

"If peace can be restored by bringing the Maoists into the democratic process then the King should be allowed to do so. This will also be a major lesson for the political leaders. We think this is the best solution at the moment to pull Nepal out of the present political crisis."

Initially, a surprisingly large percentage of Nepal's population condoned the king's move: Nothing else had worked, so why not give the king a chance to turn things around? Katawal also supported the king's takeover but not necessarily his methods. He was particularly concerned that censorship of the media would come back to haunt the king. And then there was this:

No one objected when the King took the step to bring the political parties into line but now it seemed he was concentrating power in his own hands and removing everyone who didn't agree with him. He excluded the Congress and UML from his Cabinet of Ministers and selected former office bearers from the Panchayat regime. Furthermore, there were no signs of improved governance...Less than a month after the royal takeover, seven government secretaries were dumped to a reserve pool. People who had served the monarchy were being punished, triggering fear and suspicion among government officials. Their faith in the monarchy was crumbling fast.

Ambassadors were now unwelcome at the palace. To make matters more insular, the King's inner circle of sycophants never challenged the king's mulish – if not delusional – decisions. At a time when he should have been exhibiting flexibility, the King became even more rigid. Domestically, he had turned his back on the political parties and they had countered by turning their backs on him. In fact, they had come to the conclusion that it would be far more profitable to dialogue with the Maoists, the king's archenemies.

For all practical purposes it was Gyanendra, himself, who was destroying the monarchy. Although no royalist, Katawal believed in the merits of a well-managed constitutional monarchy. Even a merely symbolic monarchy, with no real power of its own, offered historic continuity to a nation that was in dire need of unifying assets. From 2005, up until Gyanendra was dethroned and evicted from Narayanhiti Palace, Katawal sought private audiences with the king in order to shed light on the king's precarious situation. On the few occasions that he did manage to speak to the king in private, Gyanendra either left in mid-sentence or responded with a royal sneer.

The Five-Party Alliance grew into a Seven-Party Alliance and, on 22 November 2005, they officially joined hands with the Maoists. Together, they agreed to resolve the 10-year conflict through political negotiations. Without the palace's participation, they converged in Delhi and inked a 12-Point

Agreement that called for the abolishment of absolute monarchy and addressed a spate of other contentious problems, including those involving class, caste, gender and economics.

It was a game-changer. The Maoists came out of hiding and took to the streets. On 6 April 2006, they and the united parties declared the People's Movement (*Jana Andolan II*). Normal life screeched to a halt. The world watched, day after day, as the protestors swelled to the tens of thousands, while security forces in riot gear and tanks blocked the perimeters of the Royal Palace.

Finally, on 21 April, the King announced that he would restore parliament, thinking that that would solve the problem. He was deluded; it was a case of too-little-too-late. The Maoists and the Seven-Party Alliance gave him an ultimatum: The protests would continue until a Constituent Assembly was formed and the monarchy was abolished. The next day, the streets of Kathmandu swelled to hundreds of thousands of protestors. Finally, on 24 April, the King announced he was stepping down.

Six months later, on 18 September 2006, Rookmangud Katawal was sworn in as the new Chief of Army Staff (COAS). He was the first Commander-in-Chief of the Nepalese Army to come from a common family. At a time when much of the public dismissed the Army as aristocratic, reactionary and a stooge of the beleaguered monarchy, Katawal's unprecedented promotion should have sent a message that the Army was not that easy to stereotype. On the contrary, the streets were rife with the rumour that it was only a matter of time before the Army – in secret collaboration with the disgraced King – would stage a military coup. In fact, Katawal was approached on numerous occasions by leading figures to do precisely that, but he refused to act against the constitution.

The United Nations Mission in Nepal (UNMIN), arrived in Nepal in early 2007 to oversee the scheduled 2008 Constituent Elections and, more important, to monitor the 28 cantonments, which were set up to house the Maoist ex-combatants until they could be reintegrated into society. Almost from the beginning, UNMIN's presence was plagued with questions of its neutrality, as well as its ability (or inclination) to correctly cipher Maoist irregularities. Early on, UNMIN conducted a headcount of the rebels to weed out child soldiers and new people recruited *after* the peace agreement was in place. Their count was just under 20,000 combatants. The Army did everything in its power to point out the headcount discrepancies but UNMIN Director Ian Martin wasn't listening. (In 2009, however, the UNMIN's verification process became a source of embarrassment after a secret videotape of Maoist Supremo Prachanda caught him boasting to his followers that he had duped UNMIN by padding the camps with young people who didn't actually qualify. The real number of the People's Liberation Army, according to Prachanda, was actually 7,000-8,000. Even that was an inflated figure.)

The April 2008 National Elections results indicated that the Maoists had won a surprising majority of the seats in the Constituent Assembly (CA). They did not achieve a mandate, but they were clearly in a position to take over the government. In May, the CA abolished the monarchy and pronounced Nepal a republic. Ram Baran Yadav (of the opposition Nepali Congress party) became Nepal's first President. Prachanda became Prime Minister.

General Katawal spent most of his COAS tenure dealing with army bashing, with Maoist duplicity, and with formulating a practical solution to reintegrating the ex-rebels, while, at the same time, preserving the integrity of the Nepalese Army. His job became even more besieged after Prachanda became Prime Minister. With the King effectively neutralised, the Maoists turned their attention to bringing the Army to its knees.

Now it was only the Army that the Maoists needed to take care of. They knew very well that the Army was the only disciplined, coordinated and united institution in the country. They wanted to put the Army in its place as they saw it and under their control in order to complete their mission of taking over the state. They would go to any lengths to accomplish that... [They] had portrayed the Nepalese Army in a negative light as rapists and murderers and tagged them a private army.

On the other hand, the international community admired and relied on the Nepalese Army for its decades of professional participation in UN peace missions. In other parts of the world, the Nepalese Army represented the very model of an institution dedicated to maintaining peace and stability.

Nevertheless, Prachanda pushed on, dead-set on forcing the Army to integrate – wholesale – 19,000 "ex-rebels", a group with far less education, questionable skills and virtually no professional military training or experience on a par with the Nepalese Army's international standards. For Katawal, the consummate military professional, meeting Prachanda's demand would be the equivalent of allowing the army to be destroyed. That was not going to happen on Katawal's watch.

Prachanda focused on issues he thought could destroy Katawal: controversy over Katawal's alleged close affiliation with the ruling class and the Indian government; Army recruiting issues regarding replacing eight generals, who were facing retirement; and the Army's boycotting of a sports tournament that Prachanda had tried to commandeer with members of his youth group, the Young Communist League. Based on these "transgressions", Prachanda unilaterally sacked Katawal.

His autocratic ploy backfired. The Communist Party of Nepal (Unified Marxist Leninist), a pivotal party in the coalition, withdrew from the government in protest. This was followed by the President of Nepal overriding Prachanda's bold move and ordering Katawal to continue as COAS. This, in turn, resulted in Prachanda's furious resignation in May 2009, followed by the collapse of the Maoist government. This final "Prachanda vs. Katawal" battle-of-wills is recounted in the first chapter of Katawal's autobiography – a political thriller if there ever was one.

Katawal has often been portrayed as arrogant, which is a fair assessment. But after reading his life story, I don't believe he was ever conceited. He merely took pride in what he had achieved on his own. He had faith in the simple mantra that upholding one's principles was the only course of action. No doubt this had a lot to do with his soldiers' deep admiration for him. His unwavering belief in his own abilities and in his prophesised fate of becoming a "big man", nourished his conviction that his role was to safeguard Nepal's stability, to protect its constitution and rule of law – no matter who was in power.

Above all, amidst the interminable political intrigue and backstabbing, Katawal emerges as man of self-empowerment – a man who, against all odds, transcended social prejudice and rose to the top of the military at precisely the moment in history when his country most needed him. Decade after decade, his story offers an insider's view of the machinations going on behind the closed doors of Nepal's power elite.

Reading the general's autobiography is, in essence, reading the timeline of Nepal's struggle to emerge as a modern day democracy.

As might be expected, although Katawal has now retired from the Army, he keeps up an exhaustive schedule of reading, traveling, physical fitness, public functions, private ceremonies, and speaking at conferences and media programmes.

His most recent project is the launching of *The R.K. Trust*, an organisation dedicated to improving the lives of Nepali people through education and supporting social reform to better equip the nation in dealing with the international dynamics of the 21st century.

Mikel Dunham

August 16, 2015

The 16-Day War

Even before New Year, Army Headquarters were buzzing with the rumour that the Chief of Staff was about to be replaced. Then during the New Year's party, Kul Bahadur Khadka's wife was overheard saying, "We were supposed to move into Shashi Bhawan – the Chief of Staff's residence – by today. I don't know why it's taking so long."

Others told me they had also heard the rumours. Maybe they wanted me to confirm if the rumours were true. But there was no point responding to that sort of talk so I didn't pay attention to it.

The Maoists wanted to interfere in the Army and were waiting for the right moment to step in by creating an upheaval. I had regular meetings with Prime Minister Pushpa Kamal Dahal aka "Prachanda" and Defence Minister Ram Bahadur Thapa aka "Badal", even though the Defence Minister and I had our differences from time to time.

However, eventually I came to learn that the Maoists, a faction of the CPN (UML) and some Nepali Congress leaders had reached an agreement to sack me. The plan was to seek an explanation from me of certain events related to the military, an explanation which would be deemed unsatisfactory regardless of what I said. I would then be relieved of my command. They had apparently already prepared a written plan of action during a meeting in Dhulikhel. I was informed about this by well-wishers from as far away as New York and London.

"They are trying to remove you," former Prime Minister Surya Bahadur Thapa told me one day, "But hold your ground no matter what."

I had struggled against all odds to rise to the rank of Chief of Army Staff. Fifty years previously, as a youngster I had met a holy man on the banks of the Sunkoshi River. I can still hear his words to me: "Remain strong even in times of despair and you will always emerge victorious. What has been written cannot be erased."

Sunday, 19 April 2009

I was on the way to my office for my usual 8:30 am start and we were waiting at the traffic lights at Thapathali when I got a phone call from Baluwatar, the Prime Minister's residence: "The Prime Minister has summoned you."

I headed straight to Baluwatar where I was taken to the living room and served coffee. I was just taking my first sip when Prime Minister Prachanda came in, rubbing his hands. He looked cheerful as always but I noticed he wouldn't look me in the eye.

"You only have four months left," he said, "Subtract the mandatory one month's leave and you only have three months left. Let it go. Resign now and help us out."

"What wrong have I done?" I asked. "There should be a reason for my early resignation."

"It's just that you need to help us," he said evasively.

We weren't beating about the bush now. I was looking him straight in the eye, while he responded by gritting his teeth, his eyes downcast.

"Don't even think about making me resign," I said.

Defence Minister Thapa had threatened to take action against me many times but I always laughed it off.

The Prime Minister decided to speak more bluntly. "Either resign or be ready to face the consequences," he said.

"Have I broken any laws or done anything against the government? Have I betrayed my country or overstepped the Constitution?" I asked.

He didn't answer but instead ended the conversation: "Okay then, see you later."

I went back to my office. However, later that same day I met Surya Bahadur Thapa, KP Sharma Oli, Arjun Narasingha KC and other political leaders during lunch at a seminar at the Hotel Soaltee.

"How's it going, Chief?" they asked.

"Could you gentlemen come over here please?" I said and took them to a corner.

"Something surprising happened today," I said, "The Prime Minister summoned me to Baluwatar and asked for my resignation."

"So what did you tell him?" they asked.

"I told him I wouldn't resign without a reason," I replied "And the Prime Minister said he would see me again."

After lunch I returned to my office. I was almost done with some files when I got another call from the Prime Minister's Office (PMO): "Chief, could you come over at 3:30?"

Back and forth again? How many times did I have to meet the Prime Minister in one day? But he was the Prime Minister, after all, so I had to go.

"You and I have such a fantastic rapport," the Prime Minister began, "Even our families share a deep bond. We need to make our relationship even stronger."

After threatening me in the morning, now he was trying flattery. The scare tactics had failed, so now he wanted to stab me in the back while pretending to embrace me.

He acted as if he and I shared a very warm and special friendship.

"If we work together we can do wonders for this country," he went on, "We two brothers can be influential for years to come."

"A general in the army always takes orders from the legitimate government," I told him, "I am ready to assist the Prime Minister in any way I can."

"The position of head of our mission in New York becomes vacant in a month's time. Or if you want to go to France or anywhere else I can have the decision passed in Cabinet today. Or we could even make you National Security Advisor." He was dangling carrots. "It's only three months, *dai*. You have to leave the Army."

Nothing new there, I thought. He was just repeating himself with a few embellishments.

I refused to take the bait. "I'm a steadfast soldier and won't run away from the front," I said. "Furthermore, I know nothing about diplomacy."

"Come on, you already served the country for decades and you'll retire soon anyway," he said, "You need to leave now to make room for others."

"I will remain the Chief of Army Staff until the last second of my tenure," I said, trying to end the discussion. "Ambassadorships mean nothing to me. I wouldn't step down even if you offered me Lord Indra's throne."

The Prime Minister immediately sprang to his feet. Stress was visible on his face. He put his hands in his pockets, walked towards the door and then stopped for a while. He took a deep breath and walked back.

"So you won't agree?" he asked politely, his voice not betraying the emotion. I knew what he must be feeling.

Calmly I said, "You're a Brahmin's son and I'm the son of a Chhetri. We both understand Nepali. So what is it you don't understand? I've already told you my decision. How many times must I repeat myself? My decision won't change."

"Fine then. You can leave now," he said stiffly. I could finally sense mounting anger in his tone.

I thanked him and left.

The PMO was overflowing with people that day. Middle-level Maoist leaders had gathered at Singha Darbar, probably hoping to hear what had happened between me and the Prime Minister.

I went straight to my office and called lawyer, BA Kumar Sharma, the head of the Army's legal department. I told him about the possibility of the Maoist government seeking some sort of "explanations" from me. My sources in the party and Baluwatar had already given me hints about the issues which could be raised. So I asked Sharma to start formulating answers on three particular matters: recruitment, extension of the tenure of eight generals and the Army's decision to withdraw from the Fifth National Games.

That afternoon at a Cabinet meeting shortly after I left Baluwatar, it was decided, as expected, that I should be asked to explain certain decisions. The government kept this under wraps until late at night, however, I heard about it from some members of the Cabinet who supported me.

Sharma called some legal experts to come to Shashi Bhawan. We had just started brainstorming when advocate Tikaram Bhattarai got a call. UML leader, Madhav Kumar Nepal, was on the line. Tikaram *jee* handed me the phone.

I had known Madhav Kumar Nepal for quite some time. My aides had told me how concerned he was during the lead-up to my promotion to Army Chief. A police DIG had told me then that Nepal was keen to meet me but I had sent him the same message that I sent to everyone else: I wouldn't meet any political leaders to discuss my possible promotion.

Although we were neighbours at Koteshwor and had met him a few times, I didn't think it was necessary to meet him now to lobby for maintaining my position. I thought he would leave me alone but he didn't.

"So, how are you doing?" he began jokingly. He knew about the Cabinet decision, of course. "You know me," I said, "I'm upholding the Army's honour, the constitution and the law."

Before I could finish, he reassured me, "You're doing the right thing. You will have the UML's full support."

Around 10:30 that night, Defence Secretary Ganesh Raj Joshi called. The Maoists had transferred Baman Prasad Neupane from the Defence Ministry over the issue of the tenure of the eight generals and had brought in Joshi, who was actually an agricultural expert, as Acting Secretary.`

"Hello, Mr Secretary, how's it going?" I asked.

"We have to meet, Chief," he said.

I'd guessed as soon as he called that that would be the first thing he'd say.

"It's an urgent letter from the Cabinet," he added.

I could hear the anxiety in his voice. The polite Secretary was being squeezed in the tussle between the Prime Minister and the Army Chief.

"What could be so important at this hour?" I said. "Whatever it is, bring it over to the office tomorrow after 10 am. I don't receive official letters at my residence."

"I've been asked to hand it to you now. It's an emergency," he replied.

"The sentries won't let you in," I told him truthfully. "You might be humiliated because the soldiers on duty here act on very strict instructions. They have orders not to let even the Head of State come in after dark."

We were old acquaintances, so I made light of it: "Mr Secretary, your frail body might not be able to withstand the thrashing you would get if you came to Shashi Bhawan at this late hour."

Although I was joking, I knew he must be under direct orders from the Prime Minister to hand over the letter that night. I called my security staff and told them not to accept any letter from anyone or to allow anyone to attach a letter to the gate either.

There were two paths open to me. I could either stand by the constitution, the law and the democratic path to protect the Nepalese Army or I could do as the Maoists asked and resign three months ahead of schedule. I would have gained personally had I resigned. I could have become an ambassador to the country of my choice, become National Security Advisor, even a minister if the Maoists were really generous or probably a rich man. But choosing a bed of roses for myself would have put the nation's military at risk. An honourable soldier's self-respect would also have been sacrificed. If the Army leadership bowed down before the Maoists then nobody would be able to stop them using force to establish a one-party dictatorship in Nepal. The Army would be under their control.

Choosing a comfortable life would have been the easier option, of course, but I wouldn't have been able to live with myself had I taken that path. Besides, people would have accused me of being a traitor and, behind artificial smiles and the pretence of respect, my soldiers would have hated me. My family and even my descendants would have had to bear the stigma.

I was confronting the Maoists for the final showdown. They wanted to hand over the letter regarding the Cabinet's decision that night, thinking I wouldn't have time to consult anyone.

I understood this ploy and put the Secretary off, saying I would receive the letter only the next morning. This gave me time to prepare my explanation though only half a day.

To maintain a separation between my office and my home life, I didn't usually bring work home. Also my wife, Uma, wasn't the least bit interested in my work. There were lots of ups and downs in the 43 years of my military career but I always kept my family out of it. Even then, when I was facing my biggest challenge, I made sure that no one at home was aware of it. I was also careful not to let my body language betray what was going on because I believed that whatever was going to happen would happen anyway and there was no point dragging my family into it. But bottling it up inside was burdensome at times. Despite putting on a brave face, there are times when the spirit falters.

Monday, 20 April 2009

No matter how much I tried to keep things from my family, there were times when that was difficult. Uma, my son and daughter-in-law, even my daughter, Nepolina, who was in America, found out that something was happening through the TV and Internet. One good thing was that the media had not yet reported the news about the Cabinet's decision. I was surprised it was being kept under wraps.

Defence Ministry Joint Secretary Shreedhar Pokhrel came to my office in the morning and handed over the letter with the Cabinet's decision to my secretariat. Then he crept away without even seeing me. Usually, the Defence Joint Secretary wouldn't leave without calling on the Chief, so the poor man must have been in a real dilemma.

I didn't think it was necessary to read the letter so I sent it to BA Kumar Sharma, the Army's legal chief, without even looking at it. What strength does a letter hold if it's penned with insincerity? Based on information from my supporters in the Cabinet, I already knew the content of the letter. As I expected, it demanded an explanation from me about Army recruitment, the extension of the tenure of the eight generals and the Army's decision not to take part in the Fifth National Games. It also contained the threat that if I didn't answer within the stipulated time frame, or if I presented an unsatisfactory explanation, I could be dismissed as per the provisions of the Army Act.

The Maoists had created a fuss in December 2008 about the recruitment of 2,880 new personnel for the Army but that disagreement had already been resolved. The question of the extension of the tenure of the eight generals in March 2009 was before the courts, so there was no point asking me for comment on that. If the judiciary said it was legal, nothing could be done no matter how worked up the Maoists got about it.

As for the Army withdrawing from the Fifth National Games, I was firm in my decision to call our teams back when rules were flouted to allow the entry of a Maoist club. The Prime Minister's direct orders in this matter were in violation of the fundamental rules of the National Games.

The Maoists' demand that I should provide an explanation in relation to these three issues was a high-voltage confrontation that raised the heat in Kathmandu's political circles and beyond. The phones at HQ wouldn't stop ringing and some officers had to be reassigned just to take the calls.

My message to everyone was clear: "They are trying to impose a Stalinist dictatorship in Nepal but the Nepalese Army is resolutely against this and will stand by the constitution and the law. I believe the country and the people will support us. The onus is now on all of us to convince our political leaders. They can either give in to Maoist authoritarianism or support the Nepalese Army's stand and remain within the democratic system."

I also informed the Indian, American and British embassies about the Maoists' demands. I immediately called a meeting of the Principal Staff Officers, which is the Army's Cabinet of Ministers. Major General Kul Bahadur Khadka arrived 15 minutes late.

Everyone at the meeting felt we needed to move forward in accordance with the constitution and the law. We prepared a draft reply to the Cabinet and let BA Kumar Sharma take care of the legal aspects.

Sharma called some lawyers, including those who were at Shashi Bhawan the previous night, to the Army Club. I was satisfied with the final draft of the reply and sent a copy to the President's Office. I heard that the matter was extensively discussed at Sheetal Niwas. That same afternoon, the President directed the Prime Minister to proceed according to the Army Act 2006 as per the fourth and fifth amendments of the Interim Constitution. The fourth amendment states that the President is the supreme commander and the protector of constitution.

The President ordered that it would not be appropriate to take any decision regarding the Chief of Army Staff without the consensus of all political parties.

The same afternoon, Maoist Minister Baburam Bhattarai told reporters at Nepalganj airport that clarification had been sought on the legal position regarding the retirement of the Army Chief, making it clear just how prejudiced the government was towards the Army and the military leadership.

How could the Maoist leadership be considering how to force my resignation before even reading what I had to say in relation to the issues they had raised? I now had the opportunity to reveal to those people who still had some faith left in the Maoists what their intentions really were.

Despite the dizzying events of the day, I wasn't late returning to Shashi Bhawan that evening.

Uma had learnt what was happening the same morning but didn't call during the day for an update. We don't usually call each other unless it's an emergency. She was confident I wouldn't make a mistake or be afraid.

What had unsettled Uma a little, however, was a visit to Shashi Bhawan by Madam Kamala, Chhatra Man Gurung's wife. She first telephoned Uma to check how she was doing and then called around in person. Madam Kamala looked frantic and kept going on about Kul Bahadur and what he had done, and this worried Uma.

"Kul Bahadur will ruin everything. Tell the Chief to go to the courts now," Kamala said. Uma kept quiet, and Kamala repeated, "You can't just sit here doing nothing. Please call the Chief immediately and tell him to take the matter to the court."

We had heard that the Khadka and Gurung families were really close but now Kamala couldn't stop cursing Kul Bahadur and it was Uma who had to calm her down.

"The Chief won't take my call now. What happens will happen," Uma answered, "He won't give in that easily."

But Kamala wouldn't stop cursing Kul Bahadur. So Uma had to call a colonel for Kamala's sake. He said everything was fine and only then was Kamala satisfied. Her worry was understandable.

In fact, we were both worried about Chhatra Man. On the basis of seniority, qualification and long established norms, I wanted to hand over the Army Chief's responsibilities to Chhatra Man. But if the Maoists brought in Kul Bahadur then

Chhatra Man would have to retire as a three-star general and the Nepalese Army would lose the first opportunity in its modern history to have an Army Chief from an ethnic minority.

I returned to Shashi Bhawan and spent some time with the children, as I always did.

Tuesday, 21 April 2009

I was at the office by 8 am since I had to register my reply to the Cabinet by 10:30 that morning.

We were determined to deliver the letter within the stipulated time frame and didn't want to take any chances. There were three teams of officers from the Secretariat working with the letter. While one team registered it, the other would be there as backup. The first team would enter from the west gate and submit the letter. If the Maoists obstructed them, the backup team at the east gate would try to submit it there. The third team would coordinate the two approaches.

While, in theory, no one would dare stop the Army, we believed it was best to be prepared for any contingency. No matter what the mission, there were always three plans of action.

As it turned out, everything went smoothly. The first team successfully delivered the letter so we didn't need the backup team.

It was important to remain alert now. Soon after the registration, the Army's Directorate of Public Relations (DPR) and legal department informed the media that the letter had been delivered. We even put the contents online so that

Nepalis all over the world could read it, and we sent the letter to foreign embassies in Nepal as well. We took these measures to remain a step ahead – just in case the Maoists tried to create a controversy by claiming that I had not replied in time.

The letter that we sent to the Cabinet was only procedural. What mattered more to us was that people both inside and outside the country should have access to it and form their own opinions.

The Nepali Congress leader and former Prime Minister, Sher Bahadur Deuba, was convinced by what we wrote and gave us his support. "Instead of thanking the Army which helped in establishing a republic, the Maoists have tried to disgrace it. I condemn this," he said in Parliament that afternoon. He then threatened to prevent the House from sitting until the government withdrew its request for an explanation from me.

Officers from the Directorate of Military Intelligence (DMI) who were present in the Parliament that afternoon told me lawmakers from the UML and the Madhesi Janadhikar Forum also protested against what the government was doing. Nepali Congress lawmakers surrounded the rostrum while the Maoists chanted slogans against them. The Parliament was now effectively polarised over the issue.

Although UML lawmakers were protesting, the party itself was actually divided over the issue. UML leader KP Sharma Oli called a press conference at the party's headquarters in Balkhu to condemn the Maoists' attempted interference in the Army, as did Madhav Kumar Nepal. However, the UML Chairman, Jhalanath Khanal, had handed over his responsibilities to Deputy Prime Minister and Home Minister Bamdev Gautam before leaving for a visit to China, and Gautam refused to support Oli and Nepal. Gautam's ties to Prachanda were closer than to his own party leaders. He argued there was no need to make such a big issue of the whole thing because Prachanda had asked for the explanation with Khanal's agreement.

Since Gautam refused to budge on the issue, the UML's Vice-Chair, Bidya Bhandari, called all the available central members for a meeting. The Khanal faction didn't show up. The meeting demanded the withdrawal of the government's demands. According to my sources within the UML, the Khanal faction had been upset with me ever since the party's Butwal Plenary Session three months earlier because it felt I had been lobbying for Oli. When the Army was in a tough spot, Oli had spoken out against the Maoists, so back then we were in touch on a regular basis. However, it was not my job to lobby on behalf of would-be party leaders. The country's Army Chief should, I always felt, show equal respect to the leaders of all the democratic parties. I had congratulated Khanal from Sankhuwasabha when he was elected party Chairman. I refused to believe he held a grudge against me, and this was subsequently confirmed by my friends in the UML.

Members of the groups surrounding central level leaders, Ghanashyam Bhusal and Yogesh Bhattarai, called Khanal in China asking him to withdraw the letter sent to me. Khanal cut short his visit because of the crisis at home.

More and more people within the UML had begun siding with the constitution, the law and the democratic system, which unsettled the Maoists. On the same day, a Maoist Secretariat meeting decided that the Army Chief's reply amounted to insubordination and he had to be dismissed.

But other parties were coming together to oppose the

Maoists' move, which they recognised as an attempt to foist authoritarianism on the country by interfering with the Army. The President had expressed concern and, as the guardian of the constitution, sent a memo to the Prime Minister saying: Do not go beyond the Interim Constitution by removing the Chief of Army Staff.

Wednesday, 22 April 2009

I made a few calls to barrack commanders and met some of them in the morning.

Building and maintaining relationships at such an uncertain time was important to reinforce morale and maintain the troops' confidence in their leadership.

"You all know what's going on," I said, "Anything could happen, so we need to be prepared. Stay on top of unfolding developments and keep everybody else informed as well."

"We're ready, sir," they said.

I always try to call officers every week to ask how things are going. I enquire about the welfare of the men in the barracks, if they've been in touch with their families and what the overall situation is.

Under the leadership of the Nepali Congress, 16 parties stood against the Maoist move against me. They described it as an attempt by the Maoists to "interfere with the Army to enforce authoritarianism". The Madhesi Janadhikar Forum, the third partner in the coalition government, said that no decision regarding the Army would be considered valid until there was national consensus.

I knew very well how cunning Prime Minister Prachanda could be. He had demonstrated an ability to not only adapt to new situations but also to turn them to his advantage. And now he put this ability on full display.

Perhaps because he felt isolated from his coalition partners, he seemed to make an about-face. "I will only move forward with the consensus of all the parties," he told the President.

My feeling was that he said that to the President just to subdue the anger among the political leaders who were against his party's attempted interference in the Army. There was no way he could sack me as long as the parties were opposed to it, but I knew very well not to believe what he said. He had perfected the art of going back on agreements as soon as he had the upper hand.

Thursday, 23 April 2009

Since it was *Loktantra Diwas* (Democracy Day) on 24 April, we scheduled the regular Friday meeting a day early. There were 30 people, including the PSOs and the Valley Commander, at the meeting, where preparations for the next day's programme were discussed. Although the Home Ministry was the official organiser, the Army was responsible for making all the arrangements.

Reverberations from the "explanation" episode were still rankling soldiers and officers alike. Gaurav Shumsher Rana, Director General of Military Operations (DGMO), told the meeting bluntly: "The virus trying to destroy the Army is in this room." Everyone knew whom he was talking about.

Himalaya Shumsher, who headed Number One Brigade, went on to add: "The root of the problem is within us. We need to find it and get rid of it."

Even the Director General of Military Training (DGMT), Daman Ghale, said with barely-concealed anger: "Action should be taken against those who abuse the system."

I didn't want Kul Bahadur to feel he was being pushed and kicked around, so I steered the discussion to other matters.

After the meeting, the DGMO office reported that 13 soldiers had been killed while fighting a forest fire in Ramechhap. The fire had engulfed the forest near a hospital that morning and it had taken the soldiers four hours to bring it under control. This was a great loss of life and a big shock to the Army.

We are soldiers because we are ready to die fighting our enemies. We put our lives on the line and have the courage to face bullets. Here, however, the soldiers had heroically sacrificed their lives trying to save the hospital patients. I saluted them all.

After news of the deaths came through, I tried immediately to meet the Prime Minister and the Defence Minister, but I was informed they were both too busy to see me. So I went to brief the President about the incident. DGMO Gaurav Shumsher called me while I was still at Sheetal Niwas.

"The Defence Minister has demanded that he be given a helicopter to go to Ramechhap," he said.

"Make the arrangements immediately," I said, "And accompany him there."

I also directed him to take the Minister only to the site of the incident and back. I wanted to ensure that he didn't take advantage of the situation to go to the barracks and start spouting rubbish.

After returning from the President's Office, I asked the Department of the Adjutant General to arrange to honour the 13 soldiers and to immediately propose to the Defence Ministry a package of financial support for their families. The government announced this as per the Army's request on the same day and I am enormously grateful to the government for doing that.

It's every soldier's duty to risk his life for the people and we are always ready to face anything that might entail. After this incident, the Defence Minister and other Maoist leaders may have realised what the "good for nothing" Army actually did.

I had lost all interest in what was happening regarding the row with the Prime Minister but my friends in the government kept calling me all day and into the evening as I reached Shashi Bhawan.

Prachanda had not abandoned his campaign to get all the parties on board to sack me. He even went to meet UML leader, Madhav Nepal, at his residence in Koteshwor.

"The Chief only has four months to go until he retires. Why bother him now?" Nepal was said to have asked. "Our party will make a decision tomorrow."

Even Baburam Bhattarai went to meet KP Oli at his home in Balkot. "We'll decide after the Chairman returns from China," he was told and politely sent away.

I was also told about a gathering of leaders of the Oli faction at the Madan Bhandari Foundation that evening. "We won't let them execute their plan to destroy the Nepalese Army," was the common refrain there.

The Prime Minister met the Ambassadors of India, China, USA, UK, Japan and Germany at Baluwatar and asked them to support his decision to sack me. I was also informed about a separate meeting just between Indian Ambassador Rakesh Sood and the Prime Minister. This was probably their second meeting since the row flared up.

The Nepali Congress, Tarai Madhesh Loktantrik Party, Rastriya Janashakti Party and others were still blocking Parliamentary proceedings in protest at the Maoists' actions. The Nepali Congress had decided to continue its protest until the Prime Minister stopped trying to interfere with the Army.

UML Chairman Jhalanath Khanal returned after cutting his trip to China short, and the party's standing committee was set to meet the next day.

"I had to cut short my visit just to fire a general?" he apparently asked after landing at the airport.

Friday, 24 April 2009

Lokatantra Diwas was a holiday. After worshipping at the Ripumardini shrine at HQ, I left for Tundikhel to attend the day's celebrations. I sat in the first row to welcome the Prime Minister, Defence Minister and others. Maoist Chairman Prachanda might have deviated from his duty as Prime Minister but I was well aware of the importance of upholding the dignity and decorum of the position of Army Chief.

This was our first meeting since he sought the "explanation" from me. There was no conversation. I welcomed them to the programme and saw them off. That was it.

Saturday, 25 April 2009

I mostly travelled outside Kathmandu on Saturdays, visiting as many barracks as I could. It was a good opportunity to mingle with the soldiers, get to know what was happening and to feel the pulse of the force at grassroots level. I also made sure to have informal meetings with district leaders, journalists, traders, judges and other locals.

This Saturday, however, the subedar-majors from the Valley wanted to see me so I wasn't going anywhere. They said about 80 of them would come. All the PSOs were also called except Kul Bahadur. I specifically called for the soon-to-be Army Chief Chhatra Man because I wanted the future Army leadership and the troops to intermingle. It was important for the Army to remain united and I wanted them to know how crucial the relationship between the Army Chief and the subedar-majors was in achieving that.

Subedar-majors are the backbone of every regiment. They understand their units well and keep tabs on all the soldiers, their families and what's happening in their lives. Less than six months after I became the Army Chief, I hosted a dinner in their honour on 4 March 2007. Meeting them was a good opportunity to convey the message of Army unity.

I thanked them all for sacrificing their weekend to come to meet me. "The Chief is doing the right thing. We can't step back now," they told me. One of them was quick to add, "The Chief will retire soon and the next in line should also be able to provide unflinching leadership." Everyone present knew they were speaking for all the subedar-majors.

While the Army was collectively as strong as ever, the UML was dithering. It was unable to reach a decision at its standing committee meeting. After all, the UML is known for taking a position on any issue only after prolonged and profound discussion. Chairman Khanal, Vice-Chair Bamdev Gautam, General Secretary Ishwar Pokhrel and Secretary Yubaraj Gyawali were on Prachanda's side, while senior leaders Madhav Nepal, KP Oli, Vice-Chair Bidya Bhandari, and Secretaries Bishnu Paudel and Shankar Pokhrel were against it.

The chances of a unanimous decision from the UML were receding. Since many UML leaders were known for flip-flopping, there was no certainty they would support me. Moreover, Prachanda was a masterful player who could change the game. There were reports about Prachanda and Baburam meeting with Nepali Congress leader Sujata Koirala. Prachanda knew very well that Girija Prasad Koirala's weakness was his daughter and thought they could influence him through her. Prachanda must have thought that, if Sujata leaned towards him, then Girijia*babu*, pressured by his family, might influence the Congress party in his favour. I received unconfirmed reports about Prachanda offering Sujata the ministerial portfolio of her choice and the post of Deputy Prime Minister.

A recent statement from Sujata had hinted she was already leaning the Maoists' way. "Why is the Congress taking the Army's side instead of being there for the people? How can the party be democratic when it's supporting an Army Chief who is trying to create a rift between the parties?" she asked.

Sunday, 26 April 2009

I was working on some files at my desk when a general came in to speak to me.

"The Defence Minister has called for me. What should I do?" he asked.

"Go and hear what he has to say," I said.

"What do I tell him, sir?" he asked.

"Follow your conscience," I said, "And say whatever you think is right."

I was well-aware that the Maoists were lobbying everyone in the Army, from infantry to generals. They were doing everything they could to cosy up to people based on caste, ethnicity or language connections. When the Maoists tried to meet anyone in the Army, the soldiers would report it to their commanders and I would be informed.

I gave the same answer to everyone: "Meet them, and tell them what's in your mind."

The ulterior motive behind these meetings was to infiltrate and destroy the Army but I was confident that the Maoists would not be able to break our time-honoured unity.

What surprised me more was their effort to bring the eight generals on their side, the very officers whose extension of tenure they had asked me to justify. They had no scruples. Maoist ministers even met some of the generals privately and told them, "We wanted to extend your tenure but we couldn't do it because of your Chief."

They were trying to sow mistrust and garner support for their plan to oust me but none of it was working. They were shooting wildly, hoping that at least one of their bullets would hit the mark.

Amidst all this, I was informed that Prachanda was meeting the President, who had stood steadfastly behind the Army. The President said: "The efforts to remove the Army Chief should be constitutional and can proceed only with political consensus."

The Indian Ambassador to Nepal, Rakesh Sood, met the Prime Minister after returning from Delhi the day before but I couldn't find out what had transpired during that meeting. Nevertheless, the UML finally concluded its three-day standing committee meeting and agreed to go along with the President. They asked the Maoists not to move ahead unilaterally.

Monday, 27 April 2009

They say anything can happen overnight and sure enough in less than 24 hours the UML had changed its position and put forward a new proposal.

They proposed that the dispute be resolved by asking the Defence Minister to ask both Kul Bahadur Khadka and myself to resign. Some UML leaders apparently devised this compromise after Prachanda told them he wouldn't agree to anything that left me in office.

"Sacking the Chief of Staff has become a question of honour," Prachanda reportedly told the leaders. "I will agree to any proposal as long as Katawal is removed."

When some UML leaders came to me with this proposal I repeated my position: "I will remain as Chief until the last second of my tenure."

This new proposal from a faction in the UML must have boosted Prachanda's morale. He probably thought this tactic could bring me down. Prachanda even went to meet the ailing Girija*babu* at his residence in Maharajganj.

However, Girija*babu* reportedly wouldn't agree to talk about the Army at all on that occasion. The moment Prachanda uttered the words "Army Chief", Girija*babu* said: "Come back tomorrow and we'll talk about it then."

Tuesday, 28 April 2009

It had been 10 days since the Cabinet's decision to ask for my explanation on the three issues and support for the Army and for the Army Chief was growing as more people recognised that the Maoists wanted a one-party dictatorship. The controversy had become all-consuming and was taking up all my time.

As agreed, Prachanda went to meet Girija*babu* to talk about the Army, repeating his contention that his reputation was on the line if the Chief stayed on.

"Why meddle with the Army now?" Girija*babu* reportedly asked tersely. "This is not the time to take any decision without consensus."

When the Maoists were weak, Congress' bargaining power increased, so Sujata Koirala was delighted, thinking this was her time to get into government. Not surprisingly, her public statements continued to be influenced by that belief.

Wednesday, 29 April 2009

My morning began with exercise followed by a quick scan through the newspapers. Unfounded reports about various factions within the Army supporting either me or Kul Bahadur disturbed me that morning. Some party weeklies even had reports about the possibility of bloodshed at HQ as different factions supposedly fought for control.

This was not the first time such stories have been published to create disharmony within the Army. It happened almost every day. Girija*babu* and Dr Ram Sharan Mahat suggested releasing a joint statement from the Army HQ. I was waiting for the right time and today was the day to strike.

I planned to call a press conference that would be jointly organised by the top three officers in the Army. Since I didn't want to reveal my involvement, I asked a general to put forward the idea and say that, "In order to protect the Army's image, we need all of you to come together and deliver the same message."

Chhatra Man and I agreed to the proposal. Kul Bahadur also agreed without fuss. I immediately began working on the draft of the statement which was recorded for TV. The seating arrangement placed me at the centre with Kul Bahadur to my right and Chhatra Man to my left.

"There are no differences within the Army. We are always ready to provide support to the democratically elected government as set out in the constitution," the statement said. "The Army will always remain loyal to the constitutionally valid leadership and obey constitutionally valid orders."

We wanted to collectively express our commitment to the democratic process and the chain-of-command. The statement signed by the three of us sent the clear message that the Army was united and, as ever, loyal to the constitution.

Thursday, 30 April 2009

The Prime Minister visited the President, his fourth visit in 12 days, and reportedly informed him there was progress towards achieving political consensus to remove me from office.

It seemed the Maoists wouldn't budge from their position. They wanted to dismiss me even if the law didn't allow it and were only waiting for the right moment to pounce. That the Maoists had this attitude was becoming clear now, even to the UML, so the leaders of that party took a tougher stand. "We will resign from the coalition government if the Maoists take that decision on their own," they told me.

When the UML signalled that it wouldn't get on board, Prachanda and Baburam went all out to persuade Sujata. "If Congress joins the government under your leadership, then the positions of Deputy Prime Minister, Defence Minister and other important portfolios can be given to Congress," they told her.

These were the same people who had been vehemently opposed to giving the Home Ministry portfolio to the Congress party when the current Cabinet was formed. So it was quite a sight to see the Maoists doing a complete about-face in an attempt to appease the same party. I had already been informed about the meeting at Baluwatar where the Maoist leadership asked Sujata to convince her father to agree to my dismissal.

Despite all the running around, however, nobody was buying the Maoists' line. Sujata's support within the Congress party was running out of steam. The Maoists perceived this and came up with a new nationalistic argument: India was propping me up.

Several Maoist leaders including Dev Gurung told the press, "India is exerting pressure to prevent action being taken against the Army Chief. Our party has now decided that this is a matter of sovereignty and national pride." This, despite Mohan Baidya (Kiran), Krishna Bahadur Mahara, Netra Bikram Chand and Gurung having told me several times that they weren't in favour of interfering with the Army.

Mahara told me repeatedly: "We couldn't convince our leadership."

Friday, 1 May 2009

Uma left for Pokhara with her sister and brother-in-law who had come from the US. I didn't want to worry her with everything that was going on which would only worsen her blood pressure. I was glad she would be away from it all.

I left for HQ after seeing off Uma.

I had called in retired generals for a meeting. Many retired generals, including Chitra Bahadur (CB) Gurung, Pradip Pratap Bam Malla, Dilip Shumsher Rana and Dilip Rayamajhi, had come.

The majority view was that the Army leadership should stand by the law and the constitution at any cost.

Only Dilip Shumsher had a different view. "It would be better for you to resign," he said.

Before I could even respond, the other generals jumped in: "That is what they want to do. That is what they are looking for. But that is what is not going to happen."

Saturday, 2 May 2009

The generals and colonels stationed at Pokhara found out that Uma was visiting there.

"How come you're out and about while the Maoists are getting ready to hang the Chief?" they asked, trying to intimidate her.

Uma gave a carefree reply: "His stars are strong. He has stayed strong through so much. The Maoists can't touch him."

She told me about that conversation when I called her later that day. It was then that I realised that I was, always had been and always would be, in awe of her courage and drew so much strength from her.

The tussle between me and the Prime Minister put everything else on the back-burner, which was very frustrating. The Army administration was already bearing the brunt of it. It had hampered training and DGMO head, Gaurav Shumsher, had already briefed the Defence Minister about it, but nothing was done. I called the Prime Minister and Defence Minister, hoping to explain the situation to them over dinner but they turned the invitation down.

I wanted to change the common perception that the Army was an entity which only represented people of a certain class. As soon as I became Army Chief, I interacted with people from all walks of life to discuss various facets of the Army with them. As the crisis deepened, I intensified those interactions.

Sunday, 3 May 2009

My daughter, Nepolina, called early in the morning from America. She is even more blunt than I am, just like my father.

"How are things, *chhori*?" I asked.

"Keep on fighting, Dad" she said, "You're taking a stand on a constitutional issue."

To boost my morale she used to write emails like: "You are on the right side of history".

Her belief was that you couldn't be afraid to fight if you were a soldier. She continued on the phone: "Dad, if you're convinced you're right, don't give in."

My daughter-in-law, Sulakshana, was engaged on another front: to read emails, reply and document them, and monitor the Nepali and international media's reaction. My wife, Uma, was in Pokhara. My son, Shubhangad aka Darwin, a soldier like me, was in the Birendra Peace-Keeping Training Centre in Panchkhal. Like other majors in the Army, he was curious about what was happening. My grandchildren knew what was going on from watching TV.

"Prachanda Uncle and Sita Aunty used to come to visit daddy. They would take me on their laps. Why are you fighting now?" my grand-daughter asked. I didn't bring work-related matters home but, nonetheless, my family and the other members of the household were inevitably exposed to what was happening via the mass media.

Distracted by them, I was a bit late getting to the office although I was there by 8:30. "Sir, the Defence Secretary is on the line," a member of my staff said as soon as I arrived.

"Chief, could you come to Baluwatar?" he asked, "The Prime Minister wants to see you urgently."

"And where are you, Mr Secretary?" I asked.

"I'm also at Baluwatar," he replied. As soon as I hung up,

there was another call. A member of the Baluwatar security detail reported: "Kul Bahadur is with the Prime Minister and the Defence Minister at Baluwatar."

I understood what was going on because a Maoist Minister who wished me well had already told me to expect to be let go imminently. I was on the cusp of my final battle. It was win or lose.

From the car, I first called the President. "I think I'm being called to be sacked but there's no way I'm going to surrender, sir."

Then I informed Girija*babu* , and while negotiating Kathmandu's traffic, managed to call all the top leaders of the main parties to tell them what was going on. I also informed my foreign military and non-military friends. My message to them all was: "The Nepalese Army does not surrender. You do what you see fit."

I arrived at the Prime Minister's residence at 10 am with my security detail expecting the unexpected. I had taken Section Plus of the Special Forces with me, and at Baluwatar we had a company under the command of a colonel. In case the Maoists tried to detain me, I had a rescue plan in place.

I had told Chhatra Man from the car: "I'm off to Baluwatar. Apparently, Kul Bahadur is there as well. You handle things at Headquarters. Take command but don't make any decisive move unless you hear from me."

My aides-de-camp were not allowed to enter the Prime Minister's residence, so I left them on the lawn outside, under instruction to come in if they got a message from me to do so.

"Every 10 minutes I will appear where you can see me," I told them, "If you don't see me, inform those outside and storm the building."

At 10:15, I was taken inside. My old acquaintance, Om Sharma, who was the Prime Minister's Press Advisor, was there. "Hi, Mr Advisor how's everything?" I asked, "I hear you've called the Cabinet together to discuss Kul Bahadur. Why have you called me?"

He ordered some coffee and said, "Just give me a second."

Then he tried to rattle me: "Chief, I hear you've invested Rs 500 million in *Kantipur*. Is that true?"

"Sure. I've invested some of the money I looted from 63 banks," I replied, and he was too taken aback to respond. I remembered Prachanda's wife, Sita, once asking Uma in Shashi Bhawan: "They say you have a house in Noida. Is that true?" Before Uma could respond, I shot back: "Look for it, and if you find it, it's half yours and half mine."

My security staff informed me that at nearly 11 am Kul Bahadur left the Prime Minister's residence through a side door with an envelope in his hand. I immediately understood that Kul Bahadur had received the letter appointing him as Chief of Army Staff.

"I'm off," I said but, as I got up to go, the Defence Minister and Defence Secretary walked in. "One moment," the Defence Secretary said, stopping me.

"What?" I barked.

"You have to take this letter," he said.

"What letter?" I asked.

"A letter of gratitude on behalf of the government," he said.

"Am I a peon?" I said stiffly, "Did I come here to receive official letters?"

"You have the right not to receive the letter," the Defence Minister said, opening his mouth for the first time.

I strode off to my car. Kul Bahadur had left 15 or 20 minutes earlier, so I told the driver to use the siren and rush back to HQ. I was busy on the phone, informing the President, Girija*babu* and other top political leaders about the Maoists' action. I told them it was an unlawful decision and I was not going to relinquish my position.

"This isn't just a blow to the Nepalese Army. This is a blow to democracy," I said.

The President, Girija*babu* and others urged me strongly to hold my ground. It was clear the Maoists had taken a unilateral decision in the Council of Ministers while the UML, Sadbhawana and Forum ministers had boycotted the meeting, saying the move was unacceptable.

Kul Bahadur reached HQ just a few minutes before I did, around 11:30 am. He showed his letter of appointment, telling the Adjutant General to start the process of installing him as Chief of Staff.

But Nepal Bhushan Chand replied: "Whatever the decision, Chief Katawal's tenure is still valid until midnight."

All the PSOs were in the meeting room waiting under Chhatra Man's command when I got to the office. I made a few important calls but most of the people I called had already heard that I had been told to step down with Kul Bahadur replacing me.

I went to the PSOs and said that under no circumstances was I going to surrender. I was ready to fight anyone and was not going to bow down before a Maoist dictatorship.

"I'm not going to accept this unlawful decision," I told them. "According to both the constitution and the peace agreement a decision like this is supposed to be made by consensus. What do you think?"

The PSOs only said "Right, sir. Right, sir" but the meeting's conclusion was that whatever the legality of the government's decision, my tenure extended until midnight even if the PM's order was accepted.

I asked that Kul Bahadur be called to the meeting. He came in looking flustered and I immediately pounced on him: "Hey, Comrade, under whose orders did you go to Baluwatar?"

The man who only a short time before was boasting that he was the Chief looked wilted and scared. He replied: "The Defence Minister summoned me, sir."

"Don't you know the Army's chain of command, Mister? Who gave you the order to go there?" My voice had become louder.

"I tried to call you on your mobile many times," he said. "The Defence Minister called me repeatedly and I thought you had asked for me."

"Liar," I said.

"No, sir. No, sir," he said even more meekly.

"Go! Leave immediately! You have nothing to do here." I sent him off and then told Chhatra Man and Gaurav Shumsher not to let anyone out of HQ without my personal approval. "Everyone stays here," I said.

The DGMO immediately instructed all units across the country to be on alert. The Valley bases were asked to remain in barracks until further notice.

At 12 noon, the Defence Ministry sent a letter to HQ and I asked for a copy be faxed to the President along with a letter written to him saying that the coalition partners having withdrawn, it was only the Maoists' decision to replace me and, therefore, unconstitutional. Soon after, I got word that the Nepali Congress party's Sher Bahadur Deuba and Sushil Koirala were on their way to see the President. The UML leaders were also on their way to Sheetal Niwas. There were meetings at various levels in the rooms of the President's Office, with members of civil society and lawyers all there. It was the biggest crisis since the President was installed nine months earlier. I was getting information from there at regular intervals. The parties were worried that if the Chief of the Army Staff acquiesced to their demands, the Maoists would gobble up the country. "Katawal should remain. We shouldn't let the Maoists get away with this," was the common refrain.

I instructed all Army formations throughout the country to be on stand-by and apprised them of the situation. In response, the Maoists threatened to get their fighters out of the cantonments to install Kul Bahadur as Army Chief.

Even though the short-term plan of the Maoists was to replace me with Kul Bahadur, their long-term intention was to induct all 19,000 of their fighters into the Army and make one of them the Chief. Kul Bahadur was only a pawn.

There was no way I was going to let that happen but, as the clock ticked away, the country was sinking deeper into crisis. It was 9:30 pm and still there was no sign of a letter from the President.

The top generals met in a secret room and agreed to wait until midnight for word from the President. If nothing came, we were ready to fight back. We sent this message to the senior advisors surrounding the President.

Meanwhile, some UML leader apparently advised the President to ask both Kul Bahadur and me to step down. The UML was changing its stance by the hour and looked like it had no interest in defending democracy. We understood already that this proposal was just an exercise in face-saving for Prachanda. I sent word to the President that it was either Kul Bahadur or me: he had to choose one or the other.

A presidential advisor called to say how difficult it was to get all the parties to agree. It was looking like the matter would have to go to the courts for a decision. I told him it would be best if the President took a decision by midnight. I was livid at the cowardice shown by the parties and sent them my final word on the matter: "My legitimacy in this position ends at midnight but there is no way I'm going to surrender. Personally, however, I would prefer to avoid any unpleasantness."

Soon after at 11 pm, the President himself called me. "Do I have to put it in writing?" he asked me. "Can I not write it?"

I replied, "If it's not in writing, there will be a question of legitimacy. A letter will resolve the issue."

By then, KP Oli had got to Sheetal Niwas despite his ill health and called to say the President had decided to send the letter and to inform all the generals.

A few minutes later, a fax arrived from the President, giving continuity to my position as Chief of Army Staff. It was a clear and direct letter, just as we wanted. Soon after that, my mobile and all the landlines started ringing off the hook.

According to my watch it was 15 minutes to midnight. I showed the generals the letter and instructed them to inform all the barracks. I also gave the order that all new information should reach me first. The generals heaved sighs of relief and went to their rooms. But I wasn't sleepy and went to meet my soldiers outside in the HQ compound. Two or three of my personal security staff wanted to come with me but I told them to go and get some sleep.

The soldier on sentry duty asked me for the password, which everyone in the compound needs after 10 pm.

"Don't you recognise me?" I asked the soldier but he wouldn't let me through without the password.

It was only after I gave the password that he stood to attention.

"How are you? Sleepy?" I asked. "Do you know what's happening in the country?"

"Yes, I do, sir," he replied.

"Tell me," I said.

"We are fighting the Maoists, sir," he said.

"How do you know?"

"I have FM radio on my mobile and the commander also briefed us."

I asked him, "So, should I step down?"

"No, sir. If you order us to fight, we're ready to fight." I was uplifted by his answer.

Just then, the security commander arrived with his team. He also said: "Your stand is right, sir. There is no way we should run away from a fight."

I went to another post, then another. I had the impression these regular soldiers were more alert and committed than us generals.

At midnight, suddenly I remembered that Uma was on her way back from Pokhara. I hadn't had time to call her all day. I longed to speak to her but, by the time I rang, she was asleep.

Monday, 4 May 2009

It was already seven in the morning when I woke up. I went for a walk around HQ and got ready for work. After paying my respects to Ripumardini, I went into my office feeling enthused again.

I was feeling more energetic than ever and quickly began sorting out the files which had piled up on my desk over the previous two days. I decided to have lunch in the soldiers' mess. Nothing tastes better than *dāl bhāt* cooked in a soldiers' mess. It was also a way for me to gauge the mood of the soldiers. Officers ate at the mess only on Fridays, so the soldiers were surprised to see me there. The food tasted better when the conversation and company were so much fun.

I hadn't been home for more than 24 hours. I called Uma to ask how everyone was and told her that I wouldn't be able to return home just yet.

Then I was informed that the Western Divisional Headquarters in Pokhara hadn't passed on the President's letter.

"The letter was supposed to be sent last night. Why is it still pending?" the DGMO reminded the Western Division Chief, Shiva Ram Pradhan.

"I thought it was only for me so I didn't send it," he replied. There were also reports that he was delaying it on purpose.

Shiva Ram Pradhan was one of the generals who worked closely with the government side during the talks between the

Maoists and the government. Later there were rumours about his closeness with Maoist leader, Barshaman Pun. Girija*babu* once warned me: "Your general is with the Maoists."

Shiva Ram was the DGMO then. I took the warning seriously and transferred him from DGMO to the Inspector-General's office. But even at HQ, I got information about his Maoist connections several times. After that, we transferred him to Pokhara and the delay in sending such an important letter just confirmed our suspicions.

I had ordered concerned military units to keep a close watch on Prachanda, Maoist ministers and even Kul Bahadur. Baluwatar's security staff had informed me that Prachanda seemed to be deeply disturbed that morning. I was also getting information from other security and intelligence bodies.

Soon, we got information that Prachanda had left for Sankhu accompanied by members of the Young Communist League (YCL) along with state security units. Reports about Prachanda's resignation started swirling from about 11 am. Stepping down was his only option since the coalition partners had abandoned the government, leaving the Maoists in the minority.

I also learnt that legal experts had visited the President. As soon as the meeting ended, I got a call. "It's been decided that if the Prime Minister submits his resignation, it will be accepted immediately. He won't be asked to reconsider the decision."

That same afternoon Prime Minister Prachanda announced he was stepping down. At a press conference he condemned the Army, the President, the Parliamentary parties and international players, spewing venom against us all.

Many people thought this was a showdown between me and Prachanda and that I had prevailed. As the news of his resignation spread, I was flooded with congratulatory messages. There were people calling late into the night. Some civilian friends, citing the example of Bangladesh, even prodded me: "It's time to take over and run the country, then hold an election and hand over power."

But I had no such intentions. Instead, I tried to explain that the country would never progress if the military overstepped the bounds of democracy. I considered my continuing in office as a victory of the rule of law and democracy over one-party dictatorship.

I met with military officers until midnight. Most of them suggested we should court martial Kul Bahadur while others said his communication channels should be shut down. But I tried to explain that that wasn't necessary. "Just because he made some unwise choices doesn't mean we do the same," I said.

Having to spend the night at HQ again, I couldn't sleep for a while. Recent events kept playing in my mind over and over again. I was furious that the Maoists had played the nationalism card to try to delude people when they couldn't sack me. Even after the resignation, the Maoists tried to say I was only allowed to continue as Chief because of interference by "foreign lords". They even threatened to revolt to defend Nepal's "national sovereignty".

Tuesday, 5 May 2009

I had a meeting with the President and also talked to leaders from the political parties. They were already preparing to form a new coalition government and Madhav Nepal was put forward as the new Prime Minister.

There was immense pressure to discipline Kul Bahadur but I didn't want to do anything impulsively. I called foreign military attaches for a meeting during which the DMI explained the sequence of events leading up to the President's letter. They all appreciated the Army's stand. I also received a call from former Army Chief Satchit Shumsher's wife who congratulated me. "Had the Chief been alive, he would have garlanded you," she said. The late Satchit Shumsher was one of my favourite generals and it made me very emotional to think of him.

Former Chiefs Prajwalla Shumsher Rana and Pyar Jung Thapa had openly backed the Army's stand. All along, their wives had also given support to Uma.

They say history is written by the victors. I wasn't the victor. The President had simply stood his ground and made a decision based on the constitution and the law. Nevertheless, there were many people who tried to get closer to me by showering me with congratulations, the kind who would have said exactly the same things to Kul Bahadur had he become Chief. These were opportunists, only interested in position and prestige and not bothered at all about justice.

Even though things were returning to normal, I decided to stay at HQ for a little while longer.

Wednesday, 6 May 2009

All the regional divisional host formations and the units and sub-units, as well as their commanders, sent the same message: "Kul Bahadur should face court martial."

But I maintained my stance and tried to explain this to the PSOs and the legal department. I had to defend Kul Bahadur because it wouldn't have been wise to punish the person who had got entangled in this row.

I returned to Shashi Bhawan after three nights. My children were waiting near the gate. Uma and my daughter-in-law came up to me but didn't ask me anything about what had happened. I didn't feel it necessary to bring it up either. I knew they must have heard about it on the news and that was enough for the moment.

I was at complete peace while lying in my bed that night. I was confident the Maoists would not have a chance to meddle in the affairs of the Nepalese Army ever again. I closed my eyes but old memories came flooding in and kept me from sleeping. I had grown up with a reputation for audaciousness. I saw myself as a small boy, holding on to my trousers, following King Mahendra from Okhaldhunga to be a "big man".

Although I don't believe I did anything extraordinary, there are a lot of people who think the 16-day confrontation and the victory over the Maoists was a pivotal moment in Nepal's recent history.

One

He Will Ride A Horse Someday

"Son, you have to become a big man some day and ride a horse. It doesn't matter if you're a bandit, so long as you're the chief."

My mother harboured these dreams for me from the time I was four or five years old and she passed them on to me. Since I was the youngest, I was my mother's favourite. Maybe that was why she had so much faith in me. "You have to uphold the family name, dear," she always said.

Although I didn't understand what her words meant, I always nodded dutifully so I could sneak out of the house as soon as I could. But she wouldn't let me go so easily. She hugged me tightly, kissed my cheeks and said, "My *kānchhā* is blessed. He has cheated death so he'll surely become a big man, a chief, a government officer."

There was a story behind my mother always saying I was a survivor. When I was two years old and just a toddler, I had wandered into the cowshed on my own. There was a particular cow there with sharp horns and an infamously bad temper. Everyone in my village was aware of its unpredictable nature and the fact that it had attacked and injured our neighbours' livestock.

When my mother returned in the evening and didn't see me, the whole family began a frantic search. Luckily someone had seen me going into the cowshed. But that worried my mother even more. She thought the crazy cow must have crushed me to death. Everyone rushed to the cowshed only to find me happily playing beside the cow. Apparently the hated and feared animal was treating me as tenderly as it would its own calf.

Then, as a young boy I also had measles, which in Nepal can be fatal in children. Hearing my mother's stories was always a delight. I felt really fortunate to have a mother like I did.

I was born in Nisankhe in Taluwa Dharapani of eastern Nepal, which now lies in Okhaldhungha district, on 12 December 1948. Every December my mother would remind me of my age by counting the years on her fingers.

Our family had a long history of being in the military. Everyone from my great-great-grandfather to my father had been in the Army. In fact, nine generations had given their blood, sweat and youth to the Nepalese Army. My father, Khadga Dhwoj, was a sergeant, my grandfather, Dharma Dhwoj, was a lieutenant, and my great-grandfather, Shovit Man, was a warrant officer second class. We are the descendants of Dev Raj Katawal, one of Prithvi Narayan Shah's generals, who was killed during the siege of Kathmandu in 1767.

Prithvi Narayan's force was hiding in Chandragiri. Before attacking Kathmandu, he sent Dev Raj as a spy. However, Dev Raj was captured and executed in Shobhabhagwati. Another *sipahi* named Pandey, who was with Dev Raj, apparently escaped.

After that, Prithvi Narayan Shah appointed Dev Raj's descendents to his close circle. It's said that our ancestors were given responsibility for all the forts and the arsenals of every state that Prithvi Narayan conquered during his unification campaign. We were probably given that responsibility because we had proved our loyalty to king and country.

Back then, the people who protected a *kot* (fort) were called "*kotwal*". Our ancestors won the king's confidence and started writing their surname "Kotwal" which was subsequently modified until it became "Katuwal" and eventually "Katawal" which is our surname today.

During unification, our ancestors moved eastwards from Gorkha to Chyanam in Okhaldhunga and then to Nisankhe. Although our ancestors continued to choose military careers with intent to serve the King, they didn't rise up through the ranks. Instead, the career path of successive generations of Katawals in the military dipped lower and lower. My grandfather fared better than his father but my father had to console himself with a lower rank.

By the time my father joined the Army, our financial situation had also gone downhill. It wasn't just the ranks that got lower. Everything from our houses, fields, gold, utensils and cattle were reduced. Father wasn't able to stick with the Army for very long. After he lost his job, it was a struggle for him to raise his family.

"Your father is too bold for his own good," my mother used to complain.

Father had apparently become a sergeant at a very young age, thanks to my grandfather's connections. After being appointed, he was supposed to offer a coin to the general as a sign of gratitude. He went to the Palace dressed in his best *daurā suruwāl*. The general looked him up and down while he was still saluting. Later, the general angrily said to my grandfather,

"Hey, Lieutenant, your son came here all dressed up. Tell him a commoner shouldn't try to emulate us."

"Of course, Your Royal Highness," my grandfather said, saluting the general.

"I crawled to the Rana government to make you a sergeant," Grandfather scolded my father, "You'll be in trouble if you don't behave yourself."

Father was once assigned to one of the general's tours in Chautara in Sindhupalchok district. Back then only high ranking Ranas could be generals. Wherever they walked, they were accompanied by aides-de-camp. The *rani sahib*, the general's wife, had also accompanied him on the tour. This one was hoity-toity apparently and treated the soldiers like slaves. Even the soldiers and other workers under my father's command weren't spared. After a while, my father lost patience. "They joined the Army to serve the king, not you," he was audacious enough to tell her. "It's not reasonable for you to treat people as you please." The consequences of arguing with the *rani sahib*, of course, could have been serious. He could have been executed, thrown into prison or sent into exile.

Luckily the *rani sahib* chose to be kind. Father only lost his job and we lost everything with it. "You probably have a wife and children," the general said, "So I will spare your life."

Until then we lived in Asan Bahal in Kathmandu and apparently had a house there built by our grandfather. After the government took all our assets, Father had to return to Okhaldhunga. I only have a distant memory of him. He used to help the villagers with letters, agreements and other written documents. Our verandah was always filled with people queuing up to seek his help.

Father never expected anything from the villagers in return for his help but, nonetheless, they used to give whatever they could as payment, including milk, curd, ghee and vegetables. I used to be furious with people who brought pumpkin, gourd and other vegetables and hated it when mother prepared them for meals. While my brother and sister would clean their plates, I would make a grumpy face and refuse to eat.

"We have to fill our stomachs even if you don't like what's on offer, son," my mother used to say in a kind tone, tousling my hair playfully.

I hated vegetables so much that I even cut them out of our garden. Luckily, my mother and sister-in-law never found out about my antics.

"Oh no! The pests have ruined the pumpkin and gourd," my mother used to say, "How will I feed the family now?"

While my mother worried, I would just sit there feeling smug. That's how much I hated vegetables as a boy. I was picky about food from a very young age. I had to have pickles with every meal. My favourite was crushed tomatoes, even if the tomatoes were uncooked. I had such a taste for good food that the older women in the neighbourhood used to say I would be a lucky man when I grew up.

As long as my father was alive we didn't have to worry much. We never had to skip meals and almost always got a set of new clothes every year. During festivals we had plenty of meat to feast on.

Father passed away before I turned six. We were five siblings, each one a year apart. All the responsibilities now shifted to my mother's shoulders. Before she could even complete mourning my father, she was burdened with the responsibility of looking after us and running the household. She was born and raised in a wealthy family. Losing her husband and having to deal with the already shaky financial situation came as an unexpected blow.

Ainselukharka was one of Okhaldhunga's administrative units and my mother's parents lived there. It's now located in Khotang district. My maternal grandfather was a farmer and all my maternal uncles were non-gazetted officers in the government. They made a comfortable living from their jobs.

My mother was a Newar and eloped with my father when he was posted in Ainselukharka. Her family shunned her for years for eloping with a Chhetri and vowed never to see her again. She wasn't welcome in her family for many years. When my father died, she couldn't expect her family to share her sorrow at his passing. She would break down sometimes and then pick herself up. Despite the emotional turmoil and the added responsibilities, she did everything she could to ensure we had a comfortable childhood.

"If you work hard, things will turn around for sure, son," Mother used to say. My elder brothers had no interest in studying but my mother wanted me to study.

"The astrologer says Rookmangud will uphold the family name and be recognised by all," my mother liked to say, "Your stars are strong. You have to be a big man, my son."

The astrologer's words lifted my mother's spirits and she in turn lifted mine.

After hearing my mother's constant prayers for my future, the idea of becoming a "big man" started appealing to me as well. The subedar, lieutenant, captain, government officer, village chief and *khardār* were the big people I saw around me. From a very young age I understood that I had to study to become like those people. The *gurukul* tradition hadn't died out around my village yet. Since I couldn't afford formal education, I started going to a *guru* to study.

I can't recall his real name but everyone used to call him "Pokharel *guru*". I used to tag along with the older students and walk for almost an hour to reach his place. The classroom resembled an abandoned shed. We used to pay our respect to him and offer rice, lentils, vegetables or anything we could manage. But I don't remember him ever complaining about what we offered. We used to make a slate of mud and scratch letters into it with a twig. When we ran out of space, we just erased everything and started again. It was under the *guru*'s watchful eye that I learnt to write the alphabet with a twig in the mud. Some of the children from well-to-do families would bring their wood-framed slates but they were few.

Later, we were taught by Thir Prasad Koirala from Kathmandu. Like Pokharel *guru*, he too didn't have a prescribed curriculum. He would make us memorise multiplication table, verses from *Rāmāyana* , *Mahābhārata* and *Chandi*, rules of Sanskrit grammar from *Kaumudi* and stanzas from Sanskrit thesauraus *Amarakosha* among others. Back then, if someone could recite the verses of the *Mahābhārata* and write a receipt he was considered literate.

I really enjoyed the *shlokas* and *Swasthāni* stories. In two years I had learnt to recite the Swasthani. People from all over the village would gather at our home to hear the stories. My mother was happiest when she saw me recite the *Swasthāni*, *Rāmāyana* and *Mahābhārata*. Everyone was amazed to see a young boy recite the *shlokas* so fluently. There were many people who were so impressed that they even brought in marriage proposals for their daughters.

"Why force a wife on a seven year old?" my mother would tell them, politely declining the marriage proposals.

I had already become a celebrity at a young age in Nisankhe. Unlike most of my fellow students, I didn't prioritise working in the fields or herding cattle ahead of my studies. During the paddy planting season, the classroom used to be empty, while in winters we had almost 50 students. But there were times when I, too, was pressured to work in the fields. My mother never forced me but my brothers would try to send me off with the livestock every chance they got.

"I have to study," I used to plead, and cry when they told me to tend to the livestock. But my brothers would insist. Later, I had a clever idea of how I could strike a balance between my studies and my chores. Every morning I used to leave home with the goat but then I would leave it to graze in fields nearby and run off to my class.

This trick worked well until one blistering April afternoon in maybe 1956. As usual, I left the goat in a field and went off to my class. The greedy goat entered the neighbour's maize field and ate the crop.

There was huge uproar in the village. Our family had to pay compensation for the loss and when I reached home that day my brothers were waiting for me. They tied me upside down on a pole and thrashed me with a cane. They said that was the end of my studies and kept beating me until I was black and blue. Every time I was spanked, I would scream, "I will still study."

I had never seen a notebook before.

After using sticks for two years, I desperately wanted to write on paper. I begged and cried for my mother, brothers and relatives to buy me Nepali handmade paper. When I was finally able to write on paper, I felt like I owned the world.

I used to collect soot from the lamp on tin sheets and mix it with water to make my own ink. A piece of sharpened bamboo worked as a pen. I used to dip it in the soot ink and write on my new paper.

Koirala *guru* was impressed by my enthusiasm. "He would do very well if he was sent to study in Kathmandu," he used to say. My mother was encouraged and agreed to send me to the district headquarters.

Bhupendra *dai* was employed at *Goswara*, the government office, in Okhaldhunga as a 'writer'. He had returned from the Indian Army and was the most well-informed person in our village. When he visited home from the headquarters he used to teach us the English alphabet. Even he was amazed by my passion for learning. Mother convinced Bhupendra *dai* to be my guardian.

One winter afternoon, she stuffed my clothes into a tattered bag. With eyes full of tears she wished me luck and sent me off to Okhaldhunga Bazaar. I followed Bhupendra *dai* toward an unknown future.

In the town, I was as free as a bird. I was able to devour books without ever worrying about the fields and animals. *Dai* also taught me English and I could soon read and write the English alphabet.

For someone who had never stepped outside the village, reaching Okhaldhunga Bazaar was like being a frog in the well that had embarked on a round-the-world trip. I would either be buried in books or stroll around town.

It was there that I first saw a torch light. Carrying a device that could brighten up even the darkest of nights felt like holding the moon in my hand. I was so amused by the torch that I would wait for the night just so I could walk outside lighting up the place with it.

What made me even happier was being able to write effortlessly with a fountain pen. I was on top of the world when walking around with my notebook, torch, fountain pen and books in the same tattered bag that I had brought from my village. I used to think very highly of myself, as if I were a true scholar.

Sometimes I didn't have the patience to wait for the night so I would close all the windows and doors to try to create darkness. When that didn't help, I would drape the mattress and blankets over the bedframe, sneak under it and light up the torch in the pitch dark underneath. I used to imagine how easy life would be if it resembled the torch light game: switching between darkness and light whenever we wanted.

Since this was the first time I'd ever left my village, I was homesick and missed my mother terribly in the first week. I used to think how much fun it would be if I could teleport back and forth between my village and town with the click of a button, just like the button on the torch.

I couldn't share my misery with Bhupendra *dai* but he probably figured it out through my body language. "Let's go home," he suddenly said one Friday.

By the time we reached home it was already late in the evening and it was difficult recognising people by the flicker of the oil lamps.

Mother was in the kitchen making *chapatis*. When I saw her from the door, the fire illuminated her face like the sun. I bowed my head in respect.

"Oh, *kānchho* is here! How's Okhaldhunga?" she asked.

"It's fun," I said.

"What do you mean by fun?" she asked, smiling.

"Well, there are big houses where the important people live. The roads are huge and the bazaar's exciting." I told her everything in one breath.

"How can the bazaar be fun when you don't have any money?" she teased me.

"They bought me everything – a notebook, a torch and shoes." I showed her my new possessions. I didn't want the shoes to get dirty so I carried them in my bag instead of wearing them.

"Leave them. I'll look at them tomorrow," she said, looking pleased. Before sleeping I went on and on about our landlady. "She's very fond of me. She gives us good food and encourages us to study," I said.

Next day I met all my friends. I told them all about Okhaldhunga while they listened in admiration. I showed them each item from my bag. They were amazed by the torch and wanted to turn it on but I was mean and didn't let them. "No. You might break it," I said.

When they persisted I gave in. "Just once." I pushed the torch light towards them. One of them switched it on but nothing seemed to happen.

I was puzzled. I turned it on and off, looked at it from top to bottom and finally understood the problem. I took all of them to a narrow dark passage and then switched it on. They all looked stunned. They had never seen anything like it.

"Even the king probably doesn't have a light like that," one of them said.

Once before I had stolen a five paisa coin intending to go to Kathmandu (which we called Nepal) accompanied by one of my lieutenants called Kale. But we were caught after only one night in a relative's house and returned home.

Okhaldhunga Bazaar was abuzz with excitement about King Mahendra's forthcoming tour of the east. Since my cousins were government officials there, they were bustling around day and night preparing for the visit. I had learnt from the *Rāmāyana* and *Mahābhārata* about how powerful kings were.

As the date of the visit drew nearer, the excitement became more palpable. I found out through my cousins that the King would spend a night in Okhaldhunga. I was intrigued by the tents and barricades set up at Tundikhel, the parade ground, a few days before his arrival.

"Ma, they've built such a nice house made out of cloth at Tundilkhel." I used to report every single detail about the preparations to our landlady.

Everyone, from elderly people to children, could only talk about the King and how excited they were to be seeing him. The countdown for the visit had begun and everyone kept track of the days remaining. No one was allowed to go near the area where the King was scheduled to stay. But I had already made up my mind. I was going to see the King at any cost.

"We'll have to travel for few days to go to receive the King," Balaram *dai* said.

He was a clerk at the Okhaldhunga court. Although Balaram *dai* and Bhupendra *dai* were my cousins, they loved me like brothers.

I was listening intently now.

"I'll go with you," I said excitedly.

"You're too young to tag along with us," Balaram scolded, "You can see the King when he comes here to Okhaldhunga."

I was grumbling inside but didn't utter a word.

King Mahendra arrived on the scheduled date. We climbed up the trees around Tundikhel to catch a glimpse of him. At least five children were hanging off each branch, waiting to see the King.

Finally he emerged, riding a horse with a row of soldiers and aides behind him. It felt like we were seeing God. Unlike in his portraits, he didn't have a crown and his clothes weren't embellished with jewels and gemstones but even from a distance we could see his fit body and glowing face. He was wearing sunglasses and a Gorkha hat. There was a huge crowd near the ground, made up of people who looked rich, well-fed and well-dressed.

"Your Majesty, Your Majesty…" they were all saying. I was dangling from the tree and I, too, bowed my head to him from up there.

But catching a glimpse of the King wasn't enough. I wanted to meet him in person. That wasn't easy since there were a lot of people who had been registering their names to meet him. I had seen people pouring in at the office of *Badā Hākim* Yuddha Bahadur Bista, the governor of the region, asking him to arrange a time for them to see the King. If it was so difficult for the district's big shots, it would be impossible for me. When I told my friends about it everyone mocked me. But I didn't give up hope.

I walked straight towards the camp. As I came closer I grew more nervous. The house set up there was decorated like a Palace, just like something I had read about in the *Mahābhārata* and *Rāmāyana*. The camp was completely lit up. And now I couldn't contain my desire to meet the King any longer.

I began pleading with the *Badā Hākim*'s assistants to let me meet the King. They teased me and laughed. People who met the King walked out of the camp looking excited while others waited patiently outside for their turn.

The assistants had promised to let me into the King's receiving room later that night but, after I had waited for hours, they showed me the exit, saying, "Sorry. You can't meet him. Now get going."

I returned home disappointed. I told my brothers everything that night. They scolded me, "Why do you need to meet him?"

The whole night I kept thinking about different ways to meet the King. My elder cousin had mentioned that the King would leave for Rumjatar after one night in Okhaldhunga.

The next morning I got up early and wore my best *daurā suruwāl* and the red shoes that *Dai* had bought for me. I completed my look with a cap covering my long ponytail. Finally, I carried that same bag from the village with my notebook, pen and torch.

The King had already left Okhaldhunga and Balaram *dai* was in the procession. I followed them. They stopped at Rumjatar that day and people carrying Rumjatar's famous woollen blankets were in a queue to meet the King and present them to him.

The next destination was Rabuwa which lies on the banks of the Dudhkoshi, bordering Okhaldhunga and Khotang. I tried again to meet the King but my plans were foiled again.

I had seen a holy man in Okhaldhunga who seemed to be walking with the King's escorts. I greeted him.

"*Bābā*, I hope to meet the King," I said.

He gave me his blessings and put a *tikā* on my forehead.

Balaram *dai* had said that my maternal uncle, Ganesh Bahadur Rajbhandari, was among the King's escorts. I thought perhaps he could help me.

Since my mother had eloped, her relations with her family had soured. Half of her family was in Ainselukharka and the other half in Kathmandu. My uncle was travelling with the royal entourage because he was an aide to Chuda Bikram Shah, Queen Ratna's maternal uncle.

"Namaste, Uncle," Balaram *dai* had taken me to meet my uncle, Ganesh Bahadur. "This is Rookmangud, your nephew."

I greeted him. He looked strong, dressed in a knee-length top and trousers. Although we were meeting for the first time, he was neither affectionate nor polite.

"Why are you here?" he asked.

"He's very clever, Uncle, and is hell-bent on meeting the King," *Dai* said.

Uncle didn't reply. He only nodded his head.

Balram *dai* presented my request again but my uncle said, "I can't put forward an eight year old boy to meet the King." I was disappointed.

The King's entourage moved on and I followed them with my tattered old bag. Some VIPs were on horseback, and before this I had only seen my stepuncle and some local VIPs from the district headquarters on horses.

My stepuncle worked for the land revenue office. To stay in his good books, all the villagers used to bring him bananas, curd, ghee and milk. During Dasain, people would even present him with goats. But we were fighting a property case against his family, so we weren't very close.

It was his grandson who mostly boasted about the horse. He was around my age and every time his grandfather went away, he would ride around on the horse with a helper behind him. "I rode a horse. You guys climb the roof now," he would taunt us.

After seeing my stepuncle and his grandson showing off on their horse, I too began harbouring dreams of riding a horse one day.

It was only when I followed the guards that I realised how my mother's dreams for me were anything but ordinary. People who rode horses were, indeed, big shots. But even after three days I hadn't met the King.

Meeting the King

The royal entourage was making its third stop since I left Okhaldhunga on my quest to meet the King.

The entourage halted at Buipa that night. I had carefully studied the camps over the last three days and knew everything about how they were guarded, when people went in to meet the King and other details. Based on this, I had figured out a way to bypass the guards and sneak in.

It was already dark. The guards were stationed all around the tent and the whole camp was brightly lit. There were four-foot high bamboo barricades outside the tent that led to a corridor. I could hide in the shadows and sneak up this path.

Somebody had just returned after meeting the King. Before

the next person in line could enter, I sneaked in. The King was surrounded by about a dozen people. He was in military uniform, wearing woollen trousers, a vest and the Gorkha hat.

Suddenly I felt someone grab me by my neck. They were going to throw me out until a voice said "Leave him". I couldn't figure out whether it was the King himself who had spoken or someone else in the group.

There were a lot of folding chairs. King Mahendra was seated on one of them atop a raised platform in the centre. Minister Gunja Man Singh, Army Chief Toran Shumsher Rana, Aide-de–Camp (ADC) Nara Shumsher Rana, the *Badā Hākim* and some other people were seated around him.

Before the King could say anything I started reciting Madhav Ghimire's popular poem about love for the Motherland: *"Gāunchha geeta Nepāli, jyoti ko pankha uchāli, jaya jaya hey Nepāl, sundara shānta vishāl."*

King Mahendra looked impressed. He beckoned me closer and asked my name. This was yet another chance to show off my public speaking skills.

"On the 26 of Mangsir in the year 2005,

I was born on a Wednesday to the Katawal clan.

Taluwa Dharapani village Shree Purwa 3 is my birthplace,

They named me Rookmangud and my surname is Katawal."

The King smiled.

"What do you want? Why have you come here?" he asked.

I wasn't there to ask for anything but the words "I want to study" just slipped out of my mouth.

He asked, "Where do you want to study?"

"I want to study in Kathmandu," I replied.

The King discussed it with the people around him for a while.

"Take this boy to Kathmandu," he ordered.

They asked me my name and address again. After that, the Badā Hākim was ordered to inform my family.

After the King gave his orders, I was taken to the Army Chief's tent. The energetic young lad who took me there was the Chief's ADC, Lieutenant Ambika Prasad Sharma.

I was fed at the Army Chief's mess where I ate rice, lentils, vegetables, meat, fruits and curd. Never in my life had I seen so much food. They used to say that the King's meals were sumptuous and it felt like I was being served a royal banquet. I was asked to sleep in Ambika Sharma's tent that night.

What started out as a lark had now become reality. I had to leave my mother for real. My siblings, the friends I played with, the village and the forests were suddenly going to be far away. The grief of parting from my loved ones was counterbalanced by my hopes of becoming a "big man" after going to the capital.

My heart and legs felt heavy but my head told me to move forward. Teachers used to say that we have to leave our homes after the *bratabandha,* the coming of age ceremony when we turn eight, and this had become a reality in my life. I was actually leaving my home at the age of eight, in search of education.

The next morning we woke up early and headed further east. Everyone used to tease me because I was the youngest there but I was neither shy nor afraid of anyone. I spoke confidently which helped me mingle easily with the strangers in the entourage.

The next stop was Bhojpur. The King and his ADCs would be the last to leave on each leg of the journey. The rest of the entourage would go ahead and they would slowly follow on horseback.

When we reached Bhojpur, more than 40 tents were already set up at the camp. I was excited to be staying in such a lively place. Army Chief Toran Shumsher and his aides arrived shortly after us. He was corpulent and had a chubby face. A few orderlies were needed to help him get on and off his horse.

The Army was ready to welcome the King when he entered Tundikhel. The commander of the guard thought the big fat Army Chief marching towards them was the King so he immediately gave orders for the ceremonial welcome. The Army Chief tried to stop them but the guards didn't understand his signal and fired the 31 gun salute that was meant for the King. The Chief was visibly worried. His face was bright red. He was still shouting at the commander of the guard when the King entered the arena and once again the 31 gun salute was fired.

I used to note down everything I saw each day in the notebook my cousin had given me. I didn't want to run out of pages so I had to be frugal. The King found out about my daily notes and summoned me to his tent. It looked exactly the same with the folding chairs and the King surrounded by the same faces and maybe a few distinguished locals.

"What did you see today?" the King asked.

"I have it in my notes," I said.

"Let's hear it," he said.

I had struggled writing four paragraphs that day but I recited them to the tune of the *Rāmāyana* . The next morning I was told that the King had ordered me to recite my daily notes to him each evening. I was overjoyed.

I was really excited to be meeting the King every day. On the second day of the Bhojpur visit, there were a lot of sweet delicacies for us. The head cook was Pannalal who also worked at Narayanhiti Palace. He was very fond of me and let me take extra helpings.

Apparently, a Damai girl had also joined the group. We heard that some people made a sarcastic song about it in Bhojpur, saying Mahendra took away a Dalit girl.

We left for Dhankuta, walking up steep trails. Everyone from soldiers to officers would joke with me on the way.

"Hey, kid, let's hear what you've written," they'd say.

"Why should I let you hear something that I've written for the King?" I would snap back.

It was late in the evening but I hadn't written anything yet. I decided to write a poem about the holy man who had come along with us.

The King laughed out loud when I recited my verse that evening.

I enjoyed Dhankuta a lot. It was crowded with village chiefs and local government officials. They were continually jostling each other to offer the King rice, vegetables, goats and chickens. It was as if they were queuing up to give offerings to a god. Many of them believed it was a good omen if the King ate what they had offered.

During the same trip, the King laid the foundation stone for a college in Dhankuta. I was learning the nuances of the language used to address royals. My teachers were soldiers in the troop who taught me the proper words to show respect to the King and other members of the royal family whenever I wrote or spoke to them.

It was already dark by the time we reached Dharan. I had heard that a vehicle would be sent for the King. Just then I saw a big metal box with two bright eyes peeping through the darkness and inching towards us. That was the first time I had ever seen a motor vehicle.

We came across a huge tiger which was sleeping on the road we were supposed to cross. Despite all the noise, the tiger refused to budge. The soldiers were about to shoot the animal but the King told them not to do so, instead, they drove it away with burning branches.

Dharan was a big town and we stayed there for two days. The King was busier than ever. There were visitors queuing up all day. He also went on a hunting trip so I couldn't perform the evening ritual of reading to him from my notes.

"The King killed a wild boar with one shot," one eyewitness told us. "Another shot and a wild buffalo fell to the ground."

We parted ways with the King, Minister, Army Chief and other senior officers at Dharan. We didn't have to walk from Dharan to Biratnagar because we were going to take a lorry. I was curious to see what a lorry looked like. I had heard that it carried people on it but I wasn't able to picture it in my head.

We heard a loud roar. The noise got louder and all the people waiting for the lorry were craning their necks. A metal house on wheels appeared from around a bend and rolled towards us. It had a huge trunk at the front, an open space like a verandah at the back and big round tyres on its four legs.

Some soldiers hopped on to the roof and carried me with them. Within a few minutes, the lorry was racing through the forest. A man was seated in the front with a round ring like a *nānglo* to steer the bus. Soon I was nauseous. But I kept my eyes on the driver and soon figured out how he was controlling the vehicle. The metal stick beside the driver was just as important as the ring.

When I think about it now, the road was probably unpaved. Back then, what would I have known about it since I had never seen a paved road before? The lorry zigzagged through the dense forest. The faster it went, the more excited I got. Since we were sitting outside the cabin we were covered in dust, even on our eye lashes.

I got bored looking at the forest all the time, so I watched the driver intently. I looked at him closely and realised that his two legs were just as busy as his hands and eyes. It was a lot for one person to do, which I thought was amazing. He was now my superhero. If my mother had seen the lorry, she probably would have said she wanted her son to drive it someday.

"I will ride a motor vehicle not a horse," I told myself. "After I complete my studies in Kathmandu, I will drive a car."

Before I could get enough of it, the driver had brought us to Biratnagar which was an industrial town. From there we went across the border to Jogbani in India. For a village boy from the hills, everything was exciting.

We had to travel via India by train to reach the road to Kathmandu. We heard the shrieking noise of the locomotive even before we saw it. It sounded like a conch shell being blown. It kept getting shriller as it got closer. After a while we heard a loud rattling noise and saw some light. Then a monster approached us from the darkness, just like in stories. It was shaped like a python and chugged along the tracks to stop in front of us at the platform.

The station was swarming with people. There were a lot of people in red shirts with red turbans on their heads. The carriages looked like houses on wheels. They were longer than I could have imagined: like more than 50 buses in a row.

The massive train waited at the platform while people jostled to get in and out of it. Some were running to get on the train with their luggage on their heads while others were throwing their belongings out of the windows onto the platform and it looked like a fight would break out at any time. It was chaotic and no one cared about the elderly, children and women.

While others were having a tough time catching the train, the coolies were gliding past everyone, even with several pieces of luggage balanced on their heads and in their hands. They looked like circus performers. Even the passengers without any luggage had a hard time keeping up with them.

After all the chaos we finally got on. I don't remember how long it took us to reach Raxaul. It might have been a day or more. The soldiers bought me plenty of food along the way. Raxaul was just as chaotic as Jogbani. I remember seeing women running after the train with their luggage in one hand and a baby in the other and that reminded me of Jogbani.

There was a train from Raxaul to Amlekhganj in Nepal as well. While the train in India galloped like a horse, this one moved like a buffalo. Bhupendra *dai* had never told me there were trains in Nepal. This one seemed somewhat smaller and shorter than the one in India.

We passed Birganj on the way. There were scattered settlements on both sides of the railway tracks. The houses were made of mud and bamboo. The Tarai settlements there looked visibly dirty.

We passed through dense forests with big sal trees after we crossed into Jitpur. The soldiers were talking about wild animals in the jungle when we stopped in the middle of the forest after a few hours. There was a small hut covered with few tin sheets. That was Amlekhganj station.

The railway tracks built by India during the Rana regime have long since gone but the remains of the tracks around Ghantaghar in Birganj, Jitpur and Amlekhganj still bring back memories of that train ride 60 years ago.

"Hey, kid, have some lassi." One of the soldiers offered me a big glass.

That was the first time I had ever had lassi which tasted like a thick mixture of yoghurt and sugar. It was also the first time I'd seen such a huge glass. After that we boarded another lorry to travel from Amlekhgunj to Bhimphedi along Nepal's oldest road built during Chandra Shumsher's era. By the time we reached the end of the road in Bhimphedi, it was already dark.

We left early next morning. It was an uphill walk all the way from Bhimphedi to Kathmandu. On the way I asked old people how far "Nepal" was. "When we were young we used to leave early and make it there before the cannon was fired at Tundikhel," they said. I also saw the ropeway in Bhirlung, Chisapani, where the *Badā Hākim* lived. There was a checkpoint with soldiers in black uniforms.

We had to cross Chandragiri Pass to enter the Kathmandu Valley. It was already dark by the time we reached the top. All of us were drenched in sweat so we stopped for a while. The breeze on the hilltop cooled us off but after a while it got so chilly that I felt like someone had poured cold water on me.

I saw patches of bright lights twinkling down below. While some places gave off a dazzling glow others looked pitch dark as if they were behind a cloud that shielded the stars. Both the sky above and the ground below had specks of light. What a strange place Kathmandu was going to be.

"So that's Kathmadu. There's Patan and that's Bhaktapur over there." The soldiers pointed out the clusters of light below.

Back in my village we used to be delighted by the glow of an oil lamp. The well-off families used bigger lamps. After being part of the King's procession even the kerosene lamps didn't seem strange. But I wondered what exuded such dazzling brightness in the Valley below. I asked the soldiers.

"You're lucky that you're getting to see electricity when you're still so young," they said.

We descended towards Thankot in pitch darkness. My legs were starting to give way. From Thankot there were motor vehicles heading towards the city. All of us squeezed into a lorry which dropped us somewhere in town after almost an hour.

I was tired after such a long journey. Although I missed being so far from my mother, I was overjoyed about being in "Nepal". The King had taken me in so I wasn't afraid.

My hopes of being able to study further were getting stronger.

The huge house belonged to Army Chief Toran Shumsher. He had been assigned to look after me in Bhojpur so I was now his responsibility. I had heard as I travelled to Kathmandu that the Army Chief was the most powerful person in the country after the King.

I remembered how he had berated the Minister and other dignitaries during the visit in to the east. "We don't need any ministers. I can handle all the King's travel," he had once said angrily in Bhojpur.

So my first stay in Kathmandu was at the powerful Army Chief's home which was Toran Bhawan in Naxal. Everything about it, from its size to its decorations, was lavish. Back then the Army Chief didn't have a government residence. It was only during Chief Singha Bahadur Basnyat's tenure that Shashi Bhawan became the official residence of the Chief of Staff.

There were other children who, like me, had been brought to Kathmandu as a result of the King's tour. I met two of them at Toran Bhawan. I hadn't seen them on the way. They were probably with a different group. One of them was Ganesh Bahadur from the neighbouring district of Kavrepalanchok and other one was the Damai girl from Bhojpur.

The good food during the trip had spoilt me and I didn't like the food at Toran Bhawan. The rice was bland and smelly. Ganesh and the girl from Bhojpur felt the same way.

At my village I had never heard or seen, let alone tasted, *usinā chāmal* (parboiled rice). We were being fed at the infantry men's kitchen where they received parboiled rice as part of their rations. I couldn't eat a single bite for two days. We were only served one ladle of vegetables on a metal plate. The lentils were sometimes as thin as water and sometimes too coarse to swallow.

What a mistake coming here was, I thought. Everyone mistreated us and even the infantry men shouted at us. I even thought of running away but where could I run to?

The Army Chief found out about our problems. He was worried about getting into trouble because we were there on the King's orders. "Let them eat from my kitchen," he said.

We started eating well again. We were given breakfast, two additional meals and evening snacks. With so much to choose from, everyday was like Dasain.

I learnt a lot of new words for formal greetings there. Until then I didn't know the King was called *buwā sarkār* and the Queen *muwā sarkār*. After hearing others use the respectful words to address the royals, they no longer sounded strange. When he came home from the office, the Chief used to call us to his room and ask how we were getting on and whether we liked the food.

Every once in a while I would wonder if I really was on the path to becoming a big man.

Two

Student Life

Admission to Pharping Boarding School

Pharping Boarding School was established in 1951. The principal, Satyanarayan Bahadur Shrestha, had returned from Calcutta to start the school with the help of King Tribhuvan.

His whole family had been exiled during the Rana regime and, while in Calcutta, they had supported the democracy movement back home. After the success of the 1950 revolution that overthrew the Ranas, Satyanarayan returned to Nepal and King Tribhuvan offered him the position of Minister of Education. He declined and sent a message to the Palace that he'd rather open a school. "I just want to be a teacher," he wrote. King Tribhuvan donated his summer Palace in Pharping for the school.

How the Shrestha family came to be exiled was an interesting story. Satyanarayan's older brother, Bhednarayan, had returned to Nepal after completing his BA in Calcutta. He used to teach English to high-ranking Rana children in their Palaces. During these classes, he fell in love with one of the Rana daughters. They eloped to get married and the Ranas were furious. Bhednarayan didn't dare stay in Kathmandu after that, so he escaped to Calcutta and his whole family followed him. Bhednarayan's son, Japnarayan, was our senior at school.

After arriving from Okhaldhunga, we stayed at Toran Bhawan for 15 days. By then the school admission process had already begun but we were only told about it when the scholarship arrangements had been finalised by the Ministry of Education.

Ganesh Bahadur and I would be studying in Grade 5 at Pharping Boarding School. A *khardār* (non-gazetted officer) from the Palace took us to New Road to buy suits. We had never heard, seen or worn anything like this outfit called a "suit" before.

The shopkeeper started unfurling all kinds of fabric, some softer than others, some printed and a few that looked and felt like jute bags. The *khardār* seemed keen on getting us the cheapest and was negotiating with the shopkeeper. I couldn't understand their language and only found out later they were speaking Newari. When I look back on it now, I'm sure the *khardār* took a huge cut from the Rs 350 allocated for our suits, which in 1957 was a substantial sum.

Boarding school was just like the *gurukul* that Koirala *guru* had described, with classrooms, dormitories and a dining hall. There were two popular schools in Kathmandu at that time. One was St Xavier's in Godavari and the other was our Pharping School, which was officially known as Tribhuvan Adarsha School. Both were English medium schools and competed fiercely against each other in academics, sports and other activities.

I had had no formal education in my village. Whatever I learnt was based on the *guru*'s teaching. I didn't actually learn anything. We just had to memorise and recite by rote.

In Pharping, our classmates had come from good schools. They were all from well-off families and were tutored at home by subject specific teachers. I was surprised to see there were also girls in school and there were three Thakali girls in our class.

Speaking English was compulsory in the school. While I struggled with the basics, my friends spoke the language fluently. Everything at the school including the classrooms, desks, benches, dining hall and the dorms were top notch.

For someone born in a remote village, studying in such a school felt like a dream come true and I was determined to do well. There were eight students in my class. I eventually topped all the subjects in the first term exams, except English. Except for the Sanskrit teacher, Girvanyuddha Aryal, Nepali teachers, Shriraj Shashtri and Basu Shashi, and the maths teacher, Bishwanath Mathema, all the others were Anglo-Indians. The guards, gardeners and peons were Pharping locals. A school with world-class education was at their doorstep but they had no access to it. Their sons attended a government school in Pharping and the girls didn't go to school at all.

Although Pharping was on the outskirts of Kathmandu, it was no different to Nisankhe back home. The men gambled all day and only worked in the fields during the planting season or at harvest time. On the other hand, the women worked all day long. They went barefoot, toiled in all weather and gave birth once a year. Most of their children played naked in the dirt. They had limbs like sticks and protruding bellies. There were no hospitals and people died all the time. We knew someone had passed away when the guards came to the school with shaved heads. "Diarrhoea took his life. Even the shamans couldn't save him," they would sigh.

It was more than two months since I had last seen my mother. I missed her terribly and wrote a long letter home describing everything I had experienced. It took nearly two months for a reply to come. My mother was happy to hear that her son had followed the King. After that, I started sending letters home every week, although replies came only once in a while. It wasn't easy for my mother to find someone who could help her write and post letters.

I was completely devoted to my studies. Although my English had improved, it still wasn't easy for me like my other subjects. I continued topping the class in all subjects except English. I enjoyed studying Sanskrit and could quickly memorise everything but, despite getting all the answers right in exams, I never scored full marks. Back then the teachers were very stingy when it came to marking. If 50 was the full mark, they would never give me more than 47.

One day I mustered enough courage to question my Sanskrit teacher, Girvanyuddha, about it. "I got all the answers right so why didn't I get full marks?" I asked.

"Just because the answers are right doesn't mean you get full marks," he replied.

Although the answer didn't satisfy me, I hesitated to probe further.

Back then students respected teachers as much as their parents and worshipped them like gods. It wasn't just out of fear – we genuinely looked up to them. Nevertheless, no one argued with them as much as I did.

My winning streak continued into the finals and I topped Grade 5. The Principal was so happy that he promoted me directly to Grade 7. During the winter vacation, I finished studying all the books for Grade 6. We followed the Indian curriculum so all our books used to come from Calcutta. I don't know if the Nepali curriculum wasn't good enough or if it was just that the boarding school was trying to show off, but we had to study Indian history, geography and civic studies.

Despite having skipped a year, I topped Grade 7 and Ganesh Bahadur managed to pass Grade 6. From then on, I was never ranked second throughout my school life.

I took Optional Maths in Grade 9 because I wanted to study science in college and become an engineer. Krishnamurti sir, who taught the subject, was from South India and, like in my Sanskrit exam, no matter how well I did, I never got full marks in Optional Maths. Despite getting all the answers correct, I used to score 47 out of 50 in Sanskrit and 97 out of 100 in Optional Maths.

I wanted to get to the bottom of this marking issue so I asked both teachers about it. Both gave me the same answer on the same day.

"We can't give you full marks just because you get all the answers right. The three marks deducted are offered, one each, to the school, the teacher and Dakshinkali," they said.

"That's the way it is," Girvan sir ended the discussion. Even Krishnamurti sir looked miffed that I had dared to ask for an explanation. After that I never brought up this question again.

To this day, when I pass through Pharping I go to see Girvan sir. Even last year I asked him: "So, sir, tell me why you always deducted three marks?"

He didn't say anything and just smiled.

During our winter vacation, we used to stay at the school's city office in New Road. Nirmal Kumar and Kashi Prasad, who were from well-off families in Dhankuta and Pokhara, also stayed there. If they needed money, they could go to the shops in New Road, Asan or Indrachok and get Rs 200 simply by signing an account book. Rs 200 would be worth about Rs 50,000 today.

They wanted to hang out with the "first boy" while I wanted to mingle with the "rich boys". They were worried about their studies and I was worried about money, so our interests converged. In Grade 7 they used to smoke Du Maurier and Craven A cigarettes which were famous brands back then. The two boys taught me how to smoke and I was hooked. Soon, we were regulars at cinema halls too. We watched Raj Kapoor and Vaijayanti Mala in "Sangam" three times in one day.

We used to leave the hall humming the movie's song *"Bol Rādhā, Bol Sangam"* and, after taking a few puffs, would get tickets for the next session and go right back inside. Friends waiting to go back home for the holidays used to pay for me when we went out.

Cigarettes were prohibited in school. But the prohibition only made it more exciting to break the rule. I had mild withdrawal symptoms and needed to smoke desperately. I started smuggling cigarettes into school and, since the first boy was smoking, it became easier for my friends to do the same. I'd take a puff and blow it out towards the sky, enjoying the cloud of smoke that gathered around us. Inhaling the smoke deep into my lungs and then blowing it out of my nostrils like a pro made me feel confident.

But getting the cigarettes into school needed a lot of planning. We sent the school guards to get cigarettes for us but the brands they bought were cheap and didn't have the right taste.

"We'll lose our job if anyone sees us," they'd say.

They even refused to give us the cigarette that they stowed behind their ears. "I need it for the evening," they'd say. On rare occasions when they felt sorry for us, they'd sneak in some cigarettes. Our main reason for leaving the school on holidays, on the pretext of visiting Dakshinkali or getting our shoes repaired, was always to buy cigarettes.

Everyone's a poet at least once in their lives. I went through that phase too.

I scribbled verse on the last pages of my notebooks. I was very keen on reciting my poems on Radio Nepal, so I kept nagging Basu Shashi sir about it.

"Wait. I'm trying," he assured me repeatedly.

One day he called me. "You have to recite a poem on the radio tomorrow," he said. I was overjoyed and started dancing around.

"No need to be so proud," he said, "Which poem will you recite?"

"I'll get it right now," I said and dashed off to my room.

I looked for the copybooks where I had penned my poems and selected three. I took them and rushed back to Basu sir.

"Let me see," he said, snatching the poems from me and reading them.

"Okay, this is great," he said.

The next day I went to Radio Nepal with Basu sir. He sacrificed his Saturday to give me moral support.

Radio Nepal was the only source of entertainment and news that had a reach across the country. So everyone, rich, poor, King, commoner, city dweller or villagers, from the plains to the mountains, tuned into Radio Nepal. *Gorkhapatra* was limited to the educated in towns and cities. Being on the radio was like speaking to the whole country. I was more excited about saying my name and where I studied and came from on the radio than reciting the poem itself.

That was my first time inside the huge Singha Darbar complex. Basu sir took me into the recording studio. The room was completely closed and there was pin drop silence inside. I sat on a chair with a mike in front of me.

When I was told to recite my poem, I began: "My name is Rookmangud Katawal from Pharping Boarding School. I am from East Number Three, Okhaldhunga, Nisankhe. The title of my poem is '*Bādal* (Cloud)'."

My eyes were brimming with tears when I walked out of the studio. Basu sir patted me on the back and the tears rolled down my cheeks.

During King Mahendra's time, a lot of students from villages, like me, were admitted to schools in Kathmandu. Although the number dropped during King Birendra's time, the practice wasn't entirely discontinued.

Every winter vacation we had the opportunity for a brief meeting with the King. The Principal would arrange the time and take us to the Palace. He used to tell the King about how we'd progressed in our studies and sometimes the King even asked us questions. But what interested us most was the Rs 50 pocket money we always got after an audience with the King.

Since I spent my Dasain in Kathmandu, I used to go to the Palace to receive *tikā*, queuing up with the others. The royal family used to visit Dakshinkali on the eighth day of Dasain to worship the family deity and then dropped by Pharping School on their way back. We used to line up to greet them. Since I was the first boy, I'd be seated in the front row. I was also the monitor at school.

I was getting the students to straighten their rows during one such visit when King Mahendra walked past me and said, "Very smart boy."

"This is the same boy you brought from Purva Number Three," the Principal told the King.

"Oh, I see," King Mahendra said and patted my back.

The Principal and the other teachers were delighted.

"How is he?" the King asked.

"Outstanding, Your Majesty," the Principal said. "That's why he got a double promotion." The King asked what double promotion meant.

I didn't get to speak to Queen Ratna, however, and not just in school. Even after I joined the Army, I never got the chance to meet her. I had to console myself at seeing her only from a distance.

During the five years at school, I went home only once. Since I had no relatives in Kathmandu, it was very difficult to spend time alone during Dasain and the winter holidays. I went home for the winter vacation in 1958 when I was in Grade 7.

"Let's stop by my home on the way," Ganesh Bahadur said.

It didn't matter to me which route I took back home so I said yes.

He used to go home as soon as we had a break. When he was returning home in Grade 6, he spent a night on the way and eloped with a girl from the house where he stayed. Despite being married, he never stopped showing off and flirting with other girls in school.

"Let's go to my in-laws' place," Ganesh Bahadur suggested, "They'll take good care of us."

I agreed.

His in-laws' place at Tori Swara was on the banks of the Sunkoshi River. They seemed to be a well-off family and were very hospitable, serving us a hearty meal every time. The bronze plate with rice used to be surrounded by bowls full of lentils, vegetables, pickles, fish, milk, yogurt, ghee and sweet treats.

"Looks like you ate well," his mother-in-law would say, "You're very lucky."

I followed Ganesh and his father-in-law to a house perched slightly higher up the hill where I was going to sleep. Since I was guest, I couldn't complain.

Ganesh Bahadur introduced me to everyone in the family, including his father-in-law's youngest brother and his mother. There was a pretty girl sitting beside the grandmother. She must have been about 13, although she looked older dressed in *gunyu cholo* and slippers.

Ganesh dropped me there at night and went back to his in-laws' home.

The next morning, I was served another meal at the same house.

"How is it, dear?" the grandmother asked.

"Fantastic," I said.

"My granddaughter made it. She cooks very well," she said.

The girl sitting near the fireplace ran outside. I had already noticed her flushed cheeks. She was blushing but also smiling.

I didn't say anything.

After eating, everyone would go back to work except for Ganesh Bahadur and me. All we did was stuff ourselves with food, loiter around in the afternoon and come back for another round of hospitality in the evening.

We used to walk along the river which had fish traps. The fishermen told us they caught up to 200 kg of fish at a time. Some of this fish was served with our meals.

The grandmother repeated the same praise of her granddaughter after every meal. Now I understood why they were treating me so well at their home and it wasn't just the grandmother. Everyone at Ganesh's in-laws' place was trying to get me married to the granddaughter. The hospitality I was being showered with was only the bait.

I couldn't even think of getting married because I was still very young and had sacrificed my home and family to study. I had gone to Kathmandu to become a big man and I knew that marriage would hamper my studies. Most importantly, I feared it would force me back to the drudgery of village life.

However, as I had been their guest for so long, it wasn't easy to say no.

"Okay," I nodded my head.

"We can finalise it formally later," I added, trying to play it safe.

The girl was pretty, slim and looked like a prosperous Chhetri girl. But marriage was the last thing on my mind.

After staying there for eight days, I thought it was best to head home so I packed my belongings and told them I would be leaving the next day.

"Since you're leaving tomorrow, you should have *chāmre* (rice cooked in ghee). What do you want with it?" the grandmother asked.

I was only a kid after all. "Fried potatoes," I said excitedly.

But escaping the marriage proposal wasn't that simple even after I left Kavre.

The next winter, Ganesh Bahadur took me to Dhobidhara where the girl's two aunts lived and they apparently wanted to finalise the marriage arrangements.

Eventually, I had to take the sacred thread and beetle nut from the girl to formalise the engagement. But I agreed on the condition that I would marry only after the SLC, the tenth grade exams. I had no place to live in Kathmandu. How could I take a wife? This bought me time: two years to come up with a plan to get myself out of the mess.

Ganesh Bahadur visited his home and in-laws regularly. He used to boast about being the King's adopted son. He was expelled after the school received a lot of complaints about him. I was upset but, on the other hand, a part of me was jumping for joy. Now that he was gone, I thought I was finally going to be free of the forced marriage proposal to his in-law. Besides, I still hadn't finished my SLC exams.

As it turned out they must have found a better match for the girl because I never heard from them again.

I was mischievous from a very young age. I would gather all the children in the village and pretend to hold a military-style assembly. While I assigned all my friends the roles of sergeant, corporal or subedar, I would always be the superior officer. During these play sessions, I ordered a lot of my "subordinates" to thrash people with nettle leaves and water. My friends pretending to be sergeants would actually obey these orders and bully the weaker ones. The ones who were senior to me would be clerks and lieutenants.

One of my childhood friends who played a sergeant in our make-believe assemblies always used to reminisce about the good old days when I went home for holidays. He worked as a driver at Udayapur District Administration Office and passed away in 2010. We were naughty. Stealing offerings made to the priests in the village, we'd gobble down the fruits, *selroti* and pickles from the poor priest's bag and throw away the rest, including the rice, in the water. What we enjoyed even more was stealing milk from the neighbours' cows and making rice pudding with it.

There was a buffalo at Bhupendra *dai*'s home that was taken down to the pond to wallow. While the buffalo was in the mud, I would manage to milk the animal, filling up folded arum leaves that served as cups. Sometimes I even drank straight from its swollen teats.

"The calf drank the last drop of milk," my sister-in-laws would curse the animal. I used to find it hysterically funny. I was always up to something and was always planning pranks.

Everyone went to bed by 8 pm in the village so, after it got quiet, we'd sneak into people's homes and fill the *jānto* (stone grinder) with cow dung. The next day when people came to grind lentils and maize, the dung would splatter from the *jānto*, which led to a lot of cursing.

Another prank we used to play also involved nettle leaves. We'd hang a bunch of nettle leaves dipped in water on the frames of people's doors. Next morning, the first person to open the door would be stung on their forehead by the leaves. Since women woke up early, they were the ones who got whipped by the nettles the most. Their shouting and cursing would wake up the entire village, while I laughed into my pillow.

This prankster in me stayed on even after I came to Kathmandu for my studies. At Pharping School, I wasn't just ahead in studies but I used to be involved in fights over food, study times and other things. I had never tasted baked bread and didn't like it when I did.

"I don't like this," I said directly to the teacher in the school dining room when I was in Grade 9.

"That's all we have today," he replied.

"I don't like it means I don't like it," I repeated arrogantly.

He did nothing. I was so angry that I turned the table upside down. Milk spilt all over the floor and bread crumbs fell off it. The Principal happened to be coming in to the dining room just then and saw my tantrum. He asked for bread and milk.

"Take it," he said.

"I don't want to." I refused to bow down to him.

"Take it," he said again.

"I don't want to."

He said for the third time, "Take it."

I refused to budge. "I don't want to."

He ordered me to kneel down. I went down on my knees and covered my ears, ready for a boxing. This wasn't the first time I was punished. My mischievous and forthright nature landed me in trouble throughout my school life.

After the Grade 9 exams, I left for the city for my winter vacation. We used to eat at Khichapokhari's Shakti Hotel and hire a cycle to go around Kathmandu.

The annual meeting with the King was scheduled for December. "Be at the Palace's west gate by 3:30 pm," the

Principal told us. I was excited at the prospect of the customary Rs 50 we'd get after meeting the King. I left for the Palace thinking about what I would do with the money. The security personnel took me to the waiting room which was in the same building as the King's office.

I had been waiting for two hours but still no one was summoning me. The office staff went home and I was still in the waiting room. Some soldiers brought me food around 8 pm. I must have fallen asleep and was woken up around midnight by King Mahendra's ADC. Half asleep, I followed him into the King's office. The King was alone, his table scattered with papers and books. It looked like he was taking a break. His Majesty was dressed in an off-white *mayalpos* while his double breasted striped coat hung to one side. His *dhākā topi* was lying on the table. The room was filled with cigarette smoke. The ashtray was overflowing with stubs of Gold Flake cigarettes, the King's favourite brand.

He clearly wanted to get away from his work for a while and started chatting, just like in the evenings during his visit to the east. During our earlier meetings, he had mostly asked about my studies but this time he wanted to talk about romance, of all things.

"How many girlfriends do you have?"

I was too shy to say anything so he repeated the question.

"None, sir," I said but he insisted I should have a girlfriend.

"You must have one," he said with the cigarette held loosely between his fingers.

We talked for about 10 minutes and I left. By that time I was no longer sleepy. I looked around and asked a guard about the Rs 50.

"Everything is closed now," he said, "Contact the west gate at 11 am tomorrow."

As it was already midnight, a car from the Palace dropped me home.

I was impatient the whole next morning and hired a bicycle to get to the Palace. There were a lot of people queued up outside. The Volkswagen belonging to Chuda Bikram Shah, Queen Ratna's uncle, was parked outside.

"Go away. Why are you here?" a guard scolded me.

"I was asked to come here at 11 today," I said, greeting him.

"All hell has broken lose. To hell with your 11 am," he snapped. "Come back later."

I returned to my lodging, feeling dejected.

I had just taken up cycling then, at the cost of 25 paisa per day. While I was cycling back from Dillibazar to Putalisadak, I saw a lot of people gathered around a shop that had the radio on a loudspeaker. I learnt that His Majesty was going to make a major announcement at 3 pm. Like everyone else, I was curious, so I waited there to hear what it was. Although I was listening to the King' speech, I wasn't interested in what he was saying – my mind was still on the Rs 50 I hadn't managed to collect from the Palace.

A chill runs down my spine when I think of that day now. I had actually met King Mahendra the night before he made the royal putsch on 15 December 1960. The Palace had been working the whole day on the details of the 15 December coup. It was amazing that, despite all that, King Mahendra took time off at midnight to ask me about my girlfriend.

It took me a year to understand what the 1960 coup was

all about. I was neither particularly happy nor sad about the King's decision. I was just disappointed I never got my money.

I was still the top student when I graduated from Grade 9 and went into Grade 10. I was performing consistently well but the Principal was concerned that others should also do well and became very strict. He used to get guards to drag us away from class and spank us. I couldn't tolerate it and decided to lead a revolt against the Principal.

Matters came to a head when I was identified as the ringleader and expelled. Later, Satyanarayan sir came to my rescue and admitted me to the JP School in Chhetrapati, taking care of all my expenses. Since the King had brought me from a village and I was also doing so well, he probably didn't want to see me have to abandon my studies.

I now lived in a rented room and needed money to eat and to pay my rent. Satyanarayan sir had lent me around Rs 500 by then, which I was supposed to pay back. The Education Ministry had decided to provide me with a monthly scholarship of Rs 150.

After the boarding school, JP was a disappointment because the standard of instruction wasn't as high. There was a secretary from the Palace who took a weekly English class at JP and he recognised me.

"Rookmangud, why have you come down here?" he asked.

I didn't say anything but his question was like a slap in the face.

After that, I started focusing on my studies again. I passed the SLC exams from JP school in the first division in 1960. I had crossed the first hurdle to fulfil my mother's dream of me becoming a big man one day.

Public Science College

I wanted to become an engineer so I enrolled at the Public Science College which later became Amrit Science College (ASCOL). Back then, there were options after SLC for studying medicine, engineering, agriculture or forestry. I decided to take the Intermediate Level in Science (ISc) and pursue engineering under a government scholarship. It was because of His Majesty's kindness that a boy from a far-flung village got the opportunity to study in Kathmandu.

Every month I received Rs 150 from the Education Ministry and Rs 50 from the Palace which was a lot of money in those days. The problem, however, was that the money from the Ministry was often delayed and I used to get three months worth all at once. I would be already thinking about ways to spend this money and once spent it all on a famous brand of suit. After that I was in a fix. I couldn't manage my monthly expenses including paying my rent on time. Even so, I enjoyed walking around New Road in my swanky new outfit.

Around the same time I received Rs 350 from the Ministry to cover my clothing expenses for the year. I decided to get a new jacket and went to the most famous tailor in town, Jujubhai Tailor in Khichapokhari.

Although I strutted around in style, my financial situation was dire. My monthly rent was Rs 25 and meals cost Rs 40 each month. Since I had poured all my money into fancy clothes, I had a tough time meeting my daily expenses. Also, my focus was shifting from Science to other areas. Although I did well in language and literature, I was lagging behind in Chemistry, Physics and Maths.

Our winter vacation was starting and I decided to bury

myself in my books to work on my weakest subjects. Since I hadn't done so well during the academic year, I thought I could go through the whole course again in the holidays. But a rumour buzzing around diverted me from my studies.

"A Nepali movie is being made and apparently they're looking for a hero," an ISc student at Tri-Chandra, Matrika Sherchan, told me.

The first Nepali movie, called "Aama", was indeed being made.

"Buddy, even if we don't get the role of the hero, we should try for a supporting role, a villain or something," Matrika told me excitedly. His enthusiasm rubbed off on me, so I ditched my plans to study during the vacation and decided to try to pursue a career in the film industry instead.

"If I become a hero, everything will be set." I was thrilled just daydreaming about it. "I'll have name, fame and money and go everywhere with a heroine on my arm."

I decided to audition for the hero's role. Back then, tight pants were in vogue and I had cleaned and ironed all three pairs that I owned. They now had creases down the front, as sharp as a sword. I also had the suit and jacket from Jujubhai that I had splurged on.

Despite all the preparation, we were clueless about where we had to go for the auditions. We spent three days searching but couldn't find the place. On the fourth day, we heard the auditions were being held at the British Council but this turned out to be untrue. Next we rushed to the Royal Hotel (Bahadur Bhawan where the Election Commission is now housed) but there was nothing happening there either. Someone said the auditions were at the College of Education so we hurried to

Tripureshwor Guest House. But there was nothing there as well.

While we were making the rounds of Kathmandu searching for the auditions venue, the Information Department had already announced the names of the hero, heroine and the supporting cast.

For me and Matrika, from then on the hero of "Aama", Shiva Shankar, was always a villain. It took me a long time to get over my obsession with becoming a movie star. I pursued that path seriously and, in the process, even became friends with some people in the movie industry. One of them reignited my passion to appear on the silver screen when he told me about the film, "Maitighar", that was being produced in 1964 by a private company.

After I found out that Mala Sinha was going to be the heroine in the movie, I was even more excited at the idea of acting opposite that top Bollywood actress. But all my dreams were dashed. I neither became a hero nor did I do well in my exams. I knew the results wouldn't be all that great but I was confident about getting through all the papers. I later learnt that I failed the practical exams.

I made a backup plan immediately. During my second year, I signed up for Intermediate level in Arts (IA) as well. I was confident I could breeze through those exams despite being still enrolled in the science college, the trips to the cinemas, loitering around New Road, the girls and the cigarettes. Furthermore, I enjoyed literature and books on history, philosophy and politics more than Physics and Chemistry lessons. I was a member of the American Library and the British Council and devoured everything from Shakespeare's plays to Churchill's books. I had never thought of joining the Army but I was crazy about books about war.

Another reason behind my poor results in ISc was my interest in making pen friends. It was fashionable then to have pen friends and the newspapers had a whole section with pictures, names, addresses and education levels of people who wanted to make pen friends. Letters were the only way to make friends in the days before Facebook and mobile phones.

After SLC, I became so fond of pen pals that I must have written at least one letter every day throughout my ISc. My pen friends were from as far away as Burma, Assam, Meghalaya, Manipur, Nagaland, Sikkim, Dehradhun and Dharamshala. It goes without saying that I was only interested in female pen pals.

Soon there were a lot of them and some even invited me to visit them. I told them that I would come after the ISc. When the second year ended, the scholarship from the Ministry and the money from the Palace also dried up. I thought it was better to travel and live for free rather than stay in Kathmandu with no money. I decided to meet all my pen pals from India's northeastern states.

My journey started with greater Assam and Meghalaya. The society there was more open than ours. One of my female friends took me to her place and her sisters took me around the hill station there. Shillong was a very clean, beautiful and developed town. They took me to Cherrapunji, the wettest place on Earth. I also visited their relatives in Guwahati.

After Shillong, I went to Manipur. The people there were equally friendly and hospitable. I then went on to Assam after visiting Nagaland where the language, culture and clothing were similar to those of our mountain communities.

I was a big fan of Aruna Lama whose songs were popular on Radio Nepal. As I was already close to Darjeeling, I decided to pay a visit to the hometown of my favourite singer. Crossing the Tista, from Sikkim I travelled up to Darjeeling.

Aruna invited me to her place as her guest. Her house was like a temple to the arts, with the whole family devoted to music. Every evening, musicians would gather for soulful musical sessions. Hearing the enchanting voice of my favourite singer there in front of me was a treat for an awestruck fan. There was nothing more I could ask for and I will always cherish the memories of the time I was Aruna Lama's guest in Darjeeling.

Our rented place at Asan Bahal was like a university hostel. Everyone from Lokraj Baral of Jhapa to Prem Bahadur Pradhan of Ilam used to live in the same house. Baral was studying Political Science at Kirtipur and there were college students of all levels who lived there.

When I had told Prem about my planned trip to India, he invited me to his home in Ilam. "You have to drop by on your way to Darjeeling. It'll be fun. I'll take you around," he said.

So after Darjeeling, I went to Ilam.

Prem's father, Mohan Bahadur, was among the most prominent people in the village. He had already passed away but people remembered his bravery. Around the same time, the Karfok High School near Aitabare was looking for a temporary English teacher. Prem's family was asked to look for someone, so Prem boasted about how good my English was.

After that I was assigned as the English teacher for grades 9 and 10 and I used to work hard preparing for each class given that most of the students were older than me. My 12 days as a teacher passed by in the blink of an eye. The students, Principal, and the school's committee were so impressed that they wanted me to stay on. But I had to get back to Kathmandu.

Miserable days were waiting for me there. No scholarship, no job, no studies. I had wasted all my money on clothes and now no one would lend me a penny. I thought I might get something if I could meet the King and applied to see him several times. But that never worked out.

In order to cut down on expenses I started living with friends. We kept shifting from Asan to Ganeshthan, Naxal and Thamel in search of cheaper rooms. I began tutoring children for money. Some even offered me meals.

Those trying times taught me the biggest lesson of my life: be frugal even when you have resources.

Three

Army Life Begins

I knew I wouldn't fare well in my Science course in college so I sat for the IA exams and passed in 1965. But how to find a job?

I used to live in Lainchaur and eked out a living by tutoring two students sitting for the SLC exams. They paid me Rs 70 each. But I had also started applying for jobs right, left and centre, including a job with Royal Nepal Airlines. When recruitment of Army cadets was announced, my college mate, Shashi Pratap KC, talked me into applying.

Shashi was from a Kathmandu Chhetri family, the descendants of Bir Shumsher's Colonel Fauj Singh. For him, joining the Army was a matter of great prestige. His aim was not to climb the economic ladder but to uphold the family's social status by achieving the ranks of colonel and then general.

I was reluctant at first. My father was in the Army but he was too straightforward and plain-speaking, which ultimately cost him his job.

Everyone thought I took after my father and the presumption was that I would end up like him. I knew the Army's rigid hierarchy and discipline went against my forthright personality.

Shashi tried to convince me. "Filling in the form won't guarantee selection and, even you do get selected, it's up to you to decide whether or not you want to go ahead," he said. I filled out the form just for his sake. Shashi paid my application fee.

The entry exams took place at the Army Officer's Club. Although I hadn't prepared much, my results were better than I expected. Other competitors had prepared for months and supplemented their diets just to be fit enough for the physicals.

I had no particular aspirations to join the Army but, since I had already come this far, I didn't want to throw away the opportunity. I decided I should sleep the night before on a full stomach, for a change. I thought this would give me energy for the next day. But I didn't have the money. How could I eat?

I was loitering around town when I met a friend of Bhupendra *dai* in Lainchaur. He was a Joint Secretary and bumping into him there was like divine intervention. If I asked him for Rs 10, he wouldn't refuse and I'd have meat and rice that night which would give me much-needed energy the next day. Or so I thought. "I don't have that much money," he said. "Why don't you come for dinner at my place instead?"

What could I do?

I walked straight to my landlady Kalyani *bhauju's* place. She adored me and fed me plenty of *dhindo* and spinach that night. The millet paste wasn't tasty but it filled me up.

Indian Army officials had been involved since 1952 in conducting and evaluating the tests for the Nepalese Army in the British style. One of its generals lived in Shashi Bhawan. And just like that, I was selected for the final interview. Speaking was my forte so the interview went well. After a few days, Shashi told me I had been selected on merit as a cadet.

But I hadn't yet decided on the Army. I had also had an interview at the airline which had gone pretty well. Shashi and

I had been selected for basic training at the National Defence Academy (NDA) in Pune.

Reluctantly, I took steps towards joining my family's traditional line of work. I remembered the words of the holy man I had met as a young boy on the banks of the Sunkoshi River. "What's written in your destiny cannot be erased," he had said.

Before leaving for India, we were given six months' allowance in advance which was more than Rs 2,000. So Shashi and I left for India with deep pockets. There was a new batch of recruits every six months and five batches of seniors were already there.

"There'll be ragging but don't worry," those who had returned from Pune told us, "Just grin and bear it."

Some of the Nepalis in the previous batch were still in training. Among them, I only remember Lava Kumar Devkota, Ramesh Kumar Joshi and Ulendra Dhwoj Karki.

After I was selected for the cadet training and had already left for India, Royal Nepal Airlines began searching for me. The airline had a rule that I had to confirm in writing that I wouldn't be taking the job they were offering me. They somehow found out where I was and the letter reached me in Pune. I signed and sent the letter back confirming that I wouldn't be taking the airline job.

The academy at Pune had students from more than a dozen Asian and African countries. The training was conducted according to the Indian curriculum. There was no time to relax while juggling academics, sports and exercise.

We Nepalis were impressed by the facilities at the academy. It had everything: ponds and lakes, bunkers, tunnels, jungle, desert and hills. There was also a flight training ground. The academy provided basic training for the navy, air force and army. I am still amazed just thinking about the dining hall where more than 2,500 people were served at once. And the cooks were prim and proper just like in fancy hotels.

The academy was so huge that the cadets had to use bicycles to get around. We used to watch movies three times a week, twice in English and once in Hindi.

But we had heard horror stories about the ragging. In this tradition of bullying freshers, the seniors could do anything except use their hands against juniors. There were 400 of us in the first semester and the 2000 seniors could pick and choose whom they wanted to rag. It was only after graduating to the second semester that we, too, got to bully juniors. But the fear of the seniors remained until the final semester. For example, if they saw us on our bicycles, they could order us to dismount and carry our bicycles on our shoulders.

During the first six months at NDA, I never got to ride my bicycle. The bicycle rode me. My reflexes were so good that, as soon as I saw a senior, I would heave the bicycle onto my shoulders and run even before I was ordered to.

But as they say, old habits die hard. Ever since I was a young boy in my village, I couldn't stand injustice and never hesitated to raise my voice in protest. It was the same in Pune. So I had confrontations with everyone, including the senior cadets, teachers and trainers.

Hindi language classes were compulsory for students like us who didn't know the language. While everyone else relaxed after the day's rigorous training, we had to go to Hindi class where there were also South Indians. We used to be completely exhausted by the time we reached the dining hall in the evening. There, too, the bullying continued. The seniors used to tease me and other Nepalis calling us *Rājārām* and *Sitārām*.

In an absurd ritual, a new cadet was placed at each table just so the seniors could bully him. The combination of hunger and exhaustion had drained me completely by the time I got to the dining hall but every time I tried taking a bite, a senior would take away my spoon and fork and ask me to chant "Sitārām Rājārām". When he left, another senior would come along to take his place and bully me some more. This was considered part of the training in that military institution.

This was more than I could take. So, in the third term, I poked RK Sharma, a senior, with a fork. A junior behaving like that towards a senior was unthinkable. Although it was an act of bravery, my action was punishable according to the academy and I had to face the music. I was forced to do front rolls and back rolls and to crawl dozens of times on a passage covered with a jute carpet. The prickly jute stung my body like needles. At the end of the punishment, I was bleeding as if I'd been thrown into a thorn bush.

Despite knowing how severe the punishment was, I didn't stop protesting against the ragging. Shashi, on the other hand, couldn't handle it. He had never been miserable in his whole life, so the ragging took a toll on him. His eyes were full of tears. It was getting too much for him.

All the cadets had the same training for the first two years. After that they could choose between the navy, air force or army, depending on their interests and qualifications. Nepalis could opt for either land-based training or the air force. As Nepal is a landlocked country, there was no point training for the navy. The Indians were obsessed with joining the air force because the pay was better and it was considered the most prestigious service in the Indian Armed Forces. A lot of my friends from Bihar, UP, Hariyana, Punjab and others often joked that dowry rates were almost double for the air force than for the army.

Even I opted for the air force but getting in wasn't easy. Because there were so many applicants, we had to go through written, oral and practical tests to get in. It helped that I had been a Science student and I got through all the questions, moving further up the ladder.

We were all taken to Bangalore for one of the entrance tests. We were made to sit inside a simulator and it felt like we were actually flying. "If your legs don't reach the rudder pedals, you're not fit for the air force," the examiner said. Unfortunately, in the end I was deemed too short.

After that I had no choice but to take up army training. It's a coincidence that my inadequate height of 5 feet 4.25 inches actually helped me get my career back on track. Had I been selected for the air force I couldn't have gone past one-star general.

I was long done with my obsession with becoming a film hero but I was still crazy about movies. We used to travel around Bombay every weekend, hoping to catch glimpses of Bollywood stars. After the third term we could spend the whole of Saturday outside the academy, so we always took the newly-instigated Deccan Queen train to Bombay. It was one of the first electric trains in India.

Someone had once shown us a *paan* shop in Bombay which allegedly Bollywood stars used to frequent. We didn't know if this was true or not but we often lingered around the shop on our weekend trips to Bombay. Every time we saw a girl coming that way, we would pin our hopes on her. But the heroines never showed up.

We went everywhere – Marine Drive, Juhu Beach, Gateway of India, Goregaun – but we didn't catch sight of even one film star. It ended up being like a one-sided love story.

Even after a year, we still went to the same places in Bombay week after week. We were in Marine Drive one Saturday. The place was crowded as usual and suddenly a white car stopped on the side of the road. The driver got down, walked around the car and opened the left door. A girl in dark sunglasses, a long black skirt and stilettos got out. I looked carefully and thought it was Vaijayanti Mala. I walked towards her but she had already crossed the road. My eyes were still searching for her but she had disappeared into the crowd.

"We'll get a better look at them in the movies than here," we told ourselves and returned to Pune, determined not to come looking for heroines in Bombay anymore.

Our obsession with film stars was on hold but our hormones were still raging and, of course, it manifested in a craving for girls. We would make several rounds of Pune's Ferguson Girls' College. The girls there were supposed to swoon over NDA cadets.

One day, the same white car that I had seen in Marine Drive entered the NDA compound. Indeed, there was Vaijanti Mala seated in front with a man in the driver's seat. She was at NDA with her husband to visit the commandant, who was their good friend.

Vaijanti Mala was at the camp for almost a week. Sometimes

her car would drive past during our PT sessions. "Hello, boys," she used to say and wave at us. It made our hearts race.

The commandant in Pune was Air Vice-Marshal Goyal and he was married to a Rana's daughter from Nepal. He thought all Nepalis were as posh as his Rana in-laws which actually worked to our benefit, and we were treated well in Pune.

"Son, you should ride a horse one day." My mothers' words were ringing in my ears. I sent letters home less frequently but it was the memory of my mother's blessings that gave me the strength to reach the top.

Horse riding was mandatory in cadet training. We had three horse riding classes each week in the first term. We had to understand the horse's behaviour and every time I went riding it reminded me of how much I missed my mother. Sometimes I felt like she was looking at me from somewhere nearby and I used to look over my shoulder.

My mother was 1,000 km away, probably walking up a hill, carrying firewood and fodder on her back.

I never thought horse riding would be difficult. Sit on the back, pull the bridle, one whip on its rump and the horse would gallop at lightning speed, and I could always whip the horse more if it didn't obey me. But it was difficult to learn to ride without falling off. Initially, all I did was run after the horse and, even before I could climb back on, it would hurl me to the ground again. I would get up, hold on to the horse and run behind it.

Finally a week later, I learnt to ride without falling off. I thought I had mastered horse riding, so one morning I got on an Arabian horse, took the reins and kicked it. The horse ran like the wind. I was enjoying the ride and the people were praising my performance. I kicked harder to speed up and imagined myself as a prince on a flying horse. Suddenly, the horse reared up on its hind legs, I was thrown off and covered in blood.

They rushed me to hospital. My whole body was covered in bandages and I ended up spending nine days in hospital. The horse taught me a new lesson: never be too proud of your strength.

Cadets training for the army had to spend the fourth and final year at the Indian Military Academy (IMA) in Dehradun. It was established in 1932 and was renowned in the military world. Field Marshall Manekshaw was a cadet from its first batch. Pakistani Army General Niazi who fought against Bangladesh in 1971 and Indian Army General Arora were batchmates at IMA.

Shashi and I were also taken to Dehradun for our final year. Even this training centre was massive with almost 1,200 cadets. NDA students were looked upon with respect. It was easy for us to mingle there because of NDA's training, language and etiquette. But, even there, the ragging continued.

There were some Nepalis, including Yogeshwor Karki, Madhu Sapkota, Umesh Adhikari and others, who had come from Nepal for the IMA course. We were terrified when they told us about the ragging in Dehradun. There was a cadet from Nepal called Kishor Shah who ran away from the academy after being unable to tolerate the bullying.

So we tried every possible way to stay out of the sight of the seniors by hiding behind trees or under desks. They once made me run with ice inside my underwear. It was excruciatingly humiliating and painful.

Seniors were allowed to come into any room to bully. We'd lock the doors and hide inside but there was a rule that the windows had to stay open. The seniors would peer in the windows. The moment we heard the sound of seniors' marching boots, we'd run for our lives. I used to take cover under the table, hidden in a blanket near the window.

But there was only so much we could take. My habit of standing up to bullies almost got me into a fist fight in Dehradun.

"If you raise your hand, you'll be gone," my friends tried to tell me "Don't do anything to let your and your country's reputation down."

So I learnt to control my anger. After completing the course at Dehradun, we got our second lieutenant batches, that too at midnight. Bodhendra Bahadur Rayamajhi, the Military Attaché, came from Delhi to pin the badges on our uniform on behalf of the Nepalese Army.

The training in India was twice as intensive as the training in Nepal. The batches before and after us went through a maximum of two years' training in Nepal but we spent four years in Pune. Despite getting our badges two years after our batchmates, we were still thrilled about becoming second lieutenants.

The only thing I regretted was not having my family at the ceremony. A lot of my friends' families had come but my family couldn't afford to attend.

I received a letter from home just before I graduated. I jumped with joy since I rarely received letters from home. My mother used to ask others to write how she was feeling and send me those letters. Every time I opened her letters, I would be overwhelmed with emotion. And for many days I could hear my mother's sighs in those letters. But the letter I received that day continues to haunt me.

I had been missing my mother a lot so I quickly opened the letter and began reading. The words pierced my heart. My hands were trembling and the legs gave out too. I sat down on the floor weeping and then cried aloud. My mother had died.

"We've already completed the last rites so you don't have to come," my brother had written, "If you become a big man, our mother's dream will be fulfilled."

My mother's face was flashing in front of my eyes. She, who believed in my destiny, was no longer alive. She, who taught me how to hide my tears and smile, was not with me anymore. My mother, who held back her emotions and happily sent me to study, was no longer there.

Everything was becoming blurred. It seemed as if a huge surge of water was flowing in front of me. My mother always dreamt of seeing me become a big man, seeing me ride a horse. But when I was actually able to ride a horse, to put on my second lieutenant's badge, she wasn't there to share the joy. I wanted to hold her tightly, to feel loved and to forget all my pain as her loving hands touched my face. But the gods had snatched her away.

On the night when we received our badges, I could feel my mother's warmth and her hands caressing my hair. Yes, my mother was there. Even today, I feel my mother's presence with every step I take. She is always with me.

The training in Dehradun was over but we still couldn't return to Nepal. I received a letter saying I had to leave immediately for more training at the Indore Military Headquarters of War in Madhya Pradesh. Shashi was also selected and we went to Indore with three other Nepalis for the young officers' course. It was considered one of the toughest courses in the Indian Army.

After finishing the training at Pune, Dehradhun and Indore, we had already become lieutenants. My friends received hearty welcomes back in Kathmandu. I didn't have a lot of relatives there and since my mother had passed away I didn't have any garlands and *tika*.

I wanted to observe *kiriya*, the mourning rites for my mother. The priests suggested I could do it for three days straight. I had a female cousin in Kupondol who agreed, and I spent the next three days alone with the memories of my mother.

After returning to Nepal, I wanted to meet His Majesty King Mahendra. It had been seven years since I had last met him before graduating from Pharping School. I was just a wild sapling that the King had nurtured for all those years. Now, I was a sturdy tree.

I met Colonel Bhairav Bahadur Thapa. His son, Purushottam, had studied with me in Pharping. "You've become a lieutenant now. You should pay your respects and offer a gift to His Majesty," he suggested, "It won't be possible if you come through the Army. Try it from outside."

Sher Bahadur Malla was still the chief ADC. Colonel Bhairav Bahadur took me to him. I saluted.

"I've just returned after finishing my training," I said, standing at attention.

"Good," he said.

"I wanted to meet His Majesty, sir," I said, "The King would probably be happy to see the boy he brought from the east wearing a lieutenant's patch now".

"Leave an application. There's a lot of work to do," the general said.

But I didn't receive any reply. I was worried so I went to meet the general again.

"I'll let you know once everything's arranged. It's not straightforward," he said.

I waited for a reply but it never came.

Four

Junior Officer

The mantra of my teacher Basu Shashi was simple: "To tolerate oppression is also oppression." I have never wavered from that philosophy.

Four years of military training further ingrained this credo into my life. I always tried to be fair and couldn't tolerate injustice. The bullying and ragging I went through at the academy had made me as tough as steel.

After the training I was posted to Singha Darbar's Shree Shreenath Battalion where Riddhi Jung Thapa was the commander. This was the oldest battalion in Nepal and possibly in the whole of South Asia. In 2011, it chalked up 250 years of combat history.

The battalion where one first starts in the Army is called a "mother unit". Despite moving on to other battalions in the course of one's career, there's always a special bond with the mother unit – throughout their careers soldiers keep in touch with it and are invited back to it on every occasion. The battalion always regards us as one of its own.

Everyone from a private to a colonel wishes only the best for their units. When I joined the Shree Shreenath Battalion in 1969, it was lagging behind in every respect, including in sport. We were ranked one of the worst teams in football. Among my responsibilities were sports and recruit training and I was determined to change this. I set myself the goal of taking the battalion to the top.

My reforms started with sport. Soon, it was time to participate in the football tournament in the annual King's Banner competition. It was my responsibility to manage everything from selecting the players to training. We selected the best players and started practicing daily. Although I'm not a footballer, I always joined the players on the field. A subedar called Manashyam and the team captain, Subedar Durga Bikram Hamal, were the best football players in the battalion.

Our game improved steadily as we practiced. I was responsible for the players and all their requirements, from their diet, boots, shin guards, gloves, and ankle guards to bandages. I wanted to ensure that their hearts and minds were concentrated on the game. There were times when I had to fight with the accountant to get money for the players' special foods.

The first match of the league was between us and the Gorakh Bahadur Battalion which had won three successive football tournaments during the King's Banner and became permanent owners of the shield. This battalion from the Palace had every facility one could ask for. Since the first match was against such a strong team, our players' morale was already starting to falter so I came up with an idea. "If you win the match, I'll get a goat for all of you to feast on," I said. The players were ecstatic and team morale immediately shot up.

The match started at Dasharath Stadium. The spectators considered the match between Gorakh Bahadur and our battalion like a game between Brazil and Nepal. After all, Gorakh Bahadur was a three time champion while our Shree Shreenath Battalion was at the bottom of the league.

But like they say, even the most unassuming mountain stream can suddenly rage in a flash flood. It's the hard work and passion that pays off on the field and sets winners apart from losers.

Our team scored the first goal of the match, setting off a huge commotion in the stadium. Our boys then netted the second goal, registering a comfortable win against the former champions.

I think I was happier than the players after our winning shot, and we were confident we could reach the finals. Victory celebrations began at the battalion. The four companies sent a duck each as gifts to the winning team. I had already asked the battalion commander if I could present a goat to them.

I made sure to ask for his permission after hearing a story about General Aditya Shumsher, Gaurav Rana's father, who had done something similar. During a feast, General Aditya fed mutton and fine rice to his troops. But he was blamed for insulting the King by feeding the King's soldiers from his own pocket. So, I knew it was important to seek permission from the battalion commander before I gave a goat to the victorious players.

"Get the biggest goat you can find," I told the team captain, Durga. He bought a big fat goat for Rs 150, which ate a hole in my Rs 400 monthly salary. But, as a single person, I didn't indulge much in food and drink, so giving away nearly half my salary wasn't a big deal. The players had a feast and no one even looked at the ducks which we kept for another day.

A few days later, I instructed the mess to cook the ducks that had been given by the other companies. In the kitchen, everything was ready, rice, lentils, vegetables and pickles.

But when I saw the small, scrawny pieces of cooked duck in the pan, my heart sank. I assumed the players had already been fed and this was just for us. I wasn't happy because I always enjoyed eating with the soldiers rather than in the officers' mess. Food tasted better with the boys.

"The players come first. You shouldn't have set aside any meat for us," I told the cook.

He replied, "This is all there is for everyone, Lieutenant."

I got the shock of my life.

"How come four ducks look like less than one chicken?" I snapped. "Is that all there is for the boys?"

The cooked refused to meet my gaze and didn't utter a word. He started clanking the pan and this angered me even more. I thought about the players' hard work, looked at the few pieces of bony meat and couldn't restrain myself anymore.

"You moron," I growled, grabbing the cook by his collar and raising my fist.

He was petrified and blabbered, "It's not my fault, sir. The major took home the big ducks and replaced them with these skinny ones."

I was hopping mad. In the Army, it's rare for anyone to raise their voice against a senior officer no matter what they do. We tolerate it all for the sake of discipline. But I couldn't tolerate what the major, who supervised the mess, had done. I was determined to expose him no matter what the consequences might be. The major was the second in command of the unit.

That evening all the senior officers were gathered to celebrate our team's victory. I strode into the dining hall where all the officers were eating, laughing and playing cards. The major was trying his luck at the dice board.

I went over to him and grabbed his shirt.

"Don't you have enough to eat?" I demanded, "Did you have to steal the soldiers' meat?"

There was silence in the room. The officers were shocked that a newcomer, a lieutenant, had physically assaulted a major. The officers held me back. I cursed the major with all the obscenities I knew. He didn't say a single word.

They grabbed me by my hands and feet and took me to a room where they explained that such conduct was unbecoming of a soldier. As my anger cooled off it was replaced by fear. I could feel my chest tighten and I dreaded the consequences of my actions. What if they try to destroy me, I thought. But I found a new resolve: if they punished me for protesting against injustice, so be it. I was ready to face whatever repercussions there might be.

Our commanding officer, Riddhi Jung Thapa, was a devout follower of Pashupati. He would visit the temple and take a dip in the sacred Bagmati River every morning and devote hours to worship. He used to enter the office, with sandalwood *tika* on his forehead after his daily morning ritual.

Tej Bahadur Khatri, commanding officer of Sher Battalion in Baneshwor, and Thapa would compete to be holier than thou. Both walked barefoot to offer their morning prayers and, if one reached Pashupatinath at 3 am, the other had to get there earlier the next morning. I thought such a religious person would be fair-minded towards soldiers who had been cheated and who had filed a complaint against a thieving major.

The next day, I was planning to ask for a time to meet the commanding officer, when Adjuntant Major Bala Bahadur Giri summoned me to Riddhi Jung's office. I went in and saluted him. Before I could say anything, he said gruffly: "Why did you assault the major?"

I told him everything that had happened and demanded that the major be punished. But the man who looked like a pious devotee on the outside turned out to be rotten on the inside.

"Hey easterner, there are plenty of educated guys like you in the Army," he said, "Don't try to be smart and get ahead of yourself."

Needless to say, I was crestfallen.

But he hadn't finished yet. "Do you even know how to behave with senior officers?" he said, raising his voice.

There was nothing I could say when a commanding officer took sides so blatantly and unfairly. I just stared at him blankly, cursing myself for not being more assertive.

A few days later, Major Keshav Giri and Quarter Master, Captain Badri Shrestha, called me to the Army Officer's Club, which back then was still at Singha Darbar.

I vividly remember Giri saying "Why are you acting so rashly? Do you have anyone in the Army who will come to your rescue, if they decide to let you go?"

"So should I do nothing even when someone snatches food from the soldiers' plates, right under their noses?" I asked boldly.

"Yes, that's how things work in the Army. If you want to stick around you will need to stop seeing, hearing and speaking. You still need to learn the ways of the Army," he said, "After all, it's not like your salary or rations were stolen. Why do you want to act like a hero?"

I blurted out: "Turn a blind eye and tolerate thieves, then?"

"We're speaking from our own experience here, just trying to tell you how things work," Shrestha put in.

I left the room quietly despite the rage burning inside me. They were not just ignoring a wrongdoing in front of their very eyes but trying to stifle my protests against it. I kept thinking how could an Army which couldn't protect its own soldiers possibly protect the country?

The reports about a lieutenant physically threatening a major caused a stir in the Army. It was even reported to HQ. One afternoon, I was summoned by the Pay and Salary Office. Colonel Ganga Bahadur Bista was obviously hoping to knock some sense into me.

"Didn't they teach you during training that assaulting a senior officer results in court martial?" he said, trying to scare me.

"If questioning a person who steals from soldiers is punishable, then I am ready to face the music," I replied with some bravado. "I will take this issue to the Palace, even if I have to leave the Army."

That was the magic word. Colonel Bista mellowed after I mentioned the Palace.

"Listen, boy, I'm only saying this for your own good," he said, "Don't make hasty decisions."

The duck scandal nearly prompted me to resign from the Army. I had made many enemies but the saddest thing was that no action was taken against anyone. I contemplated joining the civil service, where I thought I could at least speak freely.

But no one had to tell me things weren't much better in the bureaucracy. Furthermore, my five years of rigorous training would have gone to waste and I would have had to start from scratch again.

I decided to go with the flow and leave it to fate.

Meeting Uma

The news about young women joining HQ spread like wildfire while I was still at the Singha Darbar barracks. Lieutenants and captains started frequenting HQ on various pretexts just to ogle the girls there. Finally, curiosity got the better of me and I also began visiting HQ regularly.

During my visits, I couldn't take my eyes off one of the young women. I always made excuses to meet her if I needed to get anything done at HQ. It was love at first sight and I was head over heels. I just couldn't keep her out of my mind.

When I got to HQ one day, I saw another familiar face. It was Basanta Shrestha from Bhojpur, whom I met through Bhupendra *dai* before leaving for Pune.

Basanta's family was well-known throughout the east and they owned a villa built by her grandfather. Even during the Rana regime, he was in a position to stand up to *Badā Hākim*. My younger uncle was a tenant at her house and she used to call me *dai*.

And after all these years, she also happened to be friends with the girl I was smitten with. So I had the details now, all thanks to Basanta.

Name: Uma KC. College graduate. Working city girl who had drop dead good looks. Her father was supposedly friends with the Chief Singha Bahadur Basnet.

Until then, daily rides around New Road were an unvarying part of my routine. After finishing work, I'd put on my shades, throw on my cool blazer and speed off to New Road on my bike. There wasn't much to do really, except loiter around, checking out girls and puffing on cigarettes. Back then, those who cruised around New Road on motorbikes belonged to a different league to me altogether. I used to think that was the only way to get girls.

But all that changed after meeting Uma. New Road was suddenly less exciting. All I could think of was finding an errand that would take me to HQ.

Uma had returned from Bangladesh after completing her studies. Back then, the girls who studied abroad and worked with the Army mostly belonged to distinguished families. Her father was a retired superintendent of police, highly trusted by the Inspector General of Police, Chandra Bahadur Thapa, then a terror in Kathmandu.

And there I was, a boy from the boondocks with nothing more than a lieutenant's badge. When it came to family status, we were poles apart. Just like they say in the movies: as far apart as the moon in the sky and the dust on the ground. But I was in search of a horizon where sky and earth met.

I started going to HQ daily on the pretext of meeting Basanta during her lunch breaks. Uma and Basanta used to walk back home from Bhadrakali to Putalisadak so I began taking the same route too, waiting for them and pretending to bump into them. Basanta sensed my motive.

"Hey *dai*, want to get married?" she suddenly asked me one day.

"I haven't found a girl yet. Anyone in mind?" I pretended to be naive.

"Uma," she replied. My heart leapt.

"Okay," I said quickly, trying to hide my excitement.

Now, it was up to Basanta to bring us together. One day, she called both of us to her rented room near Tukucha in Putalisadak.

While talking to Uma, I found out she was my friend Shashi's first cousin. He and I had been friends since our college and cadet training days. During our training at Pune, Shashi used to boast about his family and I used to tease him by saying I'd marry one of his sisters. "Oh you hillbilly, you don't stand a chance with my sisters," he'd say.

I had been to Shashi's home a few times during our college and NDA days. He lived with extended family and I'd seen some girls there. One of them must have been Uma.

"Since you're my friend's cousin, it'll be easy for us to be friends," I said jubilantly.

"Krishna and Sudama were also friends but forming a relationship is different," she said, playing hard-to-get. Shashi also mocked me when I told him about my feelings for Uma. "Our cousin for a hobo like you?" he laughed. But I didn't lose hope.

Basanta always supported us and used to arrange meetings at her place in the mornings and evenings. We never set a time to meet but both Uma and I would be at Basanta's place at the same time every day, before leaving for work and on our way back home.

Basanta always excused herself to leave the two of us alone. She would head towards the kitchen, do the laundry or sometimes chat with neighbours to let us have a quiet moment together.

Although we both had the same feelings for each other, neither of us had expressed it yet. Despite our frequent meetings, I hadn't been able to propose to her.

Around the same time, there were rumours that our battalion would be moved to Suparitar in Hetaunda. I wanted to convince Uma to get married before I left. I reached Basanta's room around 5 pm one evening and as always she left me alone with Uma. I could almost hear my heart pounding.

I reached for the hemline of her sari and lifted it up a little. She had tiny feet.

"Show me your hands," I said.

Even her hands were tiny, with delicate fingers.

My mother used to say that girls with small feet and hands were lucky. Uma seemed surprised by my odd behaviour. "Why do you have to snoop around inspecting the feet and hands of other people?" she asked in mock irritation.

"Mother had told me to marry a girl with tiny feet and hands because they're lucky," I replied, "I was just checking."

"So what did you find then?"

"That you really are very lucky," I said.

Uma blushed and didn't say anything but she had understood what I meant. After that I told her directly: "I have nothing more than this lieutenant's badge on my shoulder and a heart overflowing with love." I didn't see a frown of disapproval on Uma's blushing face.

That day, Uma and Basanta came right to the front door to see me off. It was only later that Uma told me this had been a test and, had I turned back after saying goodbye, I would have apparently failed.

"Men who turn back can't be relied on," Uma said. "But you walked straight to your motorbike and sped off."

Had I turned back on some impulse that day, my life would have been different. Uma believed that men who were too attracted to girls couldn't be trusted. It was sheer luck that saved me that evening because I really wasn't the kind of man Uma thought I was, at least when it came to girls.

While pursuing Uma, I was still writing regularly to a lot of my female pen pals from Burma, Manipur, Meghalaya, Assam, Delhi, Pune and even Chennai. In all the letters, I dropped hints about how attracted I was to each of them. So I wasn't exactly the type of man Uma wanted. Good thing she didn't know.

I had plenty of female friends all over India and even in Kathmandu. I had once befriended a rich man's daughter, who studied at Tri-Chandra College. She always borrowed my notes - back then that was the only excuse for boys and girls to get to know each other. Although many girls used to send letters revealing their feelings tucked inside the same note books, she never did. Instead she would sometimes slip Rs 500 into my books. For a perennially broke person like me, that was almost like Rs 100,000 would be today.

I left for Pune and she joined the medical school at AIIMS in Delhi around the same time. Our long-distance friendship blossomed and I gladly accepted her invitations to visit Delhi several times. We went to the famous coffee house at Connaught Place, Kutub Minar, all at her expense, of course.

Even on the day I proposed to Uma at Tukucha, I had written this other girl a letter but without mentioning my marriage proposal.

After getting to know Uma better, I had to tame my wild heart. The letters I used to send to other girls tapered off. The ones whom I used to write to every week got pushed back to every other week and the fortnightly letters became monthly. I wanted to be committed to Uma and only to Uma.

After more frequent rendezvous at Basanta's place, I wanted to spend more time with Uma, just the two of us. We will forever be grateful to Basanta for helping nurture our love but I felt we could now take our relationship outside her rented room.

So one day, I mustered my courage and asked her out to the cinema.

"If I don't get back home in time, they'll kill me," she replied.

That was a yes.

"Let's go for the afternoon show on Saturday then," I said.

"There's no way I'll be able to leave the house on Saturday," she said, "Also my siblings won't leave me on a weekend day."

It was annoying to see so many restrictions placed on a daughter who had just returned from studying abroad. The truth was that Uma feared being seen by others, if and when we did go out. Since her family was from Kathmandu, the chances were high that we would bump into relatives and friends. Furthermore, the Brahmin/Chhetri and Newar communities of Kathmandu were very orthodox and suspicious.

We couldn't find a single place in town to spend some quality time, so we had to get back to meeting in Basanta's room.

Uma was even reluctant to ride on my motorcycle. "People will talk about me as the girl who goes cruising around with a boy and that will be terrible," she would say as soon as she got on the bike.

We had to be very careful about when we met. It was risky in the afternoon since she could bump into her relatives. She had to reach home before it got too dark so we settled on evening dates. The setting sun was just dim enough to obscure us from prying eyes on the sidewalks as we cruised past. But the downside was that it soon got dark, and Uma had to get back. Her eyes used to be fixed on her watch and she'd get more anxious with each passing minute.

I used to try to make her stay for few more minutes but eventually had to drop her home with a heavy heart. There were other rules too. I had to leave her some distance away from her home and disappear quickly. There had to be no honking or gunning the accelerator.

I used to feel like a thief, meeting so secretively and always hiding from other people.

I was hopelessly in love with Uma and wanted to marry her as soon as possible but who would ask for her hand in marriage on my behalf? Basanta was very helpful in facilitating our meetings but wouldn't dare to take the marriage proposal to Uma's family.

"Uma's father is as fierce as a lion. I can't do it, *dai*," she told me, "Even her mother has become very suspicious."

Since there were no other options, I had to take the bull by the horns and ask for Uma's hand in marriage myself. After all, what difference would it really make if two consenting adults wanted to get married? Why was there a need for a go-between? Since Uma had already agreed, I thought asking for her hand would be a mere formality and it wouldn't matter what others said.

I was suddenly confident about taking the next step and

whizzed off on my bike from Singha Darbar barracks to Kamal Pokhari. Before stopping in front of Uma's house, I turned off the accelerator to ensure the whole neighbourhood didn't hear the sound of my roaring bike. Someone from Uma's home peeked around the main door. I signalled that I was there to visit and was asked to come upstairs.

The whole family was seated in a row in the living room, waiting for me. I began with the formal greetings, "*Namaskār* everyone," I pressed my palms together.

"*Namaskār bābu,* please take a seat," someone said, "I don't recognise where you are from."

"I'm a lieutenant. I just came from the barracks."

All eyes were on me now. There were mats on a large carpet spread across the floor. The family was seated facing two elderly gentlemen who were sitting cross-legged on the mats. They looked like brothers, so I presumed the others around them must be their sons and nephews.

The older of the two was well-built and, remembering what Basanta had said, I assumed he must be Uma's father. I was relieved to see a window beside my chair. If things went sour midway I figured I could make an emergency exit by jumping out. The gurgling of a hookah was the only sound that broke the silence in the room.

The old men smoked and looked me up and down from head to toe. I was dressed in a military jacket and had taken off my shoes. I had an army crew cut.

"Who are you and why are you here?" someone finally blurted out.

I mustered all my courage and said, "I'm here to ask for Uma's hand in marriage."

Everyone in the room was stunned. The hookah stopped gurgling.

"Whose son are you?"

"Since you don't know my father, it doesn't matter who he is," I replied bluntly, "Just think of him as some Ram Bahadur."

Going by my appearance and my abrupt ways, the men probably made up their minds that I was an insolent and immature 24-year-old. How dare he come to ask for our precious daughter's hand in marriage, they must have thought.

"Where do you live?" The interrogation continued.

"Maharajganj," I lied. I used to live in Lainchaur then and don't know why I said Maharajganj. The old man looked at his watch.

"It's seven already. Have you eaten?" he asked.

He sounded nothing like the frightening lion Basanta had described.

"No, sir," I replied politely.

"Isn't it late already?" he asked again, "Where do you normally eat?"

"Sometimes at the barracks or wherever I can, even here if you offered me a meal," I blurted out.

"Hey Sankhe, tell Gita's (Uma's sister) mother to lay the table," the old man ordered.

I was surprised.

He didn't ask me anything more and went back to his hookah. I could hear the women chatting outside. The food arrived in a while on a *khande thāl*, a big plate with several sections. Those large plates looked big but didn't hold much. I suddenly blurted, "Oh, the son-in-law cheating plate."

Sankhe came and took away the plates. After that, he brought the rice on a *jharke thāl* (bronze plate). It was surrounded by bowls of lentils, vegetables, ghee, milk and other delicacies. But they were only for me.

Sankhe also brought a bowl of water for me to wash my hands.

"Please start," Uma's mother said.

"Only for me? Please join in," I said to the old man and others in the room.

"First the guest and then it's our turn," the old man said, "If you're feeling awkward, we can leave the room."

"Not at all. I am your guest," I said, "The more the merrier, as they say. The food tastes better that way."

There were no interrogations after that. I splashed the lentils on the rice, lightly mushed it with vegetables and *achār* and shovelled a handful into my mouth.

"More rice?" Uma's mother said.

"I think I'm done," I said.

"No need to be shy," she teased me.

"I also have to eat my share in the barracks," I replied jokingly.

"First time guests have to accept a second helping," she insisted.

So I obliged.

"*Bābu*, what time do you have to get to the barracks?" the old man asked.

"At nine," I said, looking at my watch.

"About time then," he signalled that it was time for me to leave.

I got up and said my farewells. I had come there prepared to get thrashed but walked out after having a hearty meal.

I couldn't sleep the whole night, thinking about what Uma's family was going to say. It seemed like the longest night of my life. When the sun finally rose, I left for Basanta's place. Uma used to be there by 9:15 am, so I went early that morning to wait for her.

"So, what do you think happened?" I asked Basanta.

"Congrats, *dai*," she said excitedly.

I was curious and wanted to know more.

"Ask your Uma," she said and pushed me into the room where Uma was waiting. She had arrived an hour earlier.

Apparently, Uma's family discussed me after I left the previous night.

"Gita's mother, it's okay to give your daughter away to this lad," the old man gave his verdict.

"People think twice even before dumping manure," Uma quoted her mother as saying. "How can we hand over our daughter without even checking his family background?"

"I've made my decision," the old man said, "The boy looks bright. He'll take good care of Uma."

The old man, who also enjoyed a hearty meal, apparently liked the way I did justice to my dinner.

"Uma knows how he is at work," he said, ending the discussion, "Your daughter, whom you sent to school against my wishes, must have made a good choice."

Uma had run away from home to be admitted into Grade 5 at Padma Kanya School in Dillibazar. Her father hadn't planned to send his daughters to school. "They are tutored at home in English, Nepali and Maths, everything they need to know," the old man used to say, "Why do daughters, who'll have to only manage a household, need to learn anything more than that?"

Although Uma's father had already made the decision, her mother tried to find out more about me. Colonel Shailendra Bahadur Mahat and BP Koirala's ADC, Mahendra Bahadur Mahat, were their relatives and lived in Lainchaur. Uma's mother and other women in the family decided to first investigate me before agreeing to the marriage.

"There won't be good reports about me from Lainchaur," I cautioned Uma. I told her about a family there who were bent on getting their daughter married to me and how I had finally managed to shake them off. They even tried black magic but it didn't work.

Uma's sister and mother went around Lainchaur a few days later to do some door-to-door detective work. Someone told them that I used to live with a girl there and that worried Uma's family a lot.

But when Uma sensed that things weren't going right, she stepped in to fix the situation. "I refuse to believe that he lived with a girl," Uma defended me in front of her family. Having her on my side was gratifying.

A few days later, the Mahats finally set the record straight. "Despite pursuing him for so long he hasn't agreed to marry the girl here. It's best to get him married to Uma soon."

This was a lesson for me. I learnt it's best to come clean about past relationships in order to prevent future conflict and to build trust. It's much worse if a partner hears gossip and rumours from someone else.

So I told Uma all my love stories from the past. She was never jealous. In fact, she seemed to enjoy listening to them. That was how much she trusted me and I have never betrayed her.

With her family's approval, Uma was no longer reluctant to be seen with me in public. We went out on several dates until I moved to Suparitar barracks in Hetaunda. But even after moving there, I used to come to meet Uma every week, rain, hail or shine. I would spend a night in Kathmandu and rush back to Hetaunda the next day.

This weekly commute wasn't easy, so we decided it was time to get married. First, we needed to get permission from the Army HQ. Luckily, I got leave around the same time as the date the priest set for the wedding which would be Shree Panchami in 1972.

We got married in a temple and the wedding cost me Rs 350, with which I bought a *tola* of gold, a *pote* necklace and vermillion powder. There were only four people from my side at the wedding: my cousin from Kupondol, her friend and my distant cousin and his wife who worked at the French Embassy.

Uma's family had already found a rented room for us at Kamal Pokhari. It must have been a difficult transition for Uma, from a comfortable life in her spacious family home to a cramped rented room that served as kitchen, bedroom and living room. But she never complained. "You signed on for a lot of hardship by agreeing to marry me," I teased her sometimes.

Uma rarely let it show, but one day she was unable to hide her grief. A shopkeeper refused to sell her cauliflower for less than Rs 4. When she tried to bargain the price down, he'd said "You can't afford to eat them then".

That night Uma told me about what had happened, with her eyes full of tears. "Will we ever get to eat a plateful of cauliflower?" she wept. I tried to console her, but it troubled me that she was troubled. It left a gaping hole in my heart.

Let the training begin

My hard work at Suparitar paid off. The HQ's Directorate of Military Training (DMT) selected me for the three month course which was mandatory for becoming a captain. I gave it everything I had and after the training there was a party the same night.

"You've been selected as cadet DS, so you are going to Nagarkot," DMT Chief Arjun Narsingh Rana told me at the party.

I was ecstatic about my selection as a cadet trainer. From Nagarkot, Uma was now only a hop, skip and jump away. It was a huge relief.

DMT Chief Rana also told me that they needed two more trainers, but it wasn't for me to suggest names, so I just stood there.

"If you know good officers here give me their names," he said.

I suggested Umesh Adhikari and Gyan Jung Thapa. Umesh was known as a disciplined and strong officer and I was introduced to both of them in Dehradun where Gyan Jung was my junior. Rana approved both the names.

Back then Kharipati was not yet a Military Academy. It was established later on. Meher Shumsher Rana, King Tribhuvan's nephew, was the commandant at the Nagarkot Cadet Training Centre. Chief instructor and the second man was Shambhu Shumsher Rana, Dev Shumsher's grandson. All major Army training took place in Nagarkot then.

I packed my bags and left for Bhaktapur. We had to walk from Bhaktapur to Nagarkot since there were only a few vehicles that plied that road in those days. Umesh and Gyan Jung arrived a week later. Chhatra Man Singh Gurung was also one of the cadets.

All three of us had gone through the rigorous training at Dehradun. We believed that soldiers should always be ready to face any hardship, so we were strict trainers. We did our best to ensure that Chhatra Man Gurung's batch had a tough time in running, parade, obstacle courses, PT and sport. Sometimes, we made them run 40 km throughout the day, running alongside them ourselves.

Colonels Meher Shumsher and Shambhu Shumsher were worried that the training was too rigorous. They were from rich families for whom life was all about having fun, but we belonged to a different class which believed nothing was achieved without hard work.

There are lots of entertaining anecdotes about Meher Shumsher. Nagarkot had just opened its doors to tourists around that time. One day he saw two foreigners and, although he wasn't the domineering kind, he lost track of things when he got drunk.

"Bring in that *angrez* couple," he ordered Lieutenant Madhu Sapkota in broken English.

"You see, here I am the lord of all that I survey," he boasted to the foreigners. "Here, whatever I say goes."

Back then the road from Bhaktapur to Nagarkot was unpaved and dusty. There were a mule, two horses, a red one and a white one, and a jeep at the training centre. We had to tend to Meher Shumsher's horse and jeep, taking care of them like they were our children.

By the time the jeep reached his home in Chhauni from Nagarkot, it had to be cleaned twice. He was particular about using only Lux soap to clean the vehicle. The squeaky clean jeep from Bhaktapur had to be cleaned all over again, before parking it in the garage at his home. Even after returning from Kathmandu it was washed twice, once in Bhaktapur and then again in Nagarkot. The vehicle was lathered in all kinds of waxes to keep it shiny. The tyres had to be washed and scrubbed with soapy water, the same way children are bathed.

The soldiers were intrigued by this obsession with his car. There was probably no other vehicle in the Kathmandu Valley as clean as his.

I had the chance to travel in the vehicle during a visit to Birganj for the inspection of a commando course with 12 other people crammed into the small jeep. Meher Shumsher put on his red cap and started driving. He sent the driver behind to hang on to the back of the jeep. The Colonel and his wife were seated in front and they shared a bottle of local liquor as if it were water. Sometimes they would snatch the bottle from each other, before the first one was done drinking. They lit cigarettes: the Colonel's brand was Craven A, while madam lit an Asha, the cheapest Nepali brand.

The Colonel was already tipsy by the time we got to Naubise. We were now in an overloaded jeep on a treacherous road with hairpin bends with a drunk at the wheel. The Colonel also couldn't bear to see a vehicle in front of him and had to overtake everyone. He would stop moving trucks on the road, force the drivers to come down and shower them with choice obscenities. Only when everyone, including his children, begged him to stop driving did he finally agree. But even then he taunted everyone by putting his young son behind the wheel rather than the driver.

Whenever we drove over a muddy stream, the car had to be washed and waxed. After reaching Birganj, they booked a room at the Samjhana Hotel. Major Shyam and I wanted to stay in the barracks. But after seeing the tipsy Colonel force all the soldiers there to take up fighting positions, we decided the hotel would be a better option. No one could say no to him, so we just opted out. News of this alcohol-fuelled escapade even reached HQ. DMT Chief, Colonel Arjun, was hopping mad though Major Shyam finally managed to calm him down.

There are many other stories about Meher Shumsher. Food, drink and games were an everyday affair at his bungalow. One day when he was looking for a lighter with a cigarette between his lips, Pyar Jung Thapa offered to light his cigarette. He was the captain at the training centre and had brought a gas lighter from the US during a course there. But Colonel Meher took it as an insult and thought Pyar Jung was showing off, since he didn't smoke. He refused Pyar Jung's light and sent his driver to fetch his own lighter from Chhauni. After the driver brought the lighter, he called Pyar Jung over and said: "Pyar, I also have a lighter."

While he was a very fun-loving person, he knew how to get his work done by others. He understood very well to whom to assign which task. Furthermore, he trusted us and left the management of the cadets' training to us. He could choose the right man for the right job at the right time.

If the cadets made any mistakes, we would punish them as sternly as possible. Sometimes we made them count the stars or the blinking red lights in Kathmandu. Some even had to stand on Nagarkot hill in only their underwear during the winter, while others had to get soaked in pouring rain. When hailstones hammered Nagarkot, we used to make them stand still while we stuffed their underwear with hailstones.

Being punished and punishing others in the Army is passed down from one generation of cadets to the next generation of trainers. Everything we had to go through in Pune and Dehradun we simply passed on to our Nepali cadets in Nagarkot.

"The cadets are so busy they haven't even washed their socks since the new instructor came," Colonel Meher joked. Indeed, they could only rest for four to five hours each day and didn't even have time to wash their socks. That would have to wait for Saturday.

What we did to the first batch, however, was nothing compared to what we put the second batch through. Following an incident on the first day of the new batch's arrival, just the sound of my name was enough to terrify the new cadets that year.

It was already dark by the time they reached Nagarkot. I was walking around in my warm track suit that night when I saw cadets from the new batch who looked worn out after all that walking. One member of the group was acting a bit too cocky for his own good.

Most cadets behave as if they're officers already, when

in fact they've only been selected for cadet training. Unless they begin sweating it out on the training grounds, they have a tendency to look down on everyone else. That boy was probably thinking of himself as a new officer and looking for a private to carry his luggage. But it might not have been entirely his fault. Someone might have told him that since he was an officer now, there'd be helpers for him.

He walked straight towards me. I used to smoke a lot back then. What started out for the sake of being cool in school and college, kicked in as a habit and now I was addicted to smoking probably 10 cigarettes a day.

"*Dai*, give me a cigarette," he reached out towards me. Maybe he thought I was a private.

"And who are you, sir?" I asked politely.

He told me his name, which I can't remember now.

"What brought you here then?" I was even more polite now.

Hearing my subdued tone, he suddenly began acting even cockier. "I'm a second lieutenant," he said pushing his chest forward.

"Oh, you've put on the badge already?" I asked.

"No, we still have the training to do," he hesitated a little.

"So you're here for the training then?"

"Yes, *dai*," he replied.

"So take off your shoes and strip to your underwear," I ordered in a stern voice, "Stand here for two hours."

He was startled.

"Unless you pass the training you're not even a soldier, understand?" I said.

While he was braving Nagarkot's nippy winter in his underwear, I left for my warm room that night. He was struck with terror when he saw me the next day as his instructor.

After that, I didn't have to do much as word about my strictness was exaggerated as it spread. "Katawal, one day Harbaksh Singh," Colonel Meher used to tease me because of my stern nature.

Harbaksh Singh was the famous Indian Army general who set a benchmark for discipline in the military world. I was compared to him throughout the training, and it was somewhat flattering to be compared to Colonel Meher's role model.

We had to go to the field with cadets and other trainees and we once headed east from Nagarkot to the banks of the Sunkoshi for a live-fire exercise. We selected Jalbire for the practice and used two LMGs, eight rifles and smoke bombs. Every time we fired, Colonel Shambhu used to get the jitters. "This easterner will ruin everything," he used to whimper. Apparently, it was Captain Hamal who exaggerated how gruelling it was for the cadets. We reported around 2 am that the exercise went well. "Did anyone die in the firing?" Colonel Shambhu asked. When he found that none of us were bruised or injured during practice, he was genuinely relieved. He then vented his ire at Captain Hamal for getting him all worked up for nothing. "Swap your captain and lieutenant patches," he ordered, "Hamal demoted and Katawal promoted."

"Hey, Hamal give your patch to Katawal," he shouted at him, "Aren't you the one who said Katawal killed someone?"

It was difficult managing the canteen during field exercises. We used to sweat it out on the firing range but Colonel Shambhu was the one to finish all the good meaty chunks in the curry. We never got to see those chicken drumsticks. Shambhu had eaten them all and we were left with just the bony bits.

Dr Bijay Bahadur Rajbhandari used to accompany us during our practice. He was from Patan and also my classmate. "We need to think of something to get the old man away from the meat," I said. During our practice we also had a few colonels along. All they did was drink whisky and chat all day.

"Hey Colonel, looks like you finished all the chicken by yourself," Bijay said.

"Yes, doctor," Colonel Shambhu said.

"There's nothing worse than that, Colonel," Bijay said, "It looks tasty but it gives no strength."

While the Colonel looked surprised, Bijay added, "What does the leg do?"

"Walk," Colonel Shambhu said.

"What do the wings do?"

"Fly."

"So does the strength lie in the chest, the legs or the wings?" Bijay got him worked up, "These people are cheating you."

"That's true," Colonel Shambhu looked enlightened.

He immediately called the cook and ordered, "From now on, only wings and legs for me, not those chest and thigh pieces."

Only after that did we get our fair share of choice chicken pieces throughout the training. After returning to Nagarkot, he asked one of his helpers, Giri, about the relative merits of chicken pieces.

"This doctor tells me that chicken legs and wings give energy. Is that true?" he asked Giri.

"What nonsense," Giri said, "If I'm not here everyone fools you, Colonel."

Thus, Giri sabotaged our subterfuge and the juicy pieces of chicken started disappearing again.

The soldiers saw Commandant Meher Shumsher sobbing one afternoon. He was a full colonel and King Mahendra's cousin. What could possibly have happened? As people started whispering, I went straight to his bungalow and was taken aback when I saw him bawling loudly like a baby. Something very unfortunate must have happened. But how could I ask?

He looked at me affectionately and finally spoke, "Everything's over, Katawal."

I didn't understand but didn't dare ask for more information. Tears continued rolling down his cheeks, wetting his shirt.

"King Mahendra passed away," he said, sobbing.

He had found out about it before the official announcement. As soon as I heard those words, I felt dizzy too, and everything became blurry. I had gone there to give the colonel a shoulder to cry on but now I needed help to get over my own shock. I walked straight back to my room. All the memories of running behind the King in Okhaldhunga, my several attempts to meet him and travelling with his procession started flooding back. I also remembered meeting him at the school and the Palace.

King Mahendra, whom I considered my godfather, was no longer with us. Just thinking about that was very disturbing. The pain was personal and deep. Then again, I gratefully recalled his generosity to me, which had helped me get so far in life. His Majesty had carved out my destiny by plucking me from my village. He would have been so happy to hear about my promotion to lieutenant, I regretted not being able to share the news with him.

But I also remembered with bitterness all the people who stood between us and prevented me from meeting the King even one last time. I felt frustrated thinking how I couldn't visit the man who had educated me and brought me this far. A part of me wanted to believe that the reports about his death were false. If it was true, why hadn't it been announced on the radio yet?

I kept tuning the radio but all I heard was melancholy music. Radio Nepal was already in mourning. The barracks were abuzz with rumours. And shortly afterwards the radio broadcast an announcement that King Mahendra was no more. His body was being flown from Chitwan to Kathmandu.

After hearing the news confirmed, I sat on the floor feeling numb. I could hear noisy activity outside. I remembered what the old folk in my village used to say about the gods taking good people away early. It seemed true. Suddenly, I was surrounded by darkness, but how long could I lose myself in it?

I got up and walked straight to the barber. There was a long queue of people waiting to have their heads shaved. I shaved mine too and avoided salt for a few days as a sign of respect for the departed soul. The country had lost its dear King and I had lost my godfather.

My work as an instructor at the cadet training centre was appreciated. When Nripa Shumsher became the commandant he came to visit and minutely inspected my work. He was satisfied that he had posted me to the training academy. Even Colonel Meher Shumsher rewarded me with Rs 500 for my good work there.

I put on the captain's badge at Nagarkot. Later, when Bharat Keshari Simha became the DMT chief, he came to visit the training academy. He was a renowned officer who involved himself closely in all tasks under his supervision. He was strict and used to parajump himself. I was selected to make a presentation to him. Although there were several more senior officers, Colonel Nripa entrusted me with the responsibility.

We prepared a calendar of the training, encompassing everything from the cadets' entry to the passing out parade. All the reading material was translated into Nepali. We also prepared reading material on weapons training, strategy and other matters.

"I'm very impressed," Colonel Bharat Keshari said with a pat on my back. Of the three instructors, he evaluated me the highest, and after a few days I was transferred to the training directorate at HQ.

Colonel Bharat Keshari had established a division under him at the directorate to which I was assigned with responsibility for the preparation of reading materials for Army training. I would collect as much training material as possible from the Indian, British and American armies and translate, edit and adapt them to our conditions. Although I was working in the Army, my job was almost like that of a foreign affairs officer.

Since Colonel Bharat Keshari was satisfied with my performance, he started assigning me tasks in other divisions as well. This was a chance for me to prove myself, so I didn't give him any reason to complain regarding any of the tasks I was assigned to perform.

During one of the ceremonies at Tundikhel, for instance, I was given responsibility for conducting the parade. He chose me over others at DMT who had been there longer. The parade went better than he expected. After that, I was able to carve out an identity for myself at HQ and my name became synonymous with training.

Rebirth

I always dreamt of learning from powerful military forces, like those of the USA and UK, in their home countries.

In 1974-75 there was a single quota for a Ranger and Special Forces Course in the US. This was considered to be a very tough course in the Army which separated the men from the boys.

We had to fulfil all the criteria in written exams, physicals and strategy to get into the course. HQ conducted the tests. I left my competitors behind and was nominated. However, the US Embassy conducted the English exams. I had to score above 80 per cent and I failed. I felt like I had died.

Colonel Nripa was aware of my strengths and weaknesses. He wasn't satisfied with the results, so he personally requested the Americans to arrange another test. This time I passed.

The training was a collaborative effort between the US Army's Ranger Course in Fort Benning in Georgia and Fort Bragg's Special Course in North Carolina. Some of the officers before me couldn't complete this course and left partway through. Although they saved face by switching to an easier course, they left a blot on the image of the Nepalese Army in the US.

When I went to meet Colonel Nripa before leaving, he told me: "I've heard a lot of people have come back after failing that course. If you fail it too, you can drown yourself there."

"I won't return if I fail," I assured him.

During the whole journey there, I kept thinking about Colonel Nripa's warning and my words to him. I was now determined not just to pass but to top the course.

There were 90 trainees from 10 countries, including Americans, in the course. It was far more rigorous than our commando training. The first 58 days were set aside for the Ranger Course after which we had a month-long Christmas break, followed by the three month special forces training in which we had to parachute at night over unknown terrain. The aim was to teach us how to escape safely from enemy territory even when we were alone. There were soldiers on the ground posing as the enemy. After jumping from the plane we had to land safely and avoid falling into enemy hands in what was called "escape and evade". If we were caught, the whole exercise had to be repeated or our points would be deducted. It was like a real war.

There were 39 people ready to jump off the plane somewhere above the coast of the Gulf of Mexico and I was the first off the plane. "You will all jump in different places," the instructor had said, "There will be soldiers searching for you on the ground. Consider them your enemies and do not get caught at any cost."

The instructor hit my back and I leapt out the door. The plane vanished into the night sky. I was falling down in the middle of the night with the parachute billowing above me. I spotted a black spot below and assumed it must be the dense forest the instructor had told us about. I managed to control the parachute, and as I dropped, I could see something shimmering like a body of water. I thought it was a swamp and tried to avoid it. My parachute got tangled in a tree but I unfastened myself, climbed down and hid the parachute. All I had was a map, a compass and a torch. Since my Okhaldhunga days, I felt I could win the world with just a torch light.

After walking for over 20 minutes, I still hadn't run into anyone. I could see some vehicle headlights on a distant road. Suddenly, I heard a loud voice on a mike, "Officer from Nepal, come to the road."

. I was startled. I felt it was the enemy unit trying to trick me into being captured so I moved away from the road. "Officer from Nepal, come to us," the voice boomed again. I kept myself hidden in the darkness.

"Officer, don't hide," the mike blared, "This is for real." This was a combat exercise and I wasn't going to fall for that trick. I was still hiding when I suddenly found myself surrounded by powerful lights. Two helicopters hovered in the night sky, training their searchlights on the ground.

"They must have caught the rest of them," I thought, "But I won't come out at any cost."

The brigadier had come in the helicopter and the announcements on the mike began again. Something had surely gone wrong; otherwise, the entire training academy wouldn't be at the scene to look for a captain. I must have done something wrong.

I hesitantly walked out towards the road. The soldiers rushed up and grabbed me. "Oh god, You're alive!" The brigadier hugged me. I was puzzled about why they thought I was in danger. Finally, they told me what had happened. I had jumped a few seconds before I was supposed to and that had been enough to drop me several miles from the actual drop zone. The year before, a trainee from Singapore had lost his life during the same course when he jumped over the wrong spot and drowned in a marsh.

"Although he made a wrong jump, he completed the mission," the brigadier said about me. "You have been reborn." The Americans hugged and congratulated me.

The next morning, we celebrated my victory and rebirth with a big feast. My antics were talked about throughout the training period. I was selected from among the foreign trainees to speak at Duke University that year on the same stage as US Army generals as well as professors from the university.

On behalf of the trainees, I had to speak about Nepal and our region. After the formal programme, one of the professors came to talk to me during lunch. "Which part of Nepal are you from?" he asked.

"The eastern part," I replied, surprised.

"Which district in the east?"

I was even more startled.

"Okhaldhunga," I said, "Have you been there?"

"A couple of times," he said.

He asked me why the district was named Okhaldhunga. I didn't know the answer. He then told me myths about Okhaldhunga, mentioning King Prithvi Narayan Shah and Siddhicharan Shrestha. I was amazed. It was a matter of regret that I didn't know the history and geography of my own district in Nepal.

I kept my word to Colonel Nripa and topped the ranger training. I did equally well in the special forces training amongst the allied students. The US Embassy in Nepal sent a letter to the Army congratulating me. After returning to Nepal, I was posted to DMT, in the cadet selection section. My job required me to study a lot, so I kept myself occupied with all kinds of books regarding Nepali history, geography and society. I read as many books as possible by Balchandra Sharma, Grishma Bahadur Devkota, *Sardār* Bhim Bahadur Pandey and others.

I would cut down on my other expenses just to buy books and quench my thirst for knowledge. I read all the books from cover to cover. Never in my life had I read as much as I did then.

During my time in the cadet selection section, there was an invitation for the entire battalion to participate in the UN Emergency Force, UNEF-2. It was a great opportunity and a matter of pride for the entire country for the Army to take part in a UN mission.

If we could leave a good first impression then the partnership could last longer, so HQ began selecting the best officers for UNEF. Before this, only a limited number of officers from the Nepalese Army were selected for UN missions as monitoring officers or mobilised for other general work.

Our battalion's duty station was near Cairo and the battalion commander was Gadul Shumsher Rana. I was the second-in-command of one of the infantry companies and used to go to the post office everyday to receive and send the unit's mail. Colonel Gadul once saw me speeding down the road in busy traffic.

"Despite driving for all these years, I can't drive like you," he cautioned, "Be careful, all right?"

"Okay, sir," I replied, sitting up straight.

But that was only a formality.

I was driving from Ismailia to Cairo one day, speeding as usual, when I saw a Russian military truck in front of us. I stepped on the accelerator and tried to overtake it but before the truck could move away, the jeep's bonnet had already touched its rear. I veered off to the left, missed the truck by inches and went into a sandy trench by the side of the road. I blacked out and when I opened my eyes, I couldn't see the jeep, the road, the truck or my four friends who were with me in the vehicle. I looked around and realised I was in a hospital bed. The Nepali doctor was also there.

"Thank God, all four of you didn't die on the spot," the doctor said.Battalion commander Gadul Shumsher and contingent commander Arjun Narsingh Rana rushed to see us the next day. Arjun Narsingh had become a general then and was both the Nepali contingent commander and one of the brigade commanders in UNEF-2.

"I told him time and again," Colonel Gadul Shumsher sounded frustrated as he reported to General Arjun, "But this bloody man wouldn't listen."

I was able to walk out after four days' treatment at the Swedish Hospital. As a punishment, the UN seized my license for a month. The jeep was still at the camp when I was discharged from hospital. When I saw the crushed American jeep, I realised how fortunate we were to come out alive.

I remembered my mother saying, "Girls with tiny feet and hands are lucky." It was Uma's lucky stars that gave me a second chance at life.

I had the opportunity to command Kalidhoj Infantry Company in Dhankuta when I was only 27 and still just a captain. I started a plantation around the barracks with the ranger's suggestions, planting the saplings which grew the fastest. Since there was enough vegetation to provide fodder, I also brought in cows that gave us milk and other dairy products to share in the barracks.

"*Kānchhā* is lucky with cattle apparently." My mother used to keep repeating the astrologer's words about me. I also bought two roosters and three hens for Rs 39. I went on adding more hens which hatched more chicks. There was plenty of wood and stone in the village to build chicken coops and within a year there was enough chicken to feed the entire mess once a month.

Coincidentally, King Birendra and Queen Aishwarya's eastern regional visit was scheduled in the same year, 1975-76.

As it is with every royal visit, the Prime Minister, Ministers, Army Chief, IGP, security heads and other government officials were also part of the entourage. During such visits, the King, Queen and others used to stay at the regional headquarters and visit the districts from there. The chief coordinating officer for the visit was Nripa Shumsher, eastern region's general. It was he who selected me for the posting to Dhankuta.

It was, therefore, a good opportunity for me, as the head of the company, to showcase my work during the King's stay. I wanted to make the most of this time since it was also a chance to meet highflying people from all over the country. I understood it would be easier to climb up the ladder if I got in the good books of important people in the Palace, Army and civil service. Back then Surendra Bahadur Shrestha was the Eastern Zonal Commissioner, while Bhakta Bahadur Koirala was the CDO of Dhankuta. Former Prime Minister Surya Bahdur Thapa helped us a great deal to manage the visit.

The development offices used to have a tough time during the King's visit. But unlike us, their concern wasn't about welcoming the King and Queen but misleading them about progress. They'd bring in fresh tomato plants from elsewhere and produce them as success stories of model local farms. They carried out overnight tree plantations to show nonexistent afforestation and showcase better breeds of goat, cow and sheep.

The gardens in Dhankuta Palace had plenty of orange trees that used to overflow with ripe fruit hanging from their branches. Those trees would look great if they were well-maintained. Since the visit was scheduled for January-February, we tried every means from using scarecrows to placing fake eagles and dead crows on the trees, to guard them. Besides covering them with nets we did everything.

The Palace was already looking prettier, surrounded with ripe bright oranges. We also had fast-growing plants at the barracks to add to the greenery there. As the visit date came closer, we trimmed and manicured the branches of the smaller trees.

With only a few days remaining until the visit, helicopters began flying in more frequently. The Army's senior pilots used to ferry VIPs and essential items for the visit, making five or six trips per day. The barracks was responsible for providing hospitality.

One of the pilots and I were having lunch together when he made a request after the very first bite. "Katawal, you need to manage some ghee for me," the pilot said. We had been feeding him glorious golden ghee and fresh orange juice from the garden almost every day.

"Oh, we don't get that here," I tried to evade the request.

"How come?" he asked, "You've been feeding me pure ghee every day."

Now it looked like our hospitality had put me in a tight spot. The dairy products we offered him were all produced in the barracks from vet-tested best breeds of cows. I had never given anything from the barracks to our high-ranking senior officers. Instead I used to let the boys share it among themselves. But this pilot was adamant.

"I need to take a few jars home," he kept pestering me. I was annoyed at his greed.

Everyone in the Army looks the same to civilians. Although our uniforms are the same, the reality within is starkly different. The troops, ADCs and pilots from the Palace considered themselves to be a breed apart. They were closer to the King, Queen and the royal family. For them, the King and Queen didn't belong to the people of Nepal but exclusively to them, almost like their own prized possessions. It was people like us who spoiled them by sending gifts and presents in the first place. Because this pilot used to fly the King, Queen and other royal family members, he had a sense of entitlement.

I grumbled inside but didn't say a word. However, the pilot refused to give up. It reached a point where, if he ran into me at the base, he would immediately pounce on me and ask if I had sent people to fetch him his jar of ghee. I couldn't stand it anymore. "Colonel, are you here on duty or flying here just to get your ghee?" I snapped.

He turned red and didn't answer. After that I was afraid that this pilot, who flew the King and Queen regularly, wouldn't miss an opportunity to do me harm. But I also told myself that one should be fearless, do no wrong and stand by the truth.

Sure enough, I found out later that the pilot tried to befriend my staff to dig up dirt on me. When he couldn't find anything, he turned towards the orange orchard around the barracks. He was probably jealous that I would get the credit for it so he conspired to destroy all the ripe golden oranges. When landing and taking off, he would intentionally hover low over the trees to shake the fruit with his rotor wash. The oranges lay strewn about below the trees like *Pārijāt* flowers after a hailstorm.

I was furious when I found out but I didn't let my anger spiral out of control. The soldiers were heartbroken seeing their efforts go to waste. We devised a plan to save the remaining orange trees and set up bamboo poles around the helipad so that the helicopter couldn't land there.

I also complained about the pilot's actions to the zonal head and CDO. But since he was the pilot for the royal visit, no one dared say a word to him.

"This is too much, taking out your anger on the oranges," I shouted at him.

"It happens all the time while landing and taking off," he sniffed. "Or should we not ferry anything for the royal visit just to save your precious oranges?"

I then used the royals as an excuse to bring him down. "Since we were informed that His Majesty likes fresh juice, we were guarding these trees. Also they added beauty to the barracks," I said.

After hearing me, the pilot looked terror-struck. Back then the King's name was exploited to boast and threaten. But the King never knew that his name was being used like that behind his back.

The King and Queen arrived on the scheduled date. The camps were inspected on the first day. They went around looking at the rooms and tents. His Majesty was happy to see ripe oranges in the orchard even in winter.

"Looks like the oranges were guarded closely," Prince Dhirendra said.

Since it was a nippy winter evening, everyone was huddled around the bonfire. I was sitting several rows behind the VIPs. There was no way I could say anything in the presence of so many senior officers.

"I told them to protect those oranges at any cost, Your Highness," the zonal head said, trying to take all the credit.

"Don't they belong to the barracks?" ADC Shanta Kumar Malla piped in. He saw that the zonal chief's remark was only intended to curry favour with the royals.

King Birendra didn't say anything. The next morning we served them fresh orange juice and milk from the barracks. I was happy to hear everyone appreciate the oranges on the first day. But that wasn't all that made me happy. I was promoted to major and put on the insignia on the morning of the royal visit.

The entire Cabinet of Ministers and the Chief of Army Staff used to frequent the camp set up for the royal visit. The leaders and chiefs from the central, regional and zonal levels poured in as well. With all kinds of people visiting the camp, the problems were just as varied. Some couldn't do without alcohol while others couldn't stand the sight of it. There were religious visitors who were particular about not having onion and garlic in their meals, while others couldn't do without meat every meal and enjoyed gambling.

Minister Hiralal Bishwakarma visited the camp one day. He lived in Dharan and was originally from Debrebas, Dhankuta. Back then his name was mentioned on Radio Nepal news almost every day.

"If my name isn't mentioned on the radio for a few days, Her Majesty gets worried thinking I'm unwell," he used to brag to people.

Every evening he headed to Debrebas to drink and returned late at night. One had to go through the police check first and then the Army's sentry post before entering the camp. The last entry time for the base was 10 pm and, since it was the royal visit, this was strictly enforced.

One night he reached the gate completely drunk at around 11 pm. The sentry asked him for the password, without which the gates can't be opened. The passwords are changed daily. He didn't have the password, so the soldier couldn't let him in. He began boasting that he was a minister and hurling obscenities at the sentry. A soldier on duty follows his commander's orders even over those of the King.

When it was reported to me, I went running to the gate. When I got there, the Minister was lying flat on the ground.

"What happened, Minister?" I asked.

"The soldier beat me up," he said, "Are you also here to thrash me?"

"Take him to his tent on a stretcher," I said, letting him in. He started vomiting on the way.

I then called the coordinating officer Brigadier Nripa and reported everything. The Chief summoned me the next afternoon. Guna Shumsher JBR was the Army Chief at that time.

"Oh young man, there are reports that the Minister was beaten up," he said.

"I have already reported everything to the Brigade Commander (the coordinating officer), sir."

"No one raised a hand then?" he asked.

"No sir, why would a soldier beat up a minister?"

Minister Hiralal had even managed to complain to the King about it. I was called in to clarify after the King then asked the Chief about the incident.

King Birendra used to go for morning walks. He walked from the Palace to the Saraswati temple, horse stable, quarter guard and returned in exactly an hour.

The stables were thoroughly scrubbed and cleaned. They housed a strong horse and five equally healthy mules. The horse was fed plenty of mustard oil, eggs and other nutritious food. I had told the horse's groom, Dal Bahadur, to always be on duty throughout the King's visit. One morning the King went into the stables and asked Dal Bahadur, "How come the horse and mules look so well-fed?"

"Your Majesty, the Major supplements their diet with eggs and oil," he said, "He also takes care of them personally."

The same day he visited the quarter guard as well.

The King asked his ADC Tara Bahadur to call the company commander. I went running.

"What are these wooden guns for?" General Tara Bahadur asked me as soon as I got there.

The ADCs very well understood what the King's concerns were and asked me questions accordingly.

"Sir, the shape, size and weight of an SLR and this wooden gun are the same," I replied, "Using this during drills, exercises and on obstacle courses helps protect the real ones. If we can keep the SLRs in good order for longer, that will save us money."

Colonel Tara Bahadur and I were conversing in front of the King and the Chief. "Chief, why don't you tell everybody to do the same thing," the King said, apparently convinced by what I said.

Until then, all the soldiers used to practice with real SLRs during training. A gun is more precious to a soldier than his wife. He simply cannot leave his gun. It has to be carried during drills, obstacle training and running. Since they were carried everywhere during practice, there were higher chances of the guns getting damaged. They had to be banged on the ground during drills, which only meant more dents.

"And why more rations for the horse?" Colonel Tara Bahadur asked. Maybe the King wanted to know.

"Sir, I've been managing it through the canteen's profits. It hasn't affected the soldiers' rations," I said.

The horse was called Fusre and used to belong to the King of Mustang who gave it to King Birendra, and the horse somehow ended up in Dhankuta. Before I took command everyone from the zonal head to the CDO took turns riding this magnificent horse. But no one really took care of him, making him look increasingly underfed and dirty.

Since I enjoyed horse riding, I took over the responsibility for Fusre. After I started feeding him eggs, wheat gram, oil and other nutritious foods, the horse looked different in a month. I fed him grass at the stable every day. He used to jump happily and neigh excitedly and galloped like lightning. In a few months, he was back in shape and had the opportunity to serve during the royal visit.

The King and Queen flew from Dhankuta to attend programmes in the surrounding districts and then returned to the base in the evening. His Majesty met with and talked to everyone from government staff to village officials, local businessmen, social workers, teachers and the public.

During such interactions, the King used to ask them about security, administration and development in their regions. The village chiefs would ask for development projects like building roads and bridges and bringing electricity and water to their areas. The King would listen intently and immediately order the responsible bodies to implement these projects. Representatives of all ministries were also present during these interactions.

All the government officials used to be terrified during such meetings. Once, the CDO of Sankhuwasabha was so nervous that he collapsed on the ground, right before my eyes, while briefing the King.

During the visit, the King and the Queen also expressed their interest in meeting commoners. But the Palace administration and ADCs would stand in the way. Some village women with bare feet and running noses had come to meet the King in Dhankuta. They were complaining about Jhapa

Forest Administration's strict ways. But the ADCs were pulling them away saying that visiting time was over. His Majesty was furious when he saw this. "Allow them to have their say and don't judge people by their appearance," he ordered.

His Majesty was also scheduled to visit Biratnagar for the Democracy Day celebrations. The constant travelling took a toll on him and the King came down with a 103 degree fever. Military doctor Devendra Bahadur Malla, royal physician Sachhe Kumar Pahadi, Dr Gangol and other civilian doctors examined him.

"Your Majesty shouldn't travel today, you need rest," the doctors said and requested that he cancel the scheduled visit to Biratnagar.

But the King wouldn't agree. "People from all over the eastern region must have walked for days to reach Biratnagar," he apparently said, "They'll be disappointed if I don't go, so I have to get there."

The doctors could do nothing since the King had already made up his mind. He took some medicine to keep the fever in check and left for Biratnagar under the supervision of three doctors.

On the last day, General Nripa, the chief coordinating officer, hosted a dinner to officially conclude the royal visit. All the popular artists from the eastern region were invited for the dinner. There were songs, dances and poetry recitals the whole night.

I was the Master of Ceremonies that evening. After the hour-long official programme was over, it was time to dance.

"Get His Majesty to dance," General Nripa whispered to me. If the King danced, it meant he was happy and the chief coordinating officer's management was considered successful only if the King was pleased.

But His Majesty didn't want to dance and pointed towards Prime Minister Dr Tulsi Giri who passed the buck on to the Rastriya Panchayat Chairman, Khadga Man Singh.

We tried to get the King onto the dance floor again. And this time when he pointed towards the Prime Minister, Giri promptly stood up and started dancing with me.

"Where is your house in Kathmandu, Major?" the Prime Minister asked.

"I don't have one, we live in a rented room, sir," I said.

"How come majors don't have houses?" he asked.

"Even your salary isn't enough to build a house, so how can I have one," I said a bit testily.

"Who's your father?"

"You don't know him, so he could be any Ram Bahadur or Shyam Bahadur."

He tried to imply that, like many officers in the Army, I must have come from a well-to-do family.

"I'm a hillbilly from Okhaldhunga," I told him.

"Major, I know how clever you are," he said.

The party was finally getting started. Just then, the King stood up and started dancing too. I could clearly see General Nripa's face light up as the King got on the dance floor.

Some nurses surrounded the King and started dancing with him. But Colonel Mohan Bikram of the Military Secretariat and Colonel Harihar Jung Shah of the hunting section didn't let the King dance for too long.

After dinner, a select few people stayed back with the King and started a session with brandy and cigars. Poems, songs and jokes started pouring out. While hosting the programme, I had praised the Army a lot. Maybe that's why Prime Minister Giri asked for the King's permission to share an anecdote.

"Go ahead," the King said.

Prime Minister Giri began: "After the end of World War II, generals from the navy, air force and army were on a train going from Berlin to Munich. The army general said, 'We won the war.' But the navy general objected, 'If it wasn't for the Royal Navy could you have won the war? You were able to attack from the land only because of the navy's blockade.'

'If it weren't for our Royal Air Force, victory wouldn't have been possible,' the air force general said.

There was a man sitting in a corner in the same carriage. After hearing all of them, he finally spoke, 'Sit down and shut up. We told you to go to war and we ordered you to stop the war.'"

The anecdote was to illustrate civilian supremacy over the military. I had noticed that the erudite Dr Giri left all others far behind when it came to political debate and philosophy. I was seated behind General Nripa. "Sir, can I give a reply to the Prime Minister?" I asked but he pulled me by my sweater and told me to sit down. So I kept quiet.

The programme ended at midnight and soon after Military Secretary General Dan Gambhir Singh Rayamajhi summoned me to his tent.

"The King has rewarded you with Rs 12,000 for the excellent job you've done here," said Rayamajhi, handing me the money.

"Don't blow it all on alcohol and gambling," he told me and made me sign a receipt, "Use it wisely."

"Yes, sir," I saluted him and took my leave, "Good night, sir."

That night I tossed and turned in my bed for a long time but I couldn't sleep. In good times and in bad, sleep, it seems, is difficult to come by.

I was standing alongside the Zonal Commissioner, CDO, chief coordinator and other VIPs from the district to see the King off on the day of his departure.

"Thank you, Brigadier," the King told General Nripa.

"Thank you, Major," he said to me.

My work during the King's visit in Dhankuta was appreciated by everyone in the Army and I was awarded *Gorkha Dakshinbahu IV* the following year.

A lot of relatives and friends from my in-laws' side were in the Army. "Uma, your husband was apparently awarded Rs 50,000," someone got the rumour mill buzzing. I had not told Uma about the Rs 12,000 until then. I wanted to surprise her but gossipmongers spoiled the surprise and even exaggerated the sum.

I showed Uma the money and said, "It's only 12,000, not 50,000. What can we do with it?"

Back then 12,000 was a large sum of money. I had brought two motorcycles from the US. I kept one and sold the other for Rs 11,000. There was also Rs 3,300 I had saved from the UN mission. With this money we bought a plot of land in Koteshwor for Rs 14,000.

Koteshwor was a secluded area back then, far from the capital's bustling neighbourhoods, where you could hear jackals howling in the mid-afternoon. But since we got the land cheaply, we decided to make a home there because of its other plus point: a trolley bus services from 6 am to 10 pm.

Compared to other Army officers, my first property purchase came very late. But that's just my nature. I never placed importance on personal property during my military life. So much so that even building a house for my family was also never a priority for me, which earned me compliments and ridicule in equal measure.

During my posting at Dhankuta, the company had set up a private fund collected from the money that we saved from our rations and other expenses. The senior subedar and accountant told me the fund had amassed Rs 70,000.

"What should we do with this money?" I asked the soldiers during the routine Darbar parade. "What do you want?"

"Let's have blazers for everyone like the boys from the top units," they said.

When General Nripa Shumsher was the battalion commander, he provided blazers for everyone in the famous Manindra Dal Battalion.

"Everyone fine with blazers then?" I asked.

"Yes, sir," they approved the decision unanimously. Coincidentally, General Nripa was the brigade commander of the barracks we belonged to. I took the money and went with the accountant to Dharan.

It was a Saturday. The general, deputy brigade commander Madhav Shumsher and an accountant called Navin were all seated together.

I showed them our accounts, the money we had collected and said, "The boys have asked for blazers. Where should we buy them?"

"Order them from Delhi or Calcutta," General Nripa ordered Navin, "Make arrangements for the purchase."

"It's indeed true that these eastern folk don't have any brains," Madhav Shumsher suddenly blurted out. I didn't understand and looked confused.

"I've heard that he just had a son and his wife is probably living in a dark room," he said, "This money is enough to buy land and even build a house but this fool is running after blazers."

Navin looked towards the general.

"Hey, Madhav, what are you saying?" the general asked angrily. "Trying to teach people unnecessary things here?"

After that, the general thanked me and said, "Listen, Major, a soldier's blessing is all you need to be destined for better things in life."

Before leaving, he again said, "Always earn a soldier's blessings. Their curse destroys you and their blessings bring you good luck."

Whatever I have earned in my life so far, my achievements are all due to the blessings of the soldiers under my command.

Singha Pratap's glory

After I joined the Army, there were four Chiefs: Singha Pratap Shah was the fourth Army Chief after Surendra Bahadur Shah, Singha Bahadur Basnet and Guna Shumsher

JBR. Although I was a low-ranking officer, I minutely analysed their working styles based on what senior officers used to tell me.

No one could beat Singha Pratap. He didn't speak much, so no one could really decipher what he was thinking or what his intentions were. He was the Military Attaché at the Nepali Embassy in the UK when Crown Prince Birendra was studying there and served as his local guardian.

The intelligence service, the Army, and the Investigation Centre used to send reports to the Palace. Everyone thought that the military's reports were the most influential. There were rumours that if an Army report apportioned blame, it could jeopardise the job of anyone from the Prime Minister to a peon. That was why we often heard about ministers, former ministers, zonal commissioners and other dignitaries queuing up outside Shashi Bhawan every day. They would also line up with garlands to welcome the Chief during programmes. There was no doubt that all the generals were petrified of the Chief.

I used to report directly to General Bharat Keshari, the Director of Military Operations (DMO). Colonel Tika Shumsher JBR was the deputy DMO. The Directorate of Military Operations also worked as the Security Coordination Committee secretariat. It was possibly the most powerful mechanism during the Panchayat era, with the security forces and civil service as its pillars. All policy decisions related to security and administration were made through this committee. It was able to give directives not just to the ministries and zonal commissioners but also to the Prime Minister's Office. Letters signed by General Bharat Keshari used to be acted upon immediately.

I was the operations officer under the DMO, so I was

responsible for matters related to the military and civil service. This also opened doors for me to establish relationships with bigwigs in the administration and government. I used to call to invite them to the regular meetings in Army HQ, send reminders and also personally receive them. This helped expand my network of contacts.

The committee chaired by the Army Chief had the Chief Zonal Commissioner, Principal Military Secretary, Chief Secretary, Defence Secretary, Home Secretary, IGP and intelligence chief as its members. It was our office's responsibility to invite them for meetings and send them the decisions made by the committee.

I used to prepare the minutes of the meetings and the general would sign at the bottom. When I read the decisions, it looked like this committee was running Nepal and not Singha Darbar.

Either a major or colonel had to stay for night duty at HQ. I was on duty twice a week. Information would pour in from all over the country throughout the night. I had to immediately report to the general if there was anything major which required an urgent response. When I had time on my hands, I would read books and newspapers all night.

The phone rang at 11 pm.

"Good evening, Major Katawal," I heard a soft voice say, "Singha Pratap speaking."

"Good evening, sir," I got up and stood at attention, even though the Chief was on the phone and not physically present.

"How's everything going?" the Chief asked.

"The flood in Siraha has caused trouble at the barracks there," I said.

"So whom did you inform, Major?"

"Sir, I already reported it to the DMO general," I was still standing.

"Is there someone above your general in the Royal Nepal Army?" the Chief's tone was polite but firm.

"Yes, sir," I said nervously.

"From now on, can I also be informed if there is a significant incident?" he said and hung up.

It was indeed true that when Chief Singha Pratap spoke softly, it was an indication of an approaching hurricane. The conversation with the Chief left me baffled.

After a few days, General Bharat Keshari left for parajump exercises in Pokhara. He had ordered our second boss, Tika Shumsher, to call a meeting for the next day.

Around the same time, Home Secretary Sher Bahadur Shahi was also out of Kathmandu. Joint Secretary Birendra Prasad Shah was the second-in-command at the Ministry. The Chief had given specific orders to "call Bir Bahadur Shahi at the Home Ministry". But Colonel Tika probably forgot, didn't mention anything to me and only passed on to me the orders to hold the meeting. The next morning Colonel Tika entered my room smoking a cigarette.

"Hey you, the Chief had asked to speak to Bir Bahadur Shahi. Did you call him?" he asked.

By that time I had already invited the second man at the Home Ministry, according to the rules. The list of the invitees for the meeting and the agenda had already reached the Chief by then.

The Chief's ADC called me shortly afterwards.

"The Chief wants to talk to you," he said.

I was surprised.

"Singha Pratap speaking," he said quietly, "I heard there's a meeting."

"The General's in Pokhara," I said, "So we've already informed everyone, sir."

When the phone line went dead abruptly, I took a pen and notebook and went to the Chief's office. That was the first time I had entered the office of the Chief of Army Staff.

He looked me up and down. "Major, do you want to continue working in the Army?" he asked with an ominous smile.

"I do, sir," I said loudly, standing ramrod straight.

"Is everything going to work as you want it?" he sounded diplomatic.

"No, sir," I said even more loudly.

"Will everything happen as I say?" he asked.

"Yes, sir," I was still at attention.

"Whom did you call at the Home Ministry?"

"I only called as per the rules, sir."

"Didn't Colonel Tika say anything?"

"Colonel Tika only informed me about it later, sir."

His tone suddenly became normal after hearing my reply.

"I didn't know about it," I said, "It won't happen again, sir."

"Go," he ordered.

Had the Chief informed General Bharat Keshari about whom to invite, the misunderstanding could have been avoided. This was the second time I escaped the Chief's wrath.

While all the other generals were petrified of the Chief, I understood that all was not well between the Chief and General Bharat Keshari, both of whom were related to the Palace.

The Chief wanted to bring down General Bharat Keshari by pointing out faults in the DMO. But General Bharat Keshari was an upright officer, not at all scared of the Chief, and wanted to take him head-on. I was worried that I could be caught in the middle.

I was at the office one Saturday afternoon. Around 3 pm, the DMI office was buzzing with activity, the Chief having just returned after inspecting Dhankuta and Ilam.

"Is anybody working here?" the Chief asked.

Major Bhim Bahadur Thapa had said, "Rookmangud will be there if no one else is." Bhim Bahadur *dai* was like the Chief's court jester, who always accompanied him from his home to district visits. He was popular all over the country through the Army Programme on Radio Nepal.

Bhim Bahadur *dai* came to see me.

He looked happy to see me in the office and said, "I told him you'd be here and here you are. My job's safe now."

I panicked as soon as I heard about the Chief's arrival. While Bhim Bahadur *dai* was elated to have protected his job, I was worried about losing mine. I rushed off with my notebook and pen.

The Chief's secretariat was open throughout the year at all hours, so I didn't understand why he was at the DMI. I stood at attention and saluted him.

The Chief wasn't really paying much attention. Bhim Bahadur *dai* poured tea from a thermos and offered it to the Chief. He signalled Bhim Bahadur *dai* to offer me tea as well. Bhim Bahadur *dai* poured tea in the thermos lid. It was right in front of me but there was no way I could take it without the Chief's orders. I was still standing at attention.

"Relax, Major. Please sit down," the Chief said. "How's everything going? Why are you at the office on a Saturday?"

"Thirty-six prisoners have escaped from Damauli jail, sir. Soldiers under the command of Number One Brigade have gone searching for them. Reports are pouring in, so I'm working on a map based on the information as it comes to hand," I said all in one breath.

"Why on a Saturday?"

"If I have the map ready today, I can submit it tomorrow as soon as it's needed," I said, still standing straight.

"Bring me what you've made," the Chief ordered, "Let's have a look at your map."

Bhim Bahadur *dai* and I brought the map. Explaining the map was almost like giving the Chief a presentation. He listened intently.

While carrying the map back, Bhim Bahadur *dai* said, "The Chief was hopping mad the whole day. Finally he looks calm. We got lucky today."

"It was God's blessing," he told me, "There's no looking back for you now."

General Bharat Keshari and I shared a very close relationship, almost like family. He was always there for me during tough times.

In May 1979 when the Army took over in a coup in Pakistan and Zulfikar Ali Bhutto was executed, the flames engulfing Pakistan heated things up in Nepal as well. Students supporting the Nepali Congress and the Communists began protesting on the streets.

We had to prepare reports after gathering information about demonstrations from everywhere. The Security Coordination Committee also discussed the protests. The judicial commission set up by the government had to give input as well. The Chief would spend the whole night at HQ. The Palace also wanted reports frequently. The Palace's policy was not to suppress the protests but they escalated, and on 23 May 1979 the Gorkhapatra Sansthan office was torched. Although the people behind the attack weren't found, this incident led to the Army being mobilised. As per orders, Satchit Shumsher reached New Road gate with 200-300 soldiers from his Number One Brigade. We quickly received another order to immediately recall Satchit and start extinguishing the fire at the newspaper office. The Palace must have sent those orders.

I sped off to New Road on my motorcycle.

"You need to get back immediately," I told General Satchit.

But he was already marching forward and angrily snapped back, "Why should I return? I have orders to protect Gorkhapatra Sansthan and the Nepal Bank."

I refused to leave until the orders were obeyed.

"The order is to extinguish the fire, sir," I said.

He understood what I meant, so all of us started

extinguishing the fire, using only dirt and tree branches.

While I was in the field undertaking such an important task, Uma was fighting death at Shanta Bhawan after heavy bleeding. My relative and Forest Secretary Krishna Bahadur Deuja informed me that Uma was unconscious.

"Do you want your wife or your job?" he asked me on the phone.

Despite Uma's condition, I was reluctant to leave my job midway through. Furthermore, I believed that when the country was burning a soldier could not abandon his duty even for family reasons. I tried to concentrate on my job but with mixed emotions.

General Bharat Keshari found out about my situation. "Go! Leave right now," he ordered.

I reached the hospital at 6 am. Uma still had the saline drip and blood transfusion tubes attached to her. She had been given seven units of blood overnight. Everyone had given up hope when they saw her lying like a corpse, hardly breathing. It looked like she would leave us at anytime. *Muma*, Uma's mother, had also thought she might die and had brought our children, Nepolina and Darwin, to her hospital bed. At around 3 am Uma's condition had started to improve.

I was ashamed of myself when I saw the state Uma was in. No matter how important a soldier's responsibilities, a husband's duty is no less important. I sat beside Uma feeling guilt-ridden for not being there for her. I stroked her cold hands and rubbed her forehead.

She opened her eyes. When she saw me, there was a glint in her tired eyes. I gently caressed her hair. She looked at me and tears rolled down her cheeks. Tears welled in my eyes as well.

General Bharat Keshari and his wife came to see Uma at about 8 am, with a bouquet of flowers. Madam had already talked to the American doctors about Uma's situation. Having them by our side during such a difficult time was very encouraging. Even today, thinking of that day sends a chill down my spine.

Until then, I had never taken any leave during my career, except for a week at the time of my marriage. I used to go to the office even on Saturdays.

My career aim was clear: to top the Staff College and go to either the US or the UK to study. After that I wanted to work as a Military Attaché.

It wasn't difficult to get promoted to major from the rank of second lieutenant. But becoming a colonel and pushing the envelope further required getting through the iron gate of the Staff College and that was difficult because of seniority. The Staff College had strict criteria for anyone sitting the entry exam: the major had to be below 35 years of age and could only sit the exam three times.

I took four days off to prepare for it. I would jokingly tell Uma, "Get all the money you can borrow from your family and relatives and buy me lots of candles because I'll be studying by candlelight every night."

In our rented room, the owners would switch off the power at 10 pm. So Uma really did bring home a lot of thick candles to help me with my preparation. Sadeep Shah, Balananda Sharma and I were the most talked about majors sitting the exam in that batch. One afternoon Sadeep came to visit me and suggested we study together. He was from a prosperous and noble family, related to Field Marshal Kaiser Shamsher. His father was an ADC. When he saw all the candles, he asked, "What are these for?"

"You see the lights are cut off in this poor man's rented room at 10 pm," I said, "After that I have to rely on these."

When he heard this he seemed uncomfortable. "How can you study under the flickering light of a candle? Let's go to my place instead. We'll study together," he said

I thought that was good idea and we left for his bungalow, the present day Israeli Embassy in Lazimpat. With delicacies coming in at regular intervals, the study session at his place turned into a chitchat session. It wasn't working, so I decided to study in my own dark, rented room instead.

It was probably exhaustion that had me down with a high fever during the first exam. Somehow, I made it to the examination hall.

By then Colonel Tika Shusmher had already become the DMT chief. "Hey you, easterner," he said, "You've topped the exams. The Chief has asked you to choose where you want to go."

"I'll go wherever you send me," I said, "But I'd be happy if I could go to the UK."

And so I was sent there.

I was among 25 overseas students who had come from 15 countries to study in the UK. We were all divided into several syndicates and our Directing Staff (teaching staff) was a colonel.

During one of the classes, I was asked to give a talk on a certain topic. Although I didn't have a posh English accent,

I prepared well and started speaking to the class. "What is this man from Nepal yapping on about, Colonel?" a major interrupted. This same British major had also earlier mocked my English.

"Colonel, I would like to ask this major to go to my country, learn to speak my language and then do what I'm doing here," I snapped back. "Major, does your Bible say coloured people have less grey matter than others? Or has science proven it"

Suddenly, the Senior Directing Staff walked in. "You said the right thing, Major RK Chhetri," he said and looked towards the British major. "You're the host, Major, and should start treating this man accordingly."

After this incident, the major changed his ways and we started getting along quite well. "RK, can I get a copy of your home assignment?" he would come to me asking for help.

Towards the end of our term, Colonel GS, one of the most senior officers in the syndicate, told me I had come first among the overseas students but when the results came out a Nigerian student was ranked first.

I went straight to the colonel to find out what had happened. "RK, you don't have oil in Nepal," he said dryly.

It was then that I understood how and why the results had changed. After all, what could the UK possibly gain from awarding someone from Nepal the top honours?

On my return, I was posted at Number One Brigade as the Brigade Major (BM). I had saved some money from the UK, with which I built a four room house in Koteshwor named "Katawal Mahal".

Number One Brigade specialised in training during inclement weather. We were sent to ice-covered lakes in the winter and in summer we had to make the rounds of jungles full of snakes and wild animals in the Tarai. One winter we had to go to Langtang. During such trips, usually the Brigadier travelled by helicopter, while the rest of us walked. But this time, while we were still packing, there was a new order: "The Brigadier will walk with the soldiers and the Brigade Major will travel in the helicopter."

Prabhu Narasingh Rana was the brigadier commanding the Brigade then. He had a protruding belly. I was hesitant about taking the helicopter while my senior officer had to travel on foot. I raised my concerns with the office of the Brigade but it made no difference. The entire time I was only worried about what the brigadier must have thought. After flying to Langtang, I walked back for a day to meet him on his way. We also secretly used a vehicle to transport him up to Trishuli.

Back then there were only sparse settlements around Langtang. We set up a health camp there. The locals queued for checkups, carrying eggs, radishes, corn and buckwheat pancakes. We had plenty of medicine in the camp. The doctor gave cetamol tablets to everyone. Those patients who had never seen medicines before would immediately feel better after taking the pills. They thanked the Army doctor, Sigdel, and sang his praises.

We stayed there for almost a month. Chief Singha Pratap and the DMT colonel who came to inspect the camp were happy with our work. After that I was ordered to leave for Rasuwagadhi. I was assigned to conduct a field study regarding combat preparation and present a report.

We were completely burnt out after walking for so long. That afternoon a soldier started complaining and crying that he couldn't walk any further. While I carried his pack, he went berserk, crying one moment then suddenly jumping around saying he was possessed by a spirit and had to be treated by a shaman.

That same evening we took shelter at a house. "I can work as a shaman," I told him, "I've cured many people in my village."

He bought it. Since there was no turmeric, I took some grain, pretended to chant prayers over it and threw the grain in all directions. I then jumped around, acting as if I was in a trance. I sprinkled some grain on top of his woollen army cap and began blabbering nonsense again, trying to sound like I was chanting prayers. After I had acted as a shaman for half an hour, he said, "I think it's working, Major."

The next morning he woke up feeling refreshed. I had succeeded.

We were able to complete the winter training and the field study in Rasuwagadhi. With the Chief's recommendation, I received the *Gorkha Dakshinbahu* medal and *Durgam Sewa Padak*.

I had a strange relationship with Chief Singha Pratap. He began by reprimanding me and later grew very fond of me. Still, I was afraid that others would be jealous of the special bond I shared with him.

Five

Hong Kong Bound

Basanta Chhetri and I were shortlisted for the post of Royal Nepal Liaison Officer in Hong Kong. My senior, Basanta was well-educated and hardworking.

Usually it was either a colonel or a major who was sent as Liaison Officer to Hong Kong for a minimum of three years. The whole family could accompany the officer throughout his tenure. After friends and family coaxed me, I went to meet ADC Colonel Shanta Kumar Malla one morning. We had taken the course on tactics and administration together at Bhaktapur and I also knew his father, General Sher Bahadur Malla, from the time I was a young boy. He was the ADC when King Mahendra brought me from Okhaldhunga.

Basanta was also there to meet the colonel. He was walking towards his garden when he saw the two of us. "Oh, both of you at the same time?" he said.

Basanta met him first while I waited for my turn.

"We will do our best from this side," the colonel assured me but cautioned, "Be careful. Your relatives in the Palace might try to sabotage the situation for you."

Shashi was the only person whom I counted as my relative in the Palace. He was the one who encouraged me to fill in the application form to join the Army in the first place. Had it not been for him, I'd have been an engineer. After being selected as cadets we went to India together. We spent almost five years in Pune, Dehradun and Indore and became close friends. Moreover, I was his in-law. Maybe he was not happy with our relationship as in-laws?

Did Colonel Shanta mean Shashi when he told me to be cautious about my relatives in the Palace? I dismissed the idea because I doubted he would do anything to harm my interests. Nonetheless, I went to meet Shashi one morning. His wife arranged a meal. Although we were in-laws now, our relationship was just as frank and informal as it was during our days in college and as cadets.

"I've met all the criteria including seniority but everyone's telling me different things," I told him, "You guys have to see it positively in the Palace, buddy."

I was expecting he'd say it was no big deal and he'd look into it but what he said surprised me. "So you want to go to Hong Kong, huh? You need to be from a noble family and have brains and luck to go there, old chap."

I felt as if someone had punched me. It wasn't just his words but even his body language made it clear that he didn't approve of my wish to go to Hong Kong. Colonel Shanta had indeed meant Shashi when he cautioned me about my relatives. I wasn't against Basanta getting the post but then there was no reason why Shashi should oppose me but approve Basanta. He was my friend and in-law and I was furious at what he'd said.

"So you're supporting Basanta?" I said harshly.

He didn't say anything for a while.

"Has your cousin ever wished ill for you," it was all bubbling out now, "Or has her mother ever wronged you?."

My father Khadga Dhwoj and mother Dharma Kumari with my elder brother Bishnu Bahadur on her lap, before I was born.

With my sister (seated left), wife Uma and my brother (standing left).

Uma and me in Dhankuta.

Me (first from left) with Pradip KC, Kashi Prasad and Ravi Bikram Shah at Tribhuvan Adarsha Vidyalaya, Pharping, 1960. Shah went on to become a renowned artist.

With my grandson Nahushangad and granddaughter Utprerika.

With my family in Koteshwor after I was sworn in as the Army Chief. My granddaughter seated between Uma and me is holding my grandson. Son Shubhangad (Darwin), daughter Nepolina and daughter-in-law Sulakshana (standing left to right).

△ During the cadet training at National Defence Academy in Pune, India.

▽ Dressed in my sports attire at Chhauni Barrack in Kathmandu.

△ Posted as company commander while still a captain at Dhankuta in mid-1970s.

Before leaving for Egypt to participate in UNEF (United Nation Emergency

Reporting to Director General of Military Operations, Singha Pratap Shah, before flying to Egypt for UNEF in 1974.

During the Special Forces and Ranger Training in Washington DC, in April 1976.

Brigadier Bharat Keshari Simha, Singha Pratap Shah (second and third from the right) along with other high ranking officers to see off Nepal's peace keeping force.

During the junior command course at College of Combat in the Indian state of Madhya Pradesh. I was in this training during the Indian economic blockade of Nepal in 1989-90.

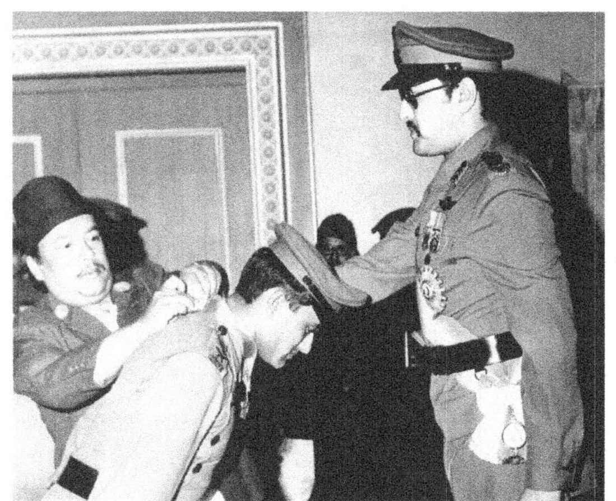

King Birendra presenting me with the 'Gorkha Dakshinbahu' medal in 1977 after his visit to eastern Nepal. King Birendra's maternal uncle Sushil Shumsher Rana is also in the picture.

Posing for a group photo with the royal family during my posting in Hong Kong. The royal family had visited Hong Kong after the United States endorsed Nepal's Zone of Peace proposal. This was also the King's birthday celebration.

Crown Prince Dipendra with me and Uma in Islamabad, Pakistan.

With Prince Gyanendra at the Royal Nepal Army's Liaison Officer's residence in Hong Kong.

With family of Prince Gyanendra and his sister Princess Shanti Singh in Hong Kong.

King Gyanendra visiting the Mid-Western Army Division with Army Chief Pyar Jung Thapa (first from left) I was the

▲ During National Defence Course (NDC) training in Pakistan.

◀ Galloping ahead: I enjoyed horse riding.

▼ Singing a folk song at NDC in Islamabad in 1997. We celebrated 'Nepal Day' with students from 15 countries along with Pakistani generals. I had gifted them traditional Nepali hat (topi).

Golf is a great game for exercise and networking. It is said that major decisions on sensitive issues are taken during games on the golf course.

Receiving the key to a Toyota car that I won at a lottery in Hong Kong.

With Deputy Prime Minister and Defence Minister Madhav Kumar Nepal, MP Narayan Man Bijukchhe of Bhaktapur, Army Chief Gadul Shumsher at the cadet graduation parade. Inviting politicians to the event was an attempt to ensure positive attitude about the Army amidst changing times.

Defence Minister Bidya Bhandari during an inspection. She was the first female Defence Minister of Nepal.

Prime Minister Girija Prasad Koirala who also had the responsibility of the Head of the State presenting me with the badge of Army Chief in August, 2006.

With UML Chairman Jhala Nath Khanal.

With Army personnel at
Kalidhoj Battalion in
Bhojpur after a Maoist
attack in the district.

With Prime Minister
Girija Prasad Koirala.
Prime Minister Koirala
began trusting me more
after he fell out with the
Maoists. Defence advisor
Ramesh Jung Thapa (left)
and Defence Secretary
Bishnu Datta Upreti
(right) also seen.

Addressing soldiers in the
Maoist stronghold of
Thawang during the
height of the insurgency.

With the local people after the Army opened the track of Surkhet-Jumla road. The Army deployed there faced frequent attacks from the Maoists.

Having lunch at a soldier's house in Ilam, eastern Nepal. I always regarded myself as a soldier first, irrespective of my rank. I made it mandatory for every officer to dine in the soldiers' mess once a week.

Consoling soldier Dinesh Shrestha's father Mohan Kaji after his son lost his life during a rescue mission.

Supreme commander of the Nepalese Army, President Ram Baran Yadav, visiting the Peace Keeping Training Centre at Panchkhal. Lieutenant General Kul Bahadur Khadka also seen.

Before flying the single engine plane of the Indian Air Force. Indian Air Force cadets had flown in the plane to Kathmandu on their study tour.

Addressing the Mid-Western Division in Surkhet after becoming the Army Chief. Divisional Commander Major General Ananta Thebe also seen.

Indian President Pratibha Patil conferring me with the title of Honorary General of the Indian Army. It is customary for the Army Chiefs of Nepal and India to receive the honorary titles of each other's forces.

Uma and me with Indian President Pratibha Patil in New Delhi.

With Indian Army Chief Deepak Kapoor. He was also my senior in Pune's cadet training.

United Nations Secretary-General Ban Ki-moon during his visit to Nepal. Foreign Minister Upendra Yadav also seen (centre).

With former US President Jimmy Carter, who was on a trip to Nepal before the Constituent Assembly elections. After I declined to meet them elsewhere, Carter's team came to the Army HQ.

With the Chief of the Indian Navy.

With President Ram
Baran Yadav and
Sri Lanka's President
Mahinda Rajapaksa.

With the Chinese
Army Chief, General
Chen Bingde.

With subedar-majors of
Kathmandu Valley who
came to show support
for my stance against
the Maoist-led
government.
Subedar-majors are
considered the
backbone of the Army.

With President Ram Baran Yadav and Prime Minister Pushpa Kamal Dahal at the Army Officers' Club.

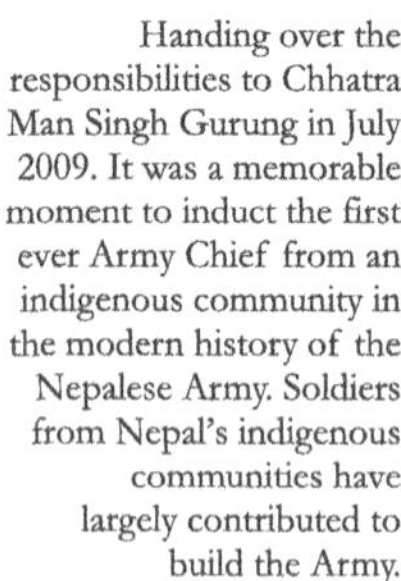

Handing over the responsibilities to Chhatra Man Singh Gurung in July 2009. It was a memorable moment to induct the first ever Army Chief from an indigenous community in the modern history of the Nepalese Army. Soldiers from Nepal's indigenous communities have largely contributed to build the Army.

A portrait painting that was gifted to me before my retirement as the Army Chief

He changed his tune when I was about to leave, "Hey buddy, I was just joking. You think I'd support anyone but you?"

"Let's go meet Colonel Shanta now," he said trying to hide his back-pedalling.

How could we go to Colonel Shanta then, asking him to resolve the issue? After a few days, I met Major Vivek Shah by chance during my morning walk. "Hey mister, be careful. Your in-law is trying to block your appointment," he told me.

"Go and meet the old man at once," he suggested.

I hesitated. How could I talk to the Chief about such a personal matter?

"Go to the Brown House on Saturday and see him there," he said.

The Army Chief Singha Pratap was Vivek's father-in-law. The Brown House was near Ravi Bhawan and I decided to go there as he suggested. Maybe Vivek had already dropped hints about me to the Chief?

But when I reached the Brown House, Basanta was already there, as well as lots of other people. I didn't want to make it more awkward for both of us. "Amazing how we always end up at the same place at the same time. Maybe because you're my senior, you're always just ahead of me," I said.

Basanta talked to the Chief for about five minutes and I could see the Chief smiling throughout their conversation.

It was my turn now. I went ahead and saluted.

"Hey, Major," he said, "I know what you've come here for and you can leave."

I saluted and left.

Basanta was immediately promoted to lieutenant colonel. The road to Hong Kong was now open for me. After that, I automatically became an acting colonel.

My ambition was to go abroad as a Military Attaché but the position as Liaison Officer in Hong Kong entailed greater responsibilities. I'd be in direct contact with the Ministry and the Secretary of Foreign Affairs, and the Palace. I would also get to know everyone from Hong Kong's governor to the diplomatic community. Meeting VIPs from Nepal, including the King was possible now.

The posting in Hong Kong was ideal for me in every way. Unlike as a Military Attaché, I didn't have to work to the Ambassador. In fact, my stature was almost equal to the Ambassador's. It was my responsibility to oversee all the passports of the Gurkha Reserve Units (GRUs) in Brunei and the Brigade of Gurkhas, including the Gurkha units in the UK and with the Singaporean Police. I had to look into issues regarding their welfare, rights, travel and other problems including family matters. We also handled the visa section of the Nepali mission's liaison office.

Although our field of operation was extensive, the status of our office was limited to Liaison Office to the Brigade of Gurkhas. It was not a formal diplomatic mission and our office was not included in Hong Kong's diplomatic list.

I've always believed in doing more than simply taking orders or getting a job done just for the sake of it. So even in Hong Kong, I wanted to do more than just maintain the status quo. I was determined to make a difference and give the Hong Kong office the status of a diplomatic mission.

The Hong Kongese protocol officer had worked alongside

the Gurkhas in Burma and was very fond of Nepalis. I invited him for lunch one day after which we started meeting frequently and became close.

"We also deal with the Hong Kong Government as representatives of Nepal. We need to be given formal diplomatic accreditation," I put to him.

"If the British Army agrees, it'll be done." He didn't seem to think it was impossible. I met the British major general and he seemed positive as well.

A week later, the Hong Kong government gave us diplomatic accreditation. I sent a photocopy of the letter to the Palace, Army HQ and the Ministry of Foreign Affairs.

King Birendra proposed that Nepal should be a Zone of Peace during his coronation on 24 February 1975 and nine years later the US endorsed the proposal. The announcement was made by US President Ronald Reagan during King Birendra's state visit to Washington DC in 1983. America's support held enormous importance for Nepal.

After this major achievement in international diplomacy, King Birendra made plans to come to Hong Kong on his way back to Nepal. Crown Prince Dipendra, Princess Shruti and Prince Nirajan would be coming from Nepal to meet their parents. The nanny, who was a Gurung from Rumjatar and who had also been King Birendra's nanny, would bring the children to Hong Kong.

The Ministry of Foreign Affairs sent the arrival schedule of the King and Queen. They were flying from Washington via Japan. I called Colonel Shanta in Japan, "We need to hold a function for Their Majesties while they're here."

"I'll send a request and let you know," he said.

He called me a little later and asked, "Can a dinner for 22 people be arranged?"

There was no way I couldn't arrange it. Welcoming the royal family was an immense opportunity for me.

"What are the brands His Majesty prefers?" I asked.

"His Majesty prefers Bardinet brandy without VSOP. The one we got from Kathmandu is about to finish so get that," Colonel Shanta said, "Her Majesty prefers wine."

I immediately sent the clerk to make the purchases but he returned empty handed – none of the shops in Hong Kong had what we were looking for. A lot of them hadn't even heard of Bardinet without VSOP. The ones who did only knew that it was French. I realised the King's drink of choice wasn't ordinary. So I went to the French Trade Commissioner.

"Without VSOP isn't a brand. It isn't available on the market," I was told. It was like our local liquors, the ones that aren't exported.

"Even a special order will take a week for preparation and delivery," he said, "Who needs it?"

I didn't reply.

After that, I talked to the Hong Kong Government regarding security arrangements for the King and Queen. I was supposed to be at the airport to meet them.

The airport is in Kowloon and I lived in the opposite direction and had to take the undersea tunnel to get there.

Unfortunately, there was an accident in the tunnel on the day they arrived. The Governor of Hong Kong and his ADC were already at the airport, but I was delayed because I had to get a few things done at the office and with the tunnel closed we were stranded halfway there. Since there was no other option, Uma and I decided to walk across the tunnel. I looked at my watch. It was hopeless. With only a few minutes left there was no way we could reach the airport in time.

I would be the only one absent from the King's reception party. My job was in serious jeopardy. The tunnel opened well past the plane's estimated time of arrival and I was drenched in sweat by that time I reached the airport. Thank goodness, the plane hadn't landed yet. It seemed like divine intervention.

I drove the vehicle and took Their Majesties to their hotel. A suite had been booked.

"Why did you book such an expensive hotel?" His Majesty asked.

"Your Majesty, it was done according to instructions from the Foreign Ministry," I said. Anything simpler and cheaper than that suite wouldn't have been suitable for a Head of State but even King Birendra felt it was unnecessarily expensive.

29 December 1983

The King's birthday celebrations would take place in Hong Kong that year. It was a hectic day full of programmes and arrangements. I organised a party for the Hong Kong diplomatic community and a few other invitees. There were around 600 people on the guest list for the party from 4-6 pm. Later, I had to pick up the King and Queen at 7 pm for another party at my residence.

There were around 25 people there including the royal family, ADC, officials from the Palace and our family. Colonel Shanta signalled that drinks should be served.

"Your Majesty, we don't have your drink of choice. We couldn't find it anywhere in Hong Kong. Even the French Consul-General couldn't get it," I told him.

"Don't worry about it. Relax," he said affably.

"What would you like, Your Majesty?"

He looked towards the Queen.

"Is there any champagne?" the Queen asked.

"Yes, there is," I said.

I had already discussed her preferred brands with the ADCs. After going through all the brands, she settled on one bottle.

"How are things with you?" His Majesty asked.

"Your Majesty, I'm the happiest man on earth."

"How come?"

"I've managed to build a four-room house in Kathmandu and my children go to the British School here," I said.

"Katawal is on a roll," Her Majesty quipped.

During our conversation, I told His Majesty about not being made fully aware of my responsibilities before I came to Hong Kong. "Even though I wanted to know, the Ministry of Foreign Affairs and the Army showed no interest," I said, "Before leaving to take up a position in a mission like this, an orientation is important, Your Majesty."

"Narayan (secretary of the Palace Narayan Prasad Shrestha), send ambassadors and others only after a proper briefing at the Ministry of Foreign Affairs for a month," King Birendra immediately ordered.

I didn't want to let go off this opportunity seeing the King was in such a good mood. Colonel Shanta was attempting to steer the conversation away from serious matters.

"Enough of requests," he said.

"Shanta, let him talk," the King smiled and gestured to the colonel to be quiet.

I understood Colonel Shanta's intention and restrained myself from bringing up other matters. The King was extremely happy that evening at the party. America's decision to endorse Nepal's proposal to be declared a Zone of Peace was a major victory for him and it was clearly reflected on his face.

Before leaving the party, His Majesty said, "Let's take a family photo." Spending this wonderful time with the royal family was one of the most memorable evenings of my life.

Hong Kong's investment and interest in border security was worth learning from. They would know even if one Chinese migrant entered their territory. I briefed King Birendra about this during his state visit to Australia.

The issue was raised again during a lunch hosted by Hong Kong's Governor and the King found it very interesting.

"My Liaison Officer is here, if you could kindly make arrangements to have him fully briefed by the relevant agency," His Majesty asked the Governor.

"Your Majesty, that will be done," the Governor promised.

They took me to their surveillance centre the very next day and showed me around. I saw the equipment used to monitor various points along the border. Based on their technical advice, I prepared a report on how the same thing might be achieved in Nepal. The initial estimate was around $39 million.

Principal Personal Secretary Narayan Prasad Shrestha and Principal Military Secretary Rishi Kumar Pandey were also with His Majesty on the visit. I informed them about the report and they thanked me.

I wanted to present the report to His Majesty in person, but the two secretaries had already started wrangling over which of them would take credit for the report I had so painstakingly prepared.

"Colonel Katawal works under the Ministry of Foreign Affairs, so I will present it," Narayan Prasad said.

"He's under the Army," General Pandey claimed.

Their heated discussion continued for a while. Later on the King's ADC Colonel Tara Bahadur Thapa made arrangements for me to present the report.

"It's the best idea but too expensive," the King said, "Send it to the concerned Ministry and let's see what we can do."

After the briefing, I invited His Majesty to dine with me. Kumar Khadga and Sharada, the King's sister, were also there.

"Your residence is quite far away," he said, "I need to prepare for my meeting."

"Your Majesty, I'll bring Nepali food here then," I said.

"Okay," His Majesty said, "But keep it simple."

I asked my staff to prepare the food at home and brought it to the hotel. I also took my children along and they were jumping up and down with excitement.

The King had to prepare for his meeting, so he started eating right away. Her Majesty, Kumar Khadga and Sharada were about to be served, when the King suddenly remembered something.

"Has the Minister been served?" he asked.

"He'll eat after you," I said.

"I'll eat only after he does," His Majesty said, "He's a senior citizen."

So I called Foreign Affairs Minister Ranadhir Subba. The Queen kept away from the wine or the meat and only tasted the spicy curries. The King wanted to have a second helping but perhaps the doctor had advised him against it, so he touched his belly and looked to the Queen for permission before saying, "I'm having another course."

The next day Her Majesty went shopping.

"Uma, choose a sari for yourself," the Queen said, "Select the one you like."

Uma was in a dilemma now. She didn't know whether to choose a cheap sari or an expensive one. What would the Queen think? That evening Uma came home with a sari worth HKD 1800 which the Queen had given her.

Meeting Gyanendra

During my stay at Hong Kong, I had the opportunity to meet almost all the members of the royal family. It was in

Hong Kong that I was introduced to Prince Gyanendra, who came there frequently. Prabhakar Shumsher, Prabhu Shumsher and Ruby Jung Rana sometimes accompanied him. On one occasion, Prince Gyanendra's family and his sister Shanti's family came to Hong Kong at the same time.

I asked Prince Gyanendra if it was okay to invite Princess Shanti and her sons for dinner along with his family.

"You're the host," he said, "It's up to you."

We invited both families on the same evening.

"They're your nephews," Princess Shanti said to Prince Gyanendra, "You also need to take care of them."

I realised that even royals discussed family matters just like anyone else.

The next time Prince Gyanendra's family visited Hong Kong, it was Chinese New Year. He invited us for dinner and I went with Uma and my children. After dinner, the men walked down to the lobby. ADC Prakash Bikram Shah was in a good mood.

After a while the Prince said, "Colonel, take us to a disco."

I thought he was trying to test me. Nepalis were highly respected in Hong Kong because of the legacy of the Gurkhas. I felt it wouldn't be fitting for a prince from Nepal to go to a disco and suggested, instead, that we have a few more rounds of drinks in his hotel suite.

But Prince Gyanendra was adamant.

"Your Royal Highness", I said "Today is Chinese New Year's Eve and I don't think it would be appropriate to go out."

"Then you can go home," he said brusquely. It was clear

from his tone that he was annoyed by my refusal to take him out.

Another day we were all having drinks in Prince Gyanendra's suite. It was the same group with Prabhu Shumsher, Anup Shumsher and Prakash Bikram. I received an urgent telex at my office from the Ministry of Foreign Affairs. It was about the deteriorating health of Bijaya Shah, Prince Gyanendra's aunt. I asked my staff to bring the telex to the hotel that night. I gave it to Prakash Bikram, who read it and gave it to Prabhu Shumsher who also read it but didn't break the news to Prince Gyanendra.

We were all having whisky and Prakash Bikram signalled to me to show the telex to the Prince who was smoking at the bar. I took the telex to him.

"Bijaya is very sick. Come as quickly as possible," the telex said.

The Prince read it and looked at me.

"Have you ever been posted in the Palace?"

"No, Your Highness," I said.

"I see. That's why they left it to you to tell me."

If it was good news, people would have fought to deliver it. However, because it was bad news, the Prince's hangers-on left it up to me to deliver the bad tidings.

Prince Dhirendra

I had been in Hong Kong for quite some time when Prince Dhirendra and his wife, Prekshya, arrived, accompanied by Keyur Shumsher, his wife and ADC Colonel Bharat Gurung.

The youngest prince was interested in dance and music and even played the *mādal*. He was a gentleman and treated his wife like a friend. They were a very down- to-earth couple.

"His Royal Highness is a gentleman," Bharat Gurung told me, "Let's do some business together."

I was never interested in business, so I didn't pay any attention to what he said.

"They'll never make you a general," he said, "If you get into business at least you'll make some money."

Prekshya came to Hong Kong twice after that. I think she came once with an Army doctor after medical treatment in the US. She was very upset at the time.

"I've realised my life could end in a flash," she said. Her anxious tone is still fresh in my memory.

Back then there were a lot of rumours about the royal family. The Queen was believed to have stashed millions of dollars in a Swiss bank account. There was similar gossip about Princes Dhirendra and Gyanendra stashing away cash in Singapore and Hong Kong. But I always felt those rumours were without foundation. During my stay in Hong Kong, I got to spend time with the royal family and to observe them closely. They liked the finer things in life but I doubted they were hoarding ill-gotten wealth. If they had so much money, why would they go looking for bargains?

Prince Dhirendra had once come to Hong Kong with his wife who wanted to go to Chongking Mansion, an Indian-owned shopping complex known for selling damaged factory goods and fake items cheaply. This was where Nepali businessmen sent their lackeys to buy "brand-name" goods to bring to Kathmandu. Ministers, Palace secretaries and other VIPs always preferred to go to posh shopping districts and Chongking Mansion certainly wasn't in that league.

I was hesitant to take Princess Prekshya there.

"It's a very simple place, not for you, Your Royal Highness," I said.

"I hear you get bargain items there, that's why I want to go," she said.

After that I was convinced that the rumours about the royal family being unduly wealthy were nothing but idle gossip.

I also remember an incident from school. Our school was housed in a building which belonged to King Tribhuvan. It used to be called the Pharping Palace and was the place where the kings would go on retreat. There were a lot of mango and litchi trees in the school compound.

"It's their personal property so we need to take these fruits to the Palace," the Principal used to say, "We should take them for the younger princes too."

The Principal would go to the King's Palace himself and send students and a driver to the Palaces of Princes Basundhara and Himalaya. I delivered those fruits once. We went to Basundhara's Palace at Tahachal in our school jeep. The guard let us in after we told him where we had come from. We handed over the sacks of fruits to a helper there. He pointed towards an elderly man walking around in a track suit.

We didn't understand.

"It's His Highness. Go and greet him," he said to us. We went towards the elderly man and bowed. Prince Basundhara asked us who we were.

"We're from Pharping School," I said.

He asked us about our studies and put his hand in his pocket.

"This is for you. Now you can go."

We held the money tightly in our fists and ran outside. When we opened our fists, all we had been given was 25 paisa. I was annoyed.

"Is the King's brother poor or what?" my friend said.

"Better to give at least Rs 2 or 3 or not give anything at all," I added.

"These people think 25 paisa is a lot of money," the driver explained.

Getting lucky

I subscribed to *Time* and *Newsweek* magazines in Hong Kong. They used to have lucky draw competitions once in a while. I lost track of all the coupons I filled in and sent away.

In 1986, I got a call from the Toyota office in Hong Kong. "Mr Katawal, congratulations. You're the winner of a Toyota car," a girl said with a Chinese accent. I thought someone was playing a joke on me. I'd never wanted a car, so I didn't believe the phone call and forgot about it.

I got a call from the same girl four days later. "Mr Katawal, we want to hand over the car to you, a Toyota 1986 model. You will have to come to collect the car. There'll be a small ceremony." I had indeed won a lottery.

I told Uma about it, "Our Toyota is coming home."

The driver brought the blue Toyota to our residence. There was a saying that if you could drive in Hong Kong, you could drive anywhere. I brushed up on my driving skills and started driving in the mornings and evenings and also on weekends. The children and I would always be in my car while Uma was more concerned with managing our home.

"We can't afford to run a car," Uma said, "Sell it, buy some land and invest in a house." I enjoyed watching her lose her temper.

"A car won't look all that bad for a colonel." I teased her. By then I had been promoted to lieutenant colonel.

"A lot of things might look good," she said, "And, if we do keep the car, what will your salary go on, the children's school fees, household expenses or the car's running costs?"

I teased her again, "It's not that we will use the car every day, just for family drives occasionally."

"Having a car is the same as raising an elephant," she argued, "What's the point of a poor person being given an elephant, even if it's for free?"

I suggested a compromise. "We'll use the car while we're in Hong Kong and sell it when we leave." Uma didn't say anything.

Some RNAC staff suggested I might ask the King to waive the import duty on the car. I thought it was a good idea but Uma soon found out about it and took a firm stand.

"If you ask the King to help you by waiving the duty, he'll think you're just as selfish as the others. You're destined for great things in life. Why do you need to be greedy about small things?"

She was right, of course. I cancelled my plans to ask for the duty to be waived.

I sold the vehicle after returning to Nepal. Home Secretary Bhakta Bahadur Koirala, who was earlier Dhankuta's CDO, helped me sell the car back to the Toyota company. Vijaya Gajananda Vaidya of Toyota bought the car for Rs 650,000. That was a huge sum in 1987, almost equivalent to 30 years of a colonel's salary. I had also saved $17,000 and had several ounces of gold. With this money we bought land in Kaushaltar and Suryabinayak.

How the two Kings met

During my tenure in Hong Kong, King Birendra made a state visit to Australia and was scheduled to stopover in Brunei en route. The Ministry of Foreign Affairs decided to send the Ambassador who was accredited to Brunei, Khilendra Raj Pandey who was based in Thailand, to oversee the arrangements for the King's visit.

The Royal Nepal Embassy in Thailand looked after Brunei and all other ASEAN countries. Khilendra Raj was a professor before his appointment, not a career diplomat. Foreign Ministry officials were always unhelpful to those they perceived as low status non-career diplomats and he was a victim of this attitude. He was a bit lost in Brunei. King Birendra's arrival was confirmed but the welcome and meetings there were not.

I received a telex from the Ministry of Foreign Affairs to go to Brunei immediately to help with the arrangements. There were some problems because the Sultan of Brunei didn't seem very keen on meeting our King. Back home, the Ministry and Palace were blaming each for this.

I was well aware of the relationship between Brunei's royal family and the Gurkhas. There were about 3,000 Nepalis working at the Brigade of Gurkhas and GRU in Brunei. The GRU was formed because the royal family there trusted Nepalis with their security. They guarded the Sultan, royal family and other VIPs. Only retired Nepalis from the British Army or Singaporean Police were accepted into the GRU.

Another reason the royal family trusted Nepalis was that the Gurkhas attached to the British Army had helped put down a Communist rebellion in the 1960s which had saved the monarchy. I was, therefore, surprised when I heard that the Sultan didn't want to meet the King of Nepal. Something didn't add up.

I called a few people in Brunei to discuss the situation. One of them was Ishwar Sherchan who had completed his SLC at Pharping School in 1958. We were still in school when we heard he went to Sandhurst after doing well as a cadet. Soldiers who studied at Sandhurst were accorded a very high status in the Nepalese Army. In 1979, he passed the entrance examination to the Staff College but resigned the very next day.

We found out later that he had gone to Brunei at the invitation of the Sultan, who was his friend at Sandhurst. During their time at Sandhurst, Ishwar *dai* had no idea he was friends with a prince. He just assumed the young Bolkiah was from a rich family.

Ishwar *dai* was probably the only person at the GRU who had served in the Nepalese Army. Back then, Brunei didn't have its own army and the British Army took care of security there. The recruitment of former Gurkhas for the security of the Sultan, royal family and VIPs was also done by the British Army. So they weren't happy when Ishwar *dai* was appointed. As a result he never became Chief of the GRU despite his seniority.

Nirmala Sherchan was another person I knew in Brunei. She was the doctor to the royal family there and also Ishwar *dai's* classmate. I also knew the Sultan's cousin, the Chief of the Brunei Air Force, with whom I was at the Staff College in the UK. The British colonel who was in command of the Garrison of Gurkhas was also my friend. I had got to know him through my regular visits to Brunei and Singapore and he was also my coursemate in Camberley, UK.

All my friends in Brunei made sure I was well taken care of as soon as I landed there and it was only after I reached Brunei that I found out the root cause of the problem. Nepalis in Brunei wanted to meet King Birendra during his visit but our Embassy in Bangkok hadn't responded positively to their request. Brunei's royal family was upset with King Birendra for not agreeing to meet with his own subjects. Sultan Bolkiah had suggested that King Birendra meet his brother instead. It was after this suggestion that the officials in the Palace and the Ministry of Foreign Affairs began panicking.

I was there to get things back on track and ensure that the Sultan himself met King Birendra. I mobilised all my contacts to help me. The Chief of the Air Force was particularly helpful, giving information for me to relay to the Ministry of Foreign Affairs.

King Birendra arrived and the Sultan's brother was at the

airport to welcome him. The King was to stay at Edinburgh Palace.

"Colonel, what's the problem here?" the King asked.

I told him everything I knew.

"Can we meet the Gurkhas in the evening?" King Birendra wanted to meet the Nepalis there. The officials at the Ministry and Palace had been reluctant for no good reason.

"Yes, Your Majesty," I replied.

I called the GRU chief, "His Majesty wants to meet the Gurkhas."

The event was held at Edinburgh Palace. There were 300 people there and it was covered by local television. The Sultan was apparently pleased when he heard about it so the same evening a bilateral meeting was arranged.

The King asked us for suggestions about issues to be raised during his meeting with the Sultan. I thought this would be a good opportunity and put forward an audacious suggestion.

"The Nepalese Army should be sent to Brunei instead of the British Gurkhas and the recruitment should be coordinated by the Government of Nepal. That way all the fees paid by the Government of Brunei for our forces would go directly to the Government of Nepal and it could be used to cover the budget of our Army," I said.

Brunei's royal family greatly trusted Nepalis and if Britain could be convinced to agree, I felt it would be a dramatic breakthrough.

The Heads of State discussed the matter that evening and the Sultan seemed positively disposed to the idea, but he didn't follow through. He enjoyed a flamboyant lifestyle and, we were told, wasn't really interested in his royal responsibilities. His brother made most of the decisions. Furthermore, the Sultan was close friends with the British Ambassador as they were both polo players. The Ambassador apparently blocked the idea and Government of Nepal failed to press the matter.

And just like that the possibility of sending soldiers from the Nepalese Army directly to Brunei, to earn billions of dollars in revenue, never went ahead.

Six

Senior Officer

After returning from Hong Kong and a stint in Number 10 Brigade as assistant brigade commander, I was posted to the Military Academy in Kharipati. I had made a name for myself in the Army through my work in Nagarkot, and once again I was back to take over the same responsibilities.

I had left the training centre in Nagarkot more than 15 years before. But even after all those years, the staff there vividly remembered the backbreaking exercises that Gyan Jung, Umesh and I put them through. I thought working there would be easy.

Colonel Prajwalla Shumsher Rana was Commandant of the Academy and I was Chief Instructor (CI), the second man down. As the Commandant had to oversee administration, public relations and other formalities, the CI was responsible for training.

I believed in making young cadets go through a gruelling process. They were like clay that could be moulded in any way, so they needed to be trained as rigorously as possible. But the Commandant was a bit soft on the cadets. "Training shouldn't be very difficult," he would say, "It shouldn't be all rough and tough."

We had a different approach not just to cadet training but on a lot of other issues as well, so our relationship never went deeper than correct formality. His lifestyle, social circles, upbringing and education were very different from mine. He was the descendant of Juddha Shumsher, once the absolute ruler of Nepal, and counted the royals as his relatives. Because of our different backgrounds, our values and worldviews differed significantly. He was obsessed about having pure cow's milk but couldn't stand the sight of cow dung, whereas I would willingly accept the presence of dung if that's what it took to get milk.

Despite our differences, both of us were focused on our duties. I was trying to maintain a balance in the cadets' physical training, sports and academics while he was busy managing the centre. It was his responsibility to oversee how the Academy's resources were spent. It wasn't my job to be concerned about his personal behaviour and financial decisions.

There were two jeeps at the Academy, one for him and the other for everyone else. We could ask his permission to use the second vehicle but that was too much for me, so I preferred taking a motorcycle to Kathmandu.

One morning, during the physical training for cadets, I got a call.

"It's from your home," the runner said, trying to catch his breath.

I didn't usually get calls from home unless it was urgent, so I was already worried and dashed off to take the call.

It was Uma. "I'm bleeding," she said, "Come home as soon as you can because I need to go to the hospital." She sounded worried.

I was concerned because she had had a similar health crisis in the past and had to quickly figure out a way to get her to hospital. My children were too young to get a taxi on their own. Moreover, our house was 15 minutes from the taxi stand and even then taxis weren't readily available. In addition, my motorbike was at a service centre in Kathmandu.

"It'll take me at least an hour to get home. There are no taxis available in Bhaktapur so I'll have to go to Suryabinayak and get the trolley bus. Even if I run, it'll take too long," I thought. Then I spotted the Academy's Land Rover and my spirits lifted. If I drove, I could reach home in 20 minutes and take Uma to hospital immediately.

Major Bharat Rayamajhi was the DS Coordinator. His office was next to mine. "I'll put forward a request," he said, after I told him about the emergency situation at my home, and he rushed off to the Commandant's quarters.

He returned looking crestfallen and I immediately understood that my request for the vehicle had been turned down.

"Apparently there's no petrol," he conveyed our boss' message.

I immediately started running towards the Suryabinayak trolley stop. Halfway there, the Land Rover from the base went past me. The driver and the boss' runner were seated in the vehicle with a dog in the backseat. The vehicle that they hadn't given me permission to use to rush my wife to hospital because the tank was supposedly empty had been, in fact, requisitioned to take the boss' dog for its shots. I was really angry but consoled told myself that was just how things worked in the Army.

"She's a good soul. God will look after her," I thought as I kept running. When I got home, the neighbours had thankfully already taken Uma to hospital.

Naturally, I was resentful towards the military for not helping me out during an emergency and even wondered if there was any point in staying on. But then again I told myself that I had chosen the job on my own. No one had forced me to join the Army.

I returned to the Academy after Uma was discharged. All the majors, captains and other staff surrounded me as soon as I reached Kharipati.

"How's Madam doing?" they asked.

"Thanks to your good wishes, she's fine now," I told them.

A lot of senior officers were also upset about what had happened regarding the vehicle. Some of the majors even raised the issue with the boss.

"Well, the dog had to get to the vet for his shots," a major told me later, quoting the boss.

One day I saw the Commandant walking around with his dog and it made me furious all over again.

"So your dog can travel in the car but I don't get to use it even when my wife's life is in jeopardy," I growled at him as he walked by.

"If you're so upset, go and report the matter to the King," the boss replied rudely, "I'm in charge here and I'll do as I please."

Although my boss at Kharipati wasn't very helpful, Army Chief Satchit Shumsher Rana trusted me. He had become the Army Chief when I returned from Hong Kong and was committed to the Army, the monarchy and the country. He was a fighter who would have given his life for the things he believed in.

The Chief called me at about 10 pm one night in 1988. "Rookmangud, you need to go to the Chinese border tomorrow morning to settle a dispute there and bring in the Army's consignment safely," he ordered.

Marich Man Singh Shrestha was the Prime Minister then and bilateral ties with India were strained over the issue of arms being imported from China. The government took a hard line and this had led to a serious crisis resulting in the border being blockaded for more than a year. We were told the policy was to not kowtow to India at any cost and everyone from King Birendra down had to adhere to it. My orders were to go to the Chinese border to make sure our consignment came across.

I was glad that the Chief trusted me enough to give me this responsibility over so many other officers at HQ and I had to inform my commander. A vehicle came to pick me up at 3 am and I headed off on the mission to the border without really understanding what it was all about.

Colonel Tula Bahadur Thapa had been there for 15-20 days with a team of drivers and mechanics. I was accompanied by a signals officer, a mechanic and driver, and some food supplies.

It was only after reaching Tatopani that I found out this was about weapons arriving from China and that I was supposed to deal with the Chinese side as we received the vehicles with the weapons. We planned to bring the trucks across the border after dark and bring them to Kathmandu the same night. It was then that I understood why the Kathmandu-Kodari Highway was strategically important.

There was a Chinese interpreter named Peter at the border who helped us communicate with the Chinese. He talked to all the Nepalis in English, so our men often teased him in Nepali thinking he didn't understand our language. But I was not convinced he didn't speak Nepali. The Chinese would never have sent an interpreter to Nepal who didn't speak Nepali.

Peter and I were having brandy in my room one day and enjoying a relaxed conversation.

"So, you did your Bachelors and Masters in Nepal," I said in Nepali, "Let's talk in Nepali, my friend."

He was taken aback at first but then began laughing. Peter replied in Nepali, "How did you find out, Colonel?"

He had studied at Tribhuvan University in Kirtipur for almost five years. "Please don't tell the others that I speak Nepali," he asked. This was a lesson to all of us not to talk about foreigners in front of them, presuming that they didn't understand our language.

I stayed at the border for 11 days to organise the transfer of all the military material. The vehicles had to descend from the high plateau where they used a different type of fuel. We had to change the fuel, and under Colonel Tul Bahadur's leadership, we completed the task and returned. The Chief was happy with our work.

The transfer of those military supplies across the border became a major reason for a further deterioration in Nepal-India relations. India said the import of Chinese military supplies breached its 1950 treaty with Nepal. The next 15 months were turbulent times for Nepal with people struggling with shortages of everything from salt to petroleum. The government even had to organise an airlift of fuel from Dhaka to Kathmandu.

Despite all of this, people still remember Marich Man's Government with fondness because he stood up to India and still managed to provide the bare essentials.

Battalion Commander in Dhangadhi

My parent unit, Shree Shreenath Battalion, was moved to the Palace from Itahari. Battalion commander Makar Bahadur Karki's tenure was about to end and there was talk that I'd be replacing him. It was a matter of great pride for me to be assigned to the Royal Palace. But after a few days, I found I had been rejected and couldn't find out why this had happened. It was decided that Makar Bahadur would continue leading the battalion for the next two years, which was very unusual in military practice.

I was then transferred to Pashupati Prasad as battalion commander at the Dhangadhi Barracks in far-western Nepal. Soon after, Shivaram Khatri came to Dipayal as the brigade commander and I used to report to him. However, despite our past acquaintance, he was very distant and not very responsive towards me.

He had just returned from Germany after going through the Staff College when I was still a lieutenant in Nagarkot. He was very affectionate towards us then and often invited us for meals. We used to be flattered to be hosted in his quarters and his two young sons were Uma's students. But in Dhangadhi, he wasn't friendly.

"Teach that lad from the east to move according to the times," he once told Uma over the phone, "Your husband won't be able to survive in the Army if he continues in this way."

"What did he do wrong, sir?" Uma asked.

"I'm telling you this because you're like a sister to me," he told her, "Food supplies used to be sent from Dhangadhi to Dipayal and Kathmandu but ever since your husband took over as battalion commander, I hear that's been stopped."

He was referring to the meat and drinks that the Dhangadhi Barracks used to send to Dipayal, an unnecessary expense which had left the battalion knee-deep in debt. I had put a stop to all such gifts in order to set the finances straight.

Uma replied with "Okay" and "Yes" but then General Khatri lost his cool: "If he doesn't shape up, he won't rise up through the ranks."

The morale at the Pashupati Prasad Battalion was possibly the lowest among all the units. It was full of officers who had been exiled there for various transgressions or those who were perceived as too old.

However, I encouraged everyone from soldiers to officers to work together to become the best battalion. "We have to prove ourselves, win the King's Banner and go to the Palace," I told them.

This battalion had never been to the Royal Palace. The Kali Bahadur and Gorakh Bahadur Battalions had been there throughout and it had become customary to believe that only they could do the Palace duties.

The practice of the victorious team taking the King's Banner to the Palace started during the reign of King Mahendra. A fight had broken out at that time during a football match between players of the Palace's regiment and a visiting regiment. General Ravi Shumsher, the son of Juddha

Shumsher after whom Ravi Bhawan was named, punched a soldier from the Palace and lost his job because of it. He was married to one of the royals but, nevertheless, a general who was in line to be Army Chief lost his job for hitting a fellow soldier. That was when the practice of alternating battalions at the Palace started.

But Pashupati Prasad Battalion had never received that opportunity. We had our eyes set on the King's Banner but we were not well-prepared to win it. I encouraged the boys, telling them how the Shree Shreenath Battalion had won the football match in the past by practicing and working hard. If we did the same, there was no reason we couldn't succeed as well.

In order to win the Banner, the battalion had to work on everything from sports, administration, organisation, tactics, hygiene and sanitation, food supplies and military skills. We would be ready for the competition only if we worked consistently throughout the year. But since many of the officers had been sent to Dhangadhi as punishment, morale was low. The second man was a major but he performed so badly that his job had to be handed over to someone else.

I decided to discuss this matter with the Chief, and one Saturday morning I called Shashi Bhawan. "Good morning, sir. Rookmangud speaking."

"Rookmangud, so tell me how's everything in Dhangadhi?" the Chief asked.

I told him about my efforts to reform the battalion.

"Good. You seem happy in Dhangadhi as well and I appreciate your efforts," he said to me flatteringly.

"Can I make a request, sir?"

"Sure, go ahead."

"This battalion seems to be a dumping ground," I said, speaking candidly, "The majors here are good for nothing."

"So why don't you conduct an inquiry?" the Chief said, "Those morons probably have families, so do it without ruining their pensions."

Around the same time, seven second lieutenants joined the battalion. With this influx of new blood, the old majors were sent for patrols or assigned as security at banks, where they possibly wouldn't mess things up.

Colonel Victory Shumsher JBR (Vikki), Chhatra Man Gurung and their team had come from HQ to inspect the battalion for the King's Banner. As the supervisor of the battalion, the rule allows the brigade commander to give up to 50 points in relation to administration. General Khatri gave us zero and our battalion came third. But I was not upset. I believed it was possible for us to climb up the ladder if we worked a bit harder.

During all this, General Khatri's son got married to Uma's cousin. "Oh Uma, where's your husband?" he asked at the ceremony. Uma came to call me.

"What's up, sir?" I asked without saluting.

"How's the battalion commander doing?" he said, taunting me.

"Fine," I said.

"And what about the battalion?"

"Nothing much to report really. My battalion doesn't even salute you. You gave us zero," I told him to his face.

To be fair, despite giving us zero, he did give me a good annual assessment. I received the highest evaluation in terms of leadership, character, professionalism, occupational knowledge, command and control, discipline and other matters.

With Kisunjee in the Maldives

I was in Kailali in the western Tarai during the People's Movement of 1990. Multiparty democracy was restored and Krishna Prasad Bhattarai became Prime Minister. The Army sent me as his security officer for the SAARC Summit in the Maldives in November 1990.

Defence Secretary Mukunda Shumsher Thapa introduced me to the Prime Minister. Kisunjee was discussing his address to the SAARC Summit and I gathered he wasn't satisfied with any of the drafts prepared by his advisors and others.

"Okay, then the Foreign Affairs Secretary will write it," he concluded. Narendra Bikram Shah was Secretary at the Ministry of Foreign Affairs then.

What he wrote was probably approved and the Prime Minister must have been trying to get the bureaucracy and the politicians onto the same page. This was the time when multiparty democracy was still being tested and the Nepali Congress and CPN (UML) regarded people in the civil service, police and Army as supporters of the Panchayat and the Royal Palace. These institutions were governed by rules, the law and the constitution, which were supposed to be immune to regime change, however, the politicians still had their doubts.

On his way to the Maldives, Kisunjee was scheduled to meet Singapore's Prime Minister Lee Kuan Yew during a transit stop in Singapore. Nepal's Ambassador to Thailand and ASEAN, Ramchandra Bahadur Singh, was also present. I accompanied Kisunjee to the reception in the evening. As the PM's chief security officer I was on duty but the Prime Minister had noted that I hadn't had even one drink. He whispered something into the ear of the Chief of Protocol Arjun Bahadur Singh who came up to me and said, "The PM says you should at least have a sip."

"I'm on duty, sir," I replied. Kisunjee was within earshot and smiled as he heard my reply. I was wearing my uniform and standing at alert.

"Where did you study, Colonel?" the Prime Minister asked informally.

"Kathmandu," I replied.

"You seem very well-educated and cultured," he said.

During the reception, the issue of irregularities in the disbursement of the Army's Welfare Fund was raised. "The Fund's money has been embezzled," the Prime Minister concluded. Even though I was just a security officer, I couldn't just stand there and let this allegation about the Army go unchallenged.

"Your Excellency, give me some time to explain and I'll tell you how it was spent," I said. "The King is the patron and not a single paisa has been embezzled. Two or three people are required to sign every cheque so there's a lot of control."

"Okay, okay," the Prime Minister said abruptly.

We left Singapore for Male and I was seated next to the Prime Minister on the flight. I helped him adjust the seat and fastened his seat belt. I thought it would be better if the

Finance Minister Devendra Raj Pandey sat beside the Prime Minister, so we swapped seats.

Professor Yadunath Khanal was also in Business Class. Khanal and the Prime Minister would switch between English, Nepali and Sanskrit, reciting verses from the Gita. This continued throughout the flight and even after we got to the hotel in Male, where it was 1 am by the time we got to bed.

Everyone left after dinner. We then helped the Prime Minister hang up his clothes after his ADC ironed them. The Gita was placed right next to his pillow.

Before leaving, I wrote my name, room number and extension in large letters on a piece of paper and placed it beside the telephone in the hall. I informed the ADC about it and left. Since we were a part of VVIP security, our room was next to the Prime Minister's. I undressed and was about to go to sleep when the phone rang.

"Answer the phone, Captain," I said.

"Sir, you may have to reply in English," my roommate said.

"Yes, Colonel Rookmangud," I picked up the phone and said with a flourish.

"Hello, *bābu*," I recognised the Prime Minister's voice.

"I'm locked out," he said, "I can't open the door."

The door separating the hall and the bedroom had got locked. I went to his rescue with my trusty Swiss army knife and took the screw off the lock from outside to open the door. I fixed it again afterwards and the Prime Minister seemed surprised by my methods.

"Wow, Colonel, are you also a mechanic?" he said with a wide smile. "You are now my best friend."

I returned after he was comfortably back in his room and his appreciation made me happy.

President Ershad of Bangladesh was at Male with his entourage. When he had come to Nepal a few years earlier, I had been assigned to his security detail. I remembered talking to Ershad, his wife, Rowshan, and their young son. In Male, I also met the security officials of the other SAARC Heads of Government.

"I'm Colonel Katawal. I met your President in Nepal during his visit," I told President Ershad's ADC one day. "If you can, please give him my best regards."

There were no formal programmes that day. Our Prime Minister and Bangladesh's President had suites near each other. The Bangladeshi ADC came to me the same afternoon. "My President would like to see you," he said. It was amazing that he remembered our casual conversation and had already arranged the meeting.

It wouldn't be respectful if I met the Head of State of another country without asking permission from my own Prime Minister. "Sir, the Bangladeshi President wants to see me," I said to Kisunjee, "May I go?"

I didn't want the Prime Minister to imagine anything untoward, so I explained how the meeting had come about. Kisunjee was quite happy about it and said: "Colonel, go and pay your respect to him."

As it turned out, there wasn't much to talk about with Ershad who was a general. "How's His Majesty?" he asked. "If you can, give him my best regards."

I said I would and the brief meeting ended but I was still struck by his kindness.

On one of the less hectic days at the Summit, the Prime Minister wanted to go to the beach in the morning. A few of us, including the ADC, Chief of Protocol Arjun Bahadur Singh and I accompanied him to the crystal clear waters. The Prime Minister stripped down to his boxer shorts and wrapped his *janai*, the holy thread, around his neck. I was worried in case he couldn't swim and he sensed my anxiety.

"Don't worry, Colonel. I'm an experienced swimmer since my Banaras days. I used to swim across the Ganges," he said.

As he entered the water, I had to too. He swam past waves and moved further out, away from the beach. He teased me from afar, "I'm old. I won't be able to rescue you, Colonel."

I was also swimming now. "Sir, don't worry. I'll do my best," I replied.

After swimming with the 67-year-old man who had been jailed for 14 years, I clambered ashore gasping for breath. "Now let's see who have their *janais*?" Kisunjee said, announcing a mock inspection. Only two of us had the sacred thread.

"The Colonel seems to be fit in every respect," Kisunjee joked again, and asked me about my father.

I repeated the same answer I had given to Prime Minister Tulsi Giri in Dhankuta once before. "What can I say, sir, you don't know him."

I told him about myself. He had assumed that I was from a noble Chhetri family. After hearing about my ordinary upbringing, he treated me with even more kindness and asked about my family, wife and children.

We returned to Kathmandu via Delhi and also visited Tirupati Balaji. After working as Prime Minister Bhattarai's security officer for 11 days, I returned home full of admiration for the man. His compassion, friendliness, simplicity and vast knowledge had impressed me. I went to drop him at Baluwatar that evening. He went to his bedroom, while I waited in the hall to seek his leave.

He couldn't find the keys to his suitcase, so he called me inside. That was the first time I had entered a Prime Minister's bedroom.

"Colonel, I think I lost my keys," he said.

I took out my Swiss army knife once more and opened the suitcase. The keys were inside. After that, I fixed the lock again.

"The Colonel is a great mechanic," he said it in his own jolly way, and I was embarrassed by the praise.

He had received a lot of gifts during the visit. "I don't have anyone to give these gifts to. They're of no use to me," he said, "You have children. You can take them home."

But I couldn't take them just because he asked me to. He understood this and distributed the wrapped gifts to everyone.

He would give away all his gifts without even finding out what was inside. He had a philosophical explanation for this: "If you take it out of the wrapping paper, you will know what the gift's worth but if you give away the gifts without knowing what they are, you won't be biased and everyone will receive whatever God decides for them."

It was already dark when I got home. Uma gave me a bundle of newspapers. I was shown with Prime Minister Bhattarai in a lot of photographs.

"Go on, be happy about my pictures," I teased Uma, "But my enemies must have already shown the pictures to the Royal Palace."

After returning from the visit, I submitted a report on the trip to HQ. In it, I included what the Prime Minister had heard regarding the Welfare Fund.

"If the Prime Minister has such perceptions about the Welfare Fund then the general public must have the same misconception," I wrote to General Gadul Shumsher, who looked after the Fund. "It's important to be sure that the rank and file don't also share those views."

After that, the Army began conducting awareness programmes about the Welfare Fund and was transparent about how the money was spent. HQ assigned me to conduct the awareness campaign and I travelled to all the barracks.

Pashupati Prasad Battalion from Dhangadhi had already started arriving at Singha Darbar in Kathmandu. Back then Singha Darbar's security wasn't very clearly delineated and I immediately tried to address that. I called for a meeting with the Home Ministry but even then there was confusion.

"Nepal's precious assets are all inside Singha Darbar and there are hundreds of families living there. In the US, even the Defence Secretary has to go through security but we've become very sloppy about it," I said.

I was playing football one day when I received an urgent summons from the Defence Secretary Mukunda Shumsher. Since we were old acquaintances, I went to his office without changing.

"What did you do, Colonel? The Prime Minister is really impressed with you," he began, "Congratulations."

"I just performed my duties," I said.

The Prime Minister had recommended that my name be put before the annual decoration committee and had spoken highly of me. CB Gurung, who had accompanied the Prime Minister to India, was also on the list.

"CB's name is here so why isn't Rookmangud, who's also a fine officer, also on the list?" the Prime Minister asked the Defence Secretary at a meeting few days after returning from Male.

He asked them to include me and wrote down my name correctly in both English and Nepali on a piece of paper. Not many people spell my name correctly.

Defence Secretary Mukunda Shumsher couldn't argue with the powerful Prime Minister who had come to office through the People's Movement. Furthermore, the constitution had been drafted within seven months, so Kisunjee's stature was at an all-time high.

"Okay, but we'll also need the recommendation to come from the Army Chief," Mukunda Shumsher said.

"Tell the Chief to submit Rookmangud's name," the Prime Minister ordered.

Chief Satchit Shumsher took advantage of this opportunity to also recommend the names of his ADC and Military Assistant.

"The Chief made the recommendation for the decoration according to the Prime Minister's orders," the Defence Secretary told me, "The PM did all this for you."

I wasn't sure how people at the office would react to the Prime Minister giving this order. What if people thought that

I went begging to the PM to put me on the decorations list? My heart was pounding as I walked towards the office.

My relationship with the Prime Minister grew even stronger over time. The PM's Office was next to ours and he would always pass by our office. Whenever his vehicle came up the driveway, I would salute him. If the Prime Minister saw me, he would always stop the car and chat with me.

"Hey Colonel, how's everything?" he would say in his friendly and informal way, "Come by to see me sometime when you're free."

I did drop by his office twice. But the rumour mills were buzzing about my closeness to the Prime Minister. "How did Katawal manage to butter up the PM?" my detractors would say, trying to undermine me because of my closeness to Prime Minister Bhattarai. This could have cost me my career but I didn't distance myself from the PM.

We had heard that the Prime Minister and the Chief had differences which began when the Chief went to submit suggestions about the new constitution on behalf of the Army. The Chief apparently went to the PM accompanied by 16 generals. "The Army should be under the King and some of his rights shouldn't be curtailed," the Chief had maintained.

"I will talk about the King's rights with the King. You needn't be unduly concerned," the Prime Minister had replied curtly.

Ever since then, there had been an undercurrent of distrust between the government and the Army. This was why my supposed closeness to the PM could have been detrimental to my military career. And sure enough, before I knew it, someone complained to the Chief that I had sympathies towards the

Nepali Congress party. Maybe the Chief didn't believe it because I was never called upon to provide an explanation.

The Prime Minister used to host a banquet and ceremony in Singha Darbar's quadrangle in honour of King Birendra's birthday. The battalion at Singha Darbar was part of the organising committee. Having that responsibility always made me nervous.

Instead of the quadrangle, I recommended the area around the pond in front of the main facade of Singha Darbar be used as the venue for the event. The Army engineers agreed that this was the most appropriate place to hold it.

The venue was elegantly decorated. Banana trunks covered with glowing lights were used as entrance gates. We brought in a special type of bush from Nagarkot to enhance the setting.

It was customary for the PM to inspect the venue before the ceremony. After all, his reputation was also on the line. The rehearsals were taking place when the PM came by. All the VIPs, including the security chiefs, secretaries, Chief Secretary, Ministers and officials from constitutional bodies, were present at the rehearsal.

As the battalion commander at Singha Darbar, I waited to welcome the Prime Minister at the main gate. I saluted him and escorted him in. He began looking around while I walked behind him.

"Make sure everything's in order, Rookmangud," he said.

Everyone present there, including the police, Army and civil service VIPs heard the PM. He shouldn't have addressed me in the presence of so many people, including the Army Chief. Three days later, the Chief called me to his office. "Please sit down, Colonel," he said sternly. I had an inkling of what was coming.

"What's really going on here, Colonel? You get recommendations for decorations from elsewhere," the Chief said, "As an Army colonel how can you ask the Prime Minister for a decoration and also be photographed with him everywhere?"

"I don't know about this, sir," I said.

"Be careful what you do. You seem to be getting around a lot. It'll be best if you stay within your limits," he said, and asked me to leave.

I saluted him and left the room.

I had never been a supporter of either the Congress or Communist parties in my life. Why would I suddenly side with any party now? The Chief had been very kind to me and I had the chance to work under him for many years, so it was utterly disheartening to see him so needlessly suspicious of me.

After Satchit Shumsher retired, Gadul Shumsher JBR became Army Chief. At about the same time, it was decided that my battalion would be deployed for UN peacekeeping duties in Lebanon. When it was time to decide on the leadership, HQ announced it would be Deepak Bikram Rana.

Even when I was expected to command the Shreenath Battalion, my name was removed at the last moment when it moved to the Palace. Everyone there from warrant officers to majors was upset. "How can they do this? We will have a word with the Chief," they said angrily, particularly the junior commissioned officers.

"You won't do anything of the kind. It will look like a mutiny," I warned them, "Just don't talk about it anymore." Instead it was me who went to talk to the Chief.

"Why wasn't my name announced, sir?" I wanted to know.

"The Palace took your name out," the Chief replied, "The orders came from His Majesty to not let you go because you're in line for promotion. Now shut up and get back to work."

After the Chief pointed to the Palace I couldn't say anything. In the end, Deepak left for Lebanon holding the flag of the battalion that I used to lead.

Nonetheless, I was happy for my friends and proud of our flag from the barracks. They had said I'd be promoted to full colonel immediately but the leadership forgot all about its promise. It took them almost a year to promote me.

After becoming a full colonel, I was posted as the acting brigade commander of Number One Brigade. A few weeks later, I was also given responsibility for overseeing the Kharipati Academy. I was now juggling twin responsibilities, between Kharipati and Mahankal. It was challenging and I was busy but I enjoyed every moment of it.

A full colonel is a first-class officer. As it was Shashi who had led me to this career path, I called to tell him about my promotion. "Oh dear, how funny is the red hat going to look on that dark face," he joked. He didn't even congratulate me.

The office of the Number One Brigade was shifted from Mahankal to Balaju, a decision which had been made before

I was appointed the acting brigade commander. This brigade was responsible for the Valley and had to contact HQ for everything. Since it was in charge of all celebrations and events at Tundikhel from New Year, Fulpati, the King's Birthday, Prithvi Jayanti, Democracy Day and Army Day to Ghode Jatra, the brigade spent virtually half its time at the Tundikhel parade ground in the city. I couldn't understand why a brigade that spent so much time at Tundikhel should be moved all the way to Balaju.

The idea of soldiers travelling back and forth in a truck from Balaju didn't make any sense at all. It would be such a hassle and a waste of time and resources. So I asked the Chief to review the decision. I told him all the reasons why the brigade shouldn't be moved to Balaju.

"Why didn't you tell me earlier?" he asked.

"Sir, I wasn't the brigade commander then," I said. "It's not too late to reverse the decision."

The Chief then disclosed why he couldn't: "I've already informed the Palace about my orders to move the battalion to Balaju. The decision can't be changed now."

I didn't see the logic to this. Why would the Palace be concerned about where the Number One Brigade was located? As long as the Army functioned professionally, the least of the King's worries would be where its barracks were. If the Palace had been told about the benefits of keeping the barracks where they were, surely it would have approved?

Actually, the problem was in the Army's decision-making processes. Once a request reached the Palace, it couldn't be withdrawn or altered even if it was all a mistake. This meant that even a wrong decision, once reported to the Palace, couldn't be corrected. It was this mindset that affected a relatively straightforward matter like whether the barracks should be moved to Balaju or not.

Around this time, the Chief decided that I would now only handle the job at the Kharipati Academy. It may have been my emphasis on strenuous training during my previous tenures there that got me appointed to Kharipati for a third time. I was pleased about being asked to head the Academy but I didn't want it to be just a job. I was determined to try some new things.

Despite the rigorous educational standards at the Academy, it wasn't recognised academically outside the Army and it seemed important to start an academic degree. Ratna Bahadur Gurung had tried to do this before but it wasn't followed through. Our officers were rigorously trained but still didn't have a formal degree. So I began working on training our cadets in a Tribhuvan University (TU)-affiliated course. The Chief was very supportive, so we went ahead.

India began providing BA/BSc degrees from the National Defence Academy (NDA) in Pune to its graduating officers. The NDA was my alma mater and was affiliated with Jawaharlal Nehru University. But in Nepal getting affiliation with TU was like fighting an uphill battle. I met the vice-chancellor, dean and other professors several times. We took them around Kharipati and briefed them several times but there was no progress.

We were finally able to convince Vice-Chancellor Kedar Bhakta Mathema's team. But before any decision was made, there were elections that brought in the UML government and everyone at the university from the vice-chancellor to the rector was replaced. The UML appointed Kamal Krishna

Joshi as the vice-chancellor and we began lobbying with him all over again.

When nothing worked, we showed TU professors how Bangaldeshi cadets were affiliated with Dhaka University. We took them to India, so they would understand the concept better. While all this was happening, Gadul Shumsher retired as Chief and Dharmapal Bar Singh Thapa replaced him. The new Chief supported my efforts to get university affiliation, as did Defence Secretary Ramesh Jung Thapa. After the Deputy Prime Minister heard about our efforts, he called Kamal Krishna Joshi and said, "The Army's proposal is good, so try to get it in place as soon as possible."

It was only then that TU started a Strategic Studies Department at Kharipati. The 18-month training period was also extended to three years. While this was a more visible achievement, the Army also gained in other ways. There were many colonels and full colonels who had always wanted to complete their undergraduate studies. Although they were highly trained, knowledgeable and experienced, not having a degree was always a liability when it came to qualifying for the NDC. And those without NDC training would have to be content with just being a single star general. So there were many senior officers who sat for the same exams as the cadets and got the opportunity to complete their undergraduate studies.

Along with this I also began organising weekly lectures for all officers from HQ and the Valley. The Chief approved my proposal for this programme. We used to invite experts like Ambassador Bhekh Bahadur Thapa, Ganesh Raj Sharma and Sridhar Khatri to speak on contemporary issues. Everyone, including Army Chief Dharmapal, attended these lectures. Such interactions with experts improved our knowledge on a lot of issues, providing Army officers with academic exposure. It also improved the Army's image in society at large.

Dipendra's cadet training

It was during Colonel Pyar Jung's tenure that Crown Prince Dipendra underwent cadet training. However, while the Crown Prince was still being trained, Pyar Jung was suddenly transferred and Ratna Gurung was called in to take his place.

The Crown Prince's training was a lot less rigorous than that of normal cadets. I heard he was treated like a prince and not like a cadet at all. He had separate quarters, he was deferred to even during classes and parades were organised only after consulting him. None of this would be to the Crown Prince's benefit and from what I understood even the King and Queen wanted his training to be more rigorous.

I remembered from my time in Hong Kong just how restless and mischievous young Dipendra and his siblings, Shruti and Nirajan, were. Dipendra would walk around with toys in his pockets and wouldn't even let his brother and sister touch them. If they did, he was quick to smack them, and he was constantly teasing his sister and making her cry. I remember thinking that even kings and queens can be exasperated by their children just like other parents. "You'll have to behave yourselves when you're sent off to St. Mary's and Kharipati," the Queen had admonished them.

I had the opportunity to spend time with the King and Queen on three occasions in Hong Kong. They were concerned that the Crown Prince could be stubborn and create problems. The cadet training could have disciplined him but, by trying to make places for themselves in the future king's good books, officials at Kharipati went against his parents' wishes and pampered him even more.

Dipendra himself would threaten trainers who were strict. "When I become king, I'll teach you a thing or two about life."

There were also rumours that a lot of trainers who had angered Dipendra left their jobs thinking their futures were in jeopardy. The Crown Prince rarely showed up at Kharipati after I became commandant but even when he did he didn't meet me. He would go there on holidays, chat with the boys, drink and smoke in the mess and leave. So I ordered the staff to inform me as soon as they saw the Crown Prince entering Kharipati.

I was home for the weekend once when I was informed that the Crown Prince had arrived at the Academy that evening. I left immediately and when I got there he was having beers with his friends and ADC. The officers' mess was filled with smoke.

I saluted him. "Colonel, sit down," the Crown Prince said, "Have some beer."

"Your Royal Highness, I think it's too early for me. I don't drink in broad daylight," I replied.

"See you," he stood up abruptly and left in his vehicle.

The next day I told the Chief what had transpired. He set the Crown Prince's beer quota at one glass per day. After that brief encounter, the Crown Prince never returned during my tenure at Kharipati. I believe he could have been a different person if his training had been as rigorous as it was for the other cadets.

Communist allegations

The graduation ceremony for cadets is a grand affair. The families of the second lieutenants flock to see their children begin a new chapter in their lives. Either the Prime Minister or the Defence Minister usually graces the ceremony as the Chief Guest along with other VIP invitees.

The guest list for the 1994 ceremony was being prepared. I asked my second-in-command, Colonel Dilip Shumsher Rana, for the list. After scanning it, I realised the list was as old as the ceremony itself. We were past the Panchayat regime, were now a democracy with two general elections and a local election behind us, yet the list was obsolete and did not reflect the country's changed political reality.

Since our academy was in Bhaktapur, I told them to add Bhaktapur's MP, Narayan Man Bijukchhe, and the town's mayor to the list. These changes were made with the best of intentions but they nearly backfired.

"What on earth is Katawal doing inviting those communists who do not respect the King or the Army to the ceremony?" someone asked HQ. Gadul Shumsher was still Chief and I went to see him.

"What's going on, Colonel? I hear that people who don't accept the monarchy are being invited." Before I could explain he went on, "Why are you doing this?"

"Can I say something, sir?" I asked.

"Go ahead," he said.

I explained my reasoning. "I'm inviting the MP because I want everyone, regardless of their rank and power, to respect the King and the Army," I said.

The Chief suddenly perked up. "How so?" he asked.

"It's important that we include people who don't like the King and the Army in our programmes. What's the point of just having our supporters there? We'll be preaching to the converted," I said.

The Chief was listening intently.

"If we can turn those who hate us into our supporters, then that will be an achievement," I said, pressing on. "By treating the new powerbrokers shabbily, we will perpetuate their hatred of the monarchy and the Army. We'll never be in touch with reality if we only surround ourselves with those who agree with us, sir. Narayan Man is so highly regarded by the locals of Bhaktapur that they won't even sell their land without consulting with him," I said.

The Chief looked visibly taken aback. "Have the invitations been distributed?" he asked.

"They're ready. We were just waiting for your approval," I replied.

"Wait till tomorrow and I'll let you know," the Chief said.

He called me the next day to tell me to invite the MP to the ceremony. He must have had to ask someone at the Palace for clearance.

Narayan Man Bijukchhe arrived before the ceremony started. He was dressed in *daurā suruwāl* and bhādgaunle cap. I had never seen him in national dress before. The formal programme had not yet started. I remember telling him: "See for yourself how feudal or how egalitarian the Army is."

Like most people, Bijukhchhe had the impression that the Army was made up of the spoilt offspring of generals, colonels and aristocratic families like the Shahs and the Ranas. After reading and hearing the list of surnames of those graduating that day, he must have changed his mind. That year a Newar boy, maybe from Bhaktapur himself, received the sword of honour for finishing at the top of his class.

"I thought there was discrimination but I didn't see any," Bijukchhe told me.

Jana Morcha and the Nepal Workers' and Peasants' Party were sharply opposed to the Army during the 1991-1994 Parliament. But after attending the ceremony Bijukchhe became a defender of the national military. Later, when the Maoist insurrection began, he was one of the first to raise his voice in Parliament calling for the Army to be mobilised.

Seven

Mixed Up With Politics

Army Chief Dharmapal Bar Singh Thapa counted me as one of his favourites not for any personal reason but because of my work at Nagarkot and Kharipati. I had recently worked under his supervision at the academy as well and he had recommended me for the prestigious *Gorkha Dakshin*bahu *III*.

It was during his tenure that I also became a one-star general (Brigadier General) and after my promotion I was posted at Number Two Brigade in Dhankuta, which looked after the entire eastern region. In the preceding few years, the generals who had gone there as brigade commanders, including Satchit Shumsher, Gadul Shumsher and Dharmapal, went on to become Army Chiefs. There was more I wanted to do than just report to HQ and direct the men under my command in the east. I didn't want to be restricted to just these aspects of my work at the barracks. So, soon after reaching Dhankuta, I decided to travel all around the east on foot which I hoped would help me better understand the society, culture, development and the overall situation in the region.

I asked Chief Dharmapal for permission.

"No matter where you go, just take care of your command," he ordered, "Take your communications gear along and keep my office informed."

I spent my winters in the Tarai and my summers in the hills and went around every unit and sub-unit. Everywhere I went

I would talk to the soldiers about what was happening and explain Army policy. I tried not to make it a one-way street and encouraged them to also speak up.

This model of handling the command from the field was very helpful. It was a good way for the soldiers and me to get to know each other. The soldiers worked at the ground level and getting to know them improved my understanding of grassroots reality.

I didn't limit myself to just military bases. Local commanders would be asked to arrange meetings with the civilian officials in the area. I always called the Chief District Officer (CDO) before heading out to any district in order to give out the message that the Army respects civilian supremacy. Such meetings were mostly arranged outside the base and also included the local Superintendent of Police, Deputy Superintendent of Police, judges, the Local Development Officer, District Education Officer and others with whom I discussed their respective areas of work.

During one visit, I went to Ilam. The battalion commanders from Itahari and Jhapa were also there and I hadn't realised that that our meeting was planned on the same day as the convention of the Federation of Nepali Journalists which was being held there. The CDO invited all the office heads for a meeting that morning and, since the timing clashed, most of the officers chose to attend our meeting. I was sorry for the inadvertent clash, after finding out about the dates.

The journalists, however, were furious with me. Most of them already had a negative attitude towards the Army and regarded us as servants of the King. That week the local papers carried sensational coverage that went: *'General orders around CDO and judges'* or *'Meeting General comes first for CDO'*.

Even the CDO and company commanders were dragged into it but I reassured them: "Don't worry. I'll field the questions if there are any."

Predictably, a few days after that there was a memo from HQ. COAS Dharmapal had written in large letters: "Beware of journalists."

Soldiers with protruding bellies almost touching the ground is one ugly sight. Everything at the Hile Brigade, from morning exercise to night duty, was rigorous. When I was running myself every morning, other officers could no longer make excuses. They, too, began arriving before the parade started.

Exercise for soldiers is determined by their age. We can't lie and hide because the tummy always tells the truth. However, there are inevitably a few people who procrastinate and have all the excuses, from headaches to toothaches, to skip exercise parade.

There was one such captain at the Brigade headquarters called Krishna Prasad Sharma who frequently fell ill. When he complained about not feeling well he would start crying, tears and all. So we couldn't even say he was just acting.

He had started out as a clerk in the Army and moved up to officer rank as a diligent accountant. His meticulous book-keeping was legendary and was talked about even at HQ. In the evenings, he blossomed into an entertainer and joked around with everyone. His dance moves and singing skills were hard to beat. Uma had come to Dhankuta with the children during their winter vacation that year. She had some relatives in Bayalbas, Sarlahi, so they decided to stop there on their way back to Kathmandu. And since Krishna Prasad also lived in Bhaktapur, he joined Uma and the children on their way back to Kathmandu.

I told Uma that he would keep them entertained throughout the ride. But instead, he apparently complained about me to Uma the whole time. "The General works way too hard. It isn't acceptable for someone of his stature. He really punishes himself," he whined.

"Why?" Uma asked, a little concerned.

"It's his first posting as a general but he isn't making the most of it. He should act like a general and enjoy the perks of office, dining in style, gambling, travelling and just having a good time. A general's stature will diminish if he starts eating with *sipahis* at the mess," he said.

"He wakes up before dawn and carries weights like a soldier. After that he goes running, leaving the others far behind," he went on. "He should take into consideration his age. What if the future Chief falls off a mountain somewhere, madam?" General Krishna Narayan Singh had told him that I was a potential COAS.

It was the first time after becoming a general that I heard anyone referring to me as a possible future Chief.

"Seeing the general panting all the way from Dhankuta to Hile is more than I can take." He wasn't done yet, Uma told me, and after going on and on about me, finally got to the point.

"We completed our exercise quota as soldiers and JCOs. After becoming officers, we hoped things would improve, better food, clothes, but the general ruined it all for us, madam.

I've lost almost eight kilos since the general started on a fitness spree," he said.

Apparently, a protruding belly was a sign of prosperity in his village and the person would be respected for it. So, when he started losing weight, everyone ridiculed him. Poor fellow, did he have problems!

Uma called me as soon as she reached Kathmandu. Before I could say anything, she was cross with me, "Why are you doing this?"

"Doing what?" I asked.

She related to me all of Krishna's tale of woe. So, when Krishna returned to Hile after the holidays, I pulled him up. "Hey you slacker, you think officers keep their jobs by sleeping all day?"

He didn't say a word.

I was selected for Pakistan's National Defence College (NDC) while I was still in Dhankuta. Kul Bahadur Khadka had already returned from Pakistan and was chosen for NDC while he was still a full colonel, which rarely happens. I bumped into him at HQ one day.

"How is it? What do I need to do to prepare?" I asked him.

"You'll need money. It's best to take around Rs 300,000," he said, "There's a lot of studying, not much different than in the US or UK."

I knew how demanding the academic pressure in India and Pakistan could be. We received only USD 1.28 daily from the Government of Nepal. Food and accommodation was provided by the Pakistanis. I asked Director of Military Training Gopal Singh Bohara for a loan from the Welfare Fund.

"Giving out loans isn't my duty, if you aren't going give a request to me in writing," he replied sternly.

I was in a classic Catch 22 situation.

Not going to Pakistan meant losing a once in a lifetime opportunity to attend the NDC. I was also worried that people would question my discipline if I made the decision not to go. However, as much as I wanted to go, I didn't have the money. I would have to reconcile myself to being just a one-star general if I didn't attend NDC. Selling off my land for money was an option but getting buyers so quickly wasn't easy.

Krishna Bahadur Gurung, whom I had known for a long time, was the Chief of General Staff then. He was our instructor in Bhaktapur when I was training to become a captain. I told him about my situation. "You should be entitled to a loan," he said, "Go see the Chief."

"What's the problem?" the Chief asked.

After I told him, he ordered that a loan of Rs 300,000 be arranged for me.

It was only after that I finally enrolled as a student of National Defence College in Pakistan which had elite officers from all over the world for its one-year course.

After returning to Kathmandu, I was posted at Number 10 Brigade near Sheetal Niwas in Maharajganj. Although I had done ranger and special forces training, I had never been part of the Special Forces which are considered a superior unit both physically and professionally. It's a special unit trained by

American and British officers. Usually, a general who has been a commander at Special Forces battalion is promoted to the post of brigade commander. But thanks to Chief Dharmapal's trust in me, I received such a prized posting.

Becoming a brigade commander twice is rare. But I had that opportunity three times. They must have taken into consideration my physical fitness and other qualities since my lieutenant days to hand me responsibility for Number 10 Brigade.

Everyone at the Special Forces, from foot soldier to general, has to take tests every six months or once a year. Depending on the rank, there are physical, professional and other tests, including para jumps in daylight and at night. The government provided a few hundred rupees allowance for the Special Forces after much lobbying with the Finance and Defence Ministries. I put forward a proposal to the Finance Ministry to increase the allowance.

"Doesn't the state need a well-equipped, well-trained and experienced force if your child is abducted or to provide security to foreign guests?" I said, "We're not asking for this money just to indulge ourselves."

After a long discussion, the increase was finally granted. The Special Forces have better weapons than others, like the Israeli *Galil*, and now the allowance came in too. But we were always performing poorly, often missing the targets at shooting competitions during the King's Banner. The Force was supposed to be the best but we faced humiliating defeat when it came to shooting.

Even the Chief was concerned about the poor shooting skills of the Special Forces personnel. At first, I couldn't figure out why the Special Forces kept shooting wildly with their *Galil*s.

I was fond of shooting and was a good shot myself. During my tenure at Number One and Number Two Brigades, they always came first in the sharpshooting competition.

Colonel Kiran Basnet of the Special Forces was the assistant brigade commander and I called him up one day and said, "Find out why they aren't hitting the targets."

I called for a meeting so we could discuss the issue.

"The *Galil* is one of the best battle-tested weapons in the world," I began, "There's no way it doesn't shoot straight. How does it kill enemies if it misses a target? We call ourselves Special Forces. The government has given us the best weapon. How can you blame the gun?" I finally convinced them that there was nothing wrong with the gun.

"It's just the fear within us that's making us nervous," I said, "Let's get rid of this fear. No one can stop us from winning. We have to win."

The officers began practicing under Kiran's supervision. The shooters were selected. Some of them started practicing short-range firing right there at Maharajganj, while some were trained at Alle, Nagarkot and Suryabinayak. We chose the best among them and made them practice a lot.

When they were ready, we finally took them to the competition.

Our brigade actually won the shooting event that year. I led three brigades and all three came first in shooting. The Chief seemed pleased about it. Tragically, Kiran was later killed by the Maoists in his house.

"The Crown Prince visits Alle almost every night on his stunt motorbike," someone from the brigade came to tell me at my residence.

There was a place called Alle in Shivapuri forest, right above Kavresthali north of Kathmandu. The barracks under my brigade were at Alle where commando training was conducted. Later it became known as the Yuddha Bhairav Battalion (Special Forces).

Yuddha Kabaj Battalion, in which armoured cars were housed, was at Sitapaila. The stunt motorbikes bought for the Ghode Jatra and Shivaratri ceremonies while I was in Hong Kong were also there. The Crown Prince and some officers used to ride these every week at Alle. The Alle commander and scout car were their partners in crime who managed these secret night rides for the Crown Prince, visiting him in Shivapuri.

Alle's company commander Colonel Baldev Shumsher Thapa hadn't informed me about any of this. I also learned that the bikes would whizz across Alle at top speed and I intended to put a stop to this because of the bad publicity in case something went wrong.

"The roads in the dense forest there are unpaved. What if there's an accident?" I told the Chief.

He agreed this was indeed dangerous and said: "I will talk to the Palace and you ask the colonel there to immediately put a stop to all of this."

I called for Colonel Thapa to come and see me.

"I hear you are encouraging the Crown Prince in bad habits," I said as soon as he entered the room. I didn't ask him to sit and didn't offer him tea. He spoke as if he was my superior just because he hobnobbed with the Crown Prince.

"Do you want to keep your job or not, general?" he asked, throwing his weight around. That was the last straw.

"Get out!" I roared.

"This officer is not fit to remain in the Army," I said in a report on Colonel Thapa to the Military Secretariat, cc-ing it to the Chief's office. General Dharmapal retired soon after and Prajwalla Shumsher Rana took over as the new Chief.

Dipendra had developed a special interest in guns and was close to the colonel and generals in the Special Forces. They had all found out about my letter regarding Colonel Thapa. This was an opportunity for some of the generals who had joined the Special Forces before me and were hell-bent on teaching me a lesson. I knew all about this but my conscience didn't let me backtrack on my decision.

Although I was firmly against Dipendra's behaviour as an individual, I still respected the position of Crown Prince. I also believed that a future king shouldn't behave in this way and no one who supported the monarchy should endorse such behaviour. Chief Prajwalla called Alle's Colonel Thapa, the Scout Car major and me into his office.

Had it been Chief Dharmapal, the decision would have been to prevent the Crown Prince from behaving recklessly. Things had changed now but still, after hearing everyone out, the Chief reprimanded them. Colonel Thapa spoke disrespectfully to Chief Prajwalla as well. In the end, the Chief supported my view and took action against him.

Colonel Thapa wanted to rise up the ranks quickly by

pleasing the Crown Prince but while doing so he forgot his duties and that eventually put a full stop to his career.

Meanwhile, the conflict was spreading. The government wasn't able to prepare and implement a security plan to deal with the insurgency, and the Army was on standby, especially the Special Forces under my command. We built a track around the compound and also set up high observation posts to keep tabs on everything around us.

We were prepared for a possible Maoist attack, even though it didn't seem likely at the time. Back then nobody ever imagined that the Maoists could attack the Army.

I met the Military Secretary at the Palace, General Shanta, at a gathering. He was my supporter and the uncle of my close friend, Sadeep Shah.

"Hey *kāji*, how's everything?" he asked.

He was acting informally to put me at ease.

"You've apparently built sentry posts and opened a perimeter track. Are we at war already?" he said jokingly.

I immediately knew someone had tattled to him. There were a lot of people who were upset when I was posted as a brigade commander for a third time. When they couldn't find anything substantial to complain about, they would latch on to an issue like my strengthening the base's defences.

"I'm only trying to keep the Special Forces secure because there will be war with the Maoists one day. Isn't it a soldier's duty to always analyse possible challenges and prepare accordingly?" I asked.

"Okay, okay, fine then," he said.

The Army had been studying the strategy of the Maoists' "People's War" in detail. When they took up arms in 1996, Dharmapal Bar Singh Thapa was the Army Chief. Back then, the Army had prepared a report on the origin, expansion and prospects of the Maoist armed conflict and presented it to the government. Political leaders who had always looked upon the Army as the King's pawns since the Panchayat years, never took our report seriously.

We had presented a plan to counter the Maoist insurgency and sought Rs 500 million to do the job. Called the Internal Security and Development Plan, it didn't just focus on a military solution to end the conflict but also emphasised development. The entire force and the Army Chief believed that addressing the issues of unemployment, disillusionment and scarcities would defuse the pressure building up in society.

Nepalese Army officers have extensive experience in peacekeeping forces in conflict areas around the world. Despite the Army's experience and our eagerness to be part of the solution to address the conflict, the government didn't believe us. Eventually, the conflict cost the country dearly, resulting in the deaths of thousands of people, destroying infrastructure and pushing development back decades. But even when hundreds of innocent fellow Nepalis were slaughtered, the Army's hands were tied. According to the constitution, the Army could be mobilised only on the government's orders. So all we could do was watch the tragedy unfold, and wait for legitimate orders.

On the other hand, Operations Romeo and Kilo Sierra 2 were carried out after a few high-ranking police officers pushed the Home Ministry. However, the police were incapable of bringing the situation under control and instead the offensives increased public anger against the state. Some police officers who were used to special privileges couldn't reform their ways, civilians were hurt and this made the counter-insurgency operations even more difficult.

Overall, the Nepal Police is a capable force. During the Panchayat years, the police force was known for its professionalism and adept handling of classified information. But after multiparty democracy was restored in 1990, politicisation and polarisation hurt the police. Even transfers and promotions of IGPs were dictated by party politics. So cosying up to political power centres, instead of focusing on its duties and the rule of law, became the norm.

It would be wrong to put all the blame on the police for the failure to counter the Maoists. The poorly-equipped force had been on the frontline of the insurgency for six years. The Army could be mobilised constitutionally only on the recommendation of the National Security Council. The Local Administration Act had provisions for the district-level Security Committee to seek the Army's assistance in times of need.

After Prajwalla Shumsher Rana took over as Army Chief in 1999, the Army repeatedly requested permission to leave the barracks. But the government and political parties refused to give us the responsibility for protecting the people. I accompanied the Chief of the General Staff (CGS) and the Director of Military Operation (DMO) for the Central Security Committee meeting at the Home Ministry several times. Both of them requested that the Army be allowed to contain the insurgency. But even after extensive loss and damage, the government didn't think it was necessary to mobilise the Army. A lot of leaders were worried that letting the Army outside the barracks might jeopardise democracy.

"If the Army is allowed to fight the Maoists, it will never return to its barracks," a leader of a national party once said publicly and in Parliament.

The Home Ministry, especially, didn't want to mobilise the Army. We had intelligence that the Home Minister and IGP had convinced the government not to mobilise the Army.

"We don't need the Army. We can do it ourselves," the IGP had said, and there were rumours that the IGP and the Army Chief didn't get along. Even King Birendra was not in favour of army mobilisation. "Whose King will I be, if people are killed?" was apparently the King's response on mobilising. He believed the root cause of the conflict should be recognised to address the problem, and that the Army should go to the villages with development programmes.

Prime Minister Girija Prasad Koirala had once visited HQ with all the ministers during Prajwalla Shumsher Rana's tenure. Mahesh Acharya was the Defence Minister then. The Chief briefed them on the situation regarding the conflict and presented a strategy. The Prime Minister and his entourage listened intently.

"The Army needs to be mobilised," the Chief said. "We'll take the Internal Security and Development Programme to the villages and implement it."

The Prime Minister gave his approval but Home Minister Govinda Raj Joshi tried to stop the Prime Minister, saying, "Army mobilisation may create turmoil and affect the results of the next local election."

"It's about the nation and the people. It doesn't matter if Congress loses. The nation and democracy cannot lose," the Prime Minister replied, standing his ground.

"The Army may move forward after formulating a plan," the PM said, "Present the budget for it."

All of us, including the Army Chief, were impressed by the Prime Minister's decisiveness. The Army then started making plans accordingly but there was no followup.

King Birendra then called all the members of the Cabinet, the Army and police chiefs to discuss the Maoist insurgency. His Majesty didn't agree with those ministers who wanted to crush the Maoists with force. After hearing everyone out, he got up to speak.

"How can Nepalis kill one another?" the King said, "We all need to remember that even the Maoists are Nepalis."

According to the King, the root causes of the conflict were poverty, illiteracy and dissatisfaction among the people and these needed to be addressed through development programmes implemented by the Army.

While Kathmandu was still wrestling with the question of whether or not to mobilise the Army, the Maoists launched a series of attacks on district headquarters and police stations. The media featured news of these attacks prominently, splashing pictures of slaughtered policemen and their mourning families. While police officers, party cadres and civil servants were being killed, it seemed the Army was doing nothing about it. So it wasn't surprising that public opinion was turning against the Army.

In October 2000, the Maoists attacked Dunai, the district headquarters of Dolpa, and turned it to ashes. Home Minister

Joshi immediately went public accusing the Army of not coming to the rescue of the police and civil servants. He later resigned.

However, the Army couldn't move until it was ordered to do so by the National Security Council. At about this time, I was transferred to HQ where I took over as head of the Directorate of Military Intelligence (DMI). My responsibility included collecting and analysing information from Nepal and abroad which was relevant to the conflict.

As Director of Military Intelligence, I came to realise that the political parties generally still viewed the Army as a royalist force. They simply refused to believe that the Army, in fact, functions on the basis of the rule of law and the constitution. Most politicians regularly questioned the Army's loyalty. The increasing distrust of the politicians led directly to the creation of the paramilitary Armed Police Force (APF). This was part of their master plan – to downsize the Army and expand the APF.

The political leadership's negative attitude towards the Army was disheartening for us. There were rumours about a split between the Army Chief and IGP so that, instead of working together to face a common threat, the Army and police were increasingly working at cross-purposes. The Army had voiced its dissatisfaction to the Supreme Commander, King Birendra, regarding the creation of the APF.

"How many security forces does a country like ours need?" the King had apparently asked in private. The civilian government held the authority on decisions relating to state mechanisms, so King Birendra, as a constitutional monarch, probably thought it was best to maintain a public silence.

When the APF was formed, it couldn't attract the best officers from the Army and the Nepal Police. Initially, it only had officers who didn't see a future for themselves in the Nepal Police or the Army, the ones who were dissatisfied with their jobs or had had disciplinary problems earlier in their careers.

The Age Factor

It was during my tenure at DMI that I was accused of lying about my age. The Palace's Military Secretary, Vivek Shah, called me to his office one day. "There are a lot of questions being asked about you at the Palace. Apparently, you lied about your age. HQ brought in files to prove it and they are even accusing you of lying to the King," he said.

This was shocking. Such enquiries wouldn't take place unless someone within the Army was aggressively pursuing it. But who? I was the most senior one-star general due for promotion and had fulfilled all the criteria regarding qualifications and experience. I knew this was all set up by a few key people in the Army who wanted to block my promotion. Accusing me of falsifying my age was all a conspiracy. I thanked Vivek profusely for his kindness.

The next day I was informed about a death in Vivek's family and went to offer my condolences. Even in the midst of mourning, Vivek raised the issue again, "There might be a problem because of your age, so gather all the evidence you have. We'll have to take care of it as soon as I'm done here." He looked more worried than I was.

My file for promotion to major general (two-star) was forwarded but had been on hold for the previous two weeks because of the controversy about my age. The truth was that I found out my true age only in 1975 when I visited my village. After hearing my brothers and relatives discuss our ages, I found out that my date of birth on paper had been incorrect the whole time. My age on paper was around five years more than my actual age and would have made me older than my elder brothers. I felt this mistake had to be corrected, so I presented the necessary certification from the Village Panchayat and District Panchayat at HQ. The Army sought information from my school as well. Furthermore, a committee under the auspices of HQ had been formed to look into my case. The request was presented to the Chief who sent my files to the Palace. The Principal Military Secretary at the Palace, Sher Bahadur Malla at that time, went through all the documents and apparently presented it to the King. No one would have dared to present documents to the King unless the information they contained was verified.

After a convoluted process, my age was corrected on orders from King Birendra himself. Finally, my actual age and my age on the Army's files were the same.

Vivek was back at work after observing the 13 days of customary mourning. I got his call, "Send in all the documents you have regarding your age."

"All the evidence is at the Military Secretariat. I have nothing," I told him. "Only those who cheat keep evidence to 'prove' things. Honest people don't feel they need it."

"I'll ask them to look for it," Vivek assured me.

The issue of my age even came up in discussions between the Chief and the King and I heard that the Chief's views were not in my favour. Now, all I could rely on was the reputation I had built up and earned through my hard work.

I remembered what the ascetic I met on the banks of the Sunkoshi had told me when I was a child: "What is fixed by fate must come to pass."

As a young boy, I was always told that my planetary alignments would bring challenges throughout my life and I felt this was just another test. I was determined to face everything that would be thrown at me.

The ones who accused me of falsifying my age wanted to send me into retirement. Had I not corrected my age in 1975, I would have retired by 2000. Colonel Bharat Gurung who had accompanied Prince Dhirendra in Hong Kong had said, "They won't make you the Chief anyway. If you look after our business in Hong Kong, you can at least make some money."

He had implied that I should make arrangements to facilitate the Prince's various business dealings in Hong Kong but I had directly refused to be part of that.

He had been persistent in trying to convince me, "You won't be made the Chief, so think about it."

Back then I had just become an acting colonel. The idea of me becoming the Chief one day was such a farfetched notion that I couldn't even dream about it. General was the highest rank I thought I could reach.

"How do you know who will be made Army Chief?" I had asked Bharat Gurung, just to shut him up.

"There was an unwritten agreement between the King and the Ranas in 1950," he replied, "Only members of the Shah and Rana families would be made Army Chiefs and, if that wasn't possible, arrangements would be made so the post went only to their kinfolks, including the Thapas, Basnets and Pandeys. We also heard there was a gentleman's agreement that the future Shah kings would only marry Rana girls."

Whether what he said was literally true or not, my promotion was now obviously being held up because of historical issues relating to power and class. Some people in the Palace were lobbying against me and so was HQ. According to some of my supporters, if I were to be promoted to a two -star general I would then be in line to be Army Chief and that was, in fact, the root cause of all the drama.

For a boy who walked barefoot from Okhaldhunga, not becoming a two- star general was never an issue. What disturbed me most was that my reputation had been tarnished, all because of a false accusation.

Nevertheless, I put on a brave face.

"Let me have a spare room here," I told Uma one evening.

"Why?" she asked.

"I won't be promoted, so I'll start teaching," I said, "I need to start doing something."

Being a security guard wouldn't befit an ex-general. So I thought tutoring students in the mornings and evenings would be a better option since it would pay me enough to get by. My salary was around Rs 15,000 and I could easily make that through tutoring.

Koteshwor had changed completely since we built our house there 20 years previously. Back then, it was rice fields and a few scattered buildings. Now it was densely packed with houses. I spread the word in my neighbourhood that I'd soon be giving tuition. A few students had already signed up. So I was glad that I could still make a living even if I lost my job in the Army.

The issue of my promotion remained undecided. The file that was presented to the Palace hadn't been returned with a decision one way or the other.

"List and present all the charges against Katawal," the King ordered the Chief. The King was apparently enraged when he realised what HQ was trying to do me. His Majesty called Vivek after the Chief left the Palace and said, "I don't give orders without seeing factual evidence. There should be grounds to support what you say, so start looking for them."

Vivek and a few other officers began a frantic search and finally, after three days, found my files with the records of the formal correction of my age. The letter sent by the Defence Ministry in 1975 had been at the Palace all along. The file explained the grounds for correcting my age and it was all there in black and white.

Vivek presented all the evidence to the King, who ordered him to promote me. The King's vehicle was about to leave but Vivek said he was still bowing.

"What else?" the King asked.

"What about Balananda, Your Majesty?"

"Fine then. Promote Bala as well," he ordered.

The posts of two major generals were vacant. So Vivek wanted Balananda to be promoted as well. Balananda's age had been corrected by the Army Secretariat seven years previously. The conspiracy to sabotage my promotion soon fizzled out, after which Balananda and I were promoted in the last week of May in 2000.

The Royal Massacre

I was returning from an embassy dinner on 1 June when I got a call from home.

"It's urgent. You need to go to HQ immediately," Uma said.

I went to HQ around 10.30 pm, still in my uniform. Maybe the Maoists had launched a major attack somewhere, I thought. As the vehicle entered HQ, I could sense that something was terribly wrong. Even the duty officer didn't know exactly what had happened.

"Sir, everyone's upstairs. I don't know what it's all about," he said.

Dilip Rayamajhi was at the Army Chief's office. He gave it to me straight: "There was bloodshed in the Palace apparently and the royal family has been killed." I fell back on my chair, unable to speak a word. The Chief and some others were at the Chhauni Hospital but we knew nothing more.

"The King was shot and is in the hospital now," someone said, "The entire family has been wiped out, they say."

I was in a dilemma over whether or not to go to the hospital. We didn't have the orders, which meant going to the hospital was out of bounds for officers like me. But at that moment the consequences didn't matter. The King was a father-figure to me, so I couldn't hold back my desire to see him one last time.

I rushed out on a motorcycle. Going in there as a uniformed general in a military car would only have drawn unnecessary attention. Chhauni Hospital was heavily guarded. Members of the extended royal family were going in with stunned looks on their faces. Despite so many people milling about, the hospital was eerily quiet. The Chief, Shanta Kumar Malla, and other generals were gathered in the lobby.

I went to see the Chief. "Go away," the Chief said, showing me out. "Why are you even here?"

So I went back to my office. The order was to remain on standby. After midnight there were continuous phone calls from friends and family, who probably thought a general would know what had happened. But we were told nothing, so we knew nothing. We just heard rumours, like everyone else. Some were saying that King Birendra, Queen Aishwarya, Princess Shruti, Prince Nirajan and five others had died while others said that the King was seriously injured. Rumours had been rife about discord within the royal family relating to Crown Prince Dipendra's marriage. We spent the whole night at HQ.

I couldn't contain myself so, despite being ordered not to, I went to the hospital again the next day. Crown Prince Dipendra's ADC, Raju Karki, was sitting near the special ward, looking pale.

"What happened?" I asked.

"The Crown Prince's condition is very serious," he said.

By then the news about the death of all the immediate royal family members had spread across the city.

"Can I see His Royal Highness?" I asked. I was led in and saw Dipendra with his head completely covered in bandages. His motionless body lay on the bed and I gave up hope of him coming out alive.

"It's all over, sir," Raju said in an anguished voice.

That morning the nation woke up in shock as word spread. Not including Dipendra, nine members of the royal family were dead. Soldiers were discouraged from displaying emotion. We needed to be strong. So, when the whole country was mourning the death of our beloved King, Queen, Princess Shruti and Prince Nirajan, I couldn't shed tears and grieve for the loss like other Nepalis.

I was assigned to take charge of the arrangements for the funeral procession. In the evening, I took my position and walked beside King Birendra's body in the procession. Some hooligans near Swayambhu threw stones at Prime Minister Girija Prasad Koirala's car. Their anger was directed at the Prime Minister and Prince Gyanendra.

During the funeral procession, I remembered Princess Shruti most fondly. She was my daughter's senior at St. Mary's School. Every time we visited our daughter on weekends, she used to talk about Shruti, with whom she shared her food.

"Shruti *didi* is very protective of us," my daughter used to say.

The King and Queen couldn't come to see their daughter like the rest of us did so, whenever possible, we used to talk to Shruti.

Prince Gyanendra's daughter, Prerana, also went to the same school. "Uncle and aunt visit us occasionally," I remember Shruti telling me. Her voice kept ringing in my ears. As the funeral procession marched forward, these memories flashed in front of my eyes.

I remembered King Birendra and was overwhelmed thinking about the generosity and trust he displayed towards me from behind the scenes. Queen Aishwarya's motionless body and serene face reminded me of the time she spent in Hong Kong. I clearly remembered how she went around shopping with Uma on an empty stomach and bought my wife a sari. She had wanted stringent cadet training for Dipendra. If that had happened, maybe things wouldn't have turned out so tragically for the royal family.

We let him be a prince instead of a commoner during training which has lead to this, I remember thinking. The ADCs also spoilt the Crown Prince which only made things worse. Despite my attempts to put on a brave soldier's face, I could no longer hold back my tears. Close to Aryaghat, my eyes brimmed up and the tears ran down my cheeks uncontrollably.

"The Crown Prince's ADCs should have been a lot more senior than him, instead of young boys his own age whom he could boss around," I thought.

During King Mahendra's time, his sons apparently used to fear their ADCs. But King Birendra couldn't be as strict with his own son. Later on at Kharipati, Dipendra apparently threatened the strict Directing Staff (DS) officer yelling, "Am I a cadet or a crown prince?"

The DS should have firmly replied that in Kharipati he was just a cadet but he didn't dare. If only the DS had been given the right to wield his authority then maybe Dipendra wouldn't have ended up so spoilt. Alas, none of this could undo what happened that night. What's written in one's fate is written and can't be erased.

After King Birendra and his descendants were wiped out, Gyanendra was named King by *Raj Parishad,* the Royal Privy Council. The formalities of his coronation were completed at Hanuman Dhoka Palace. Everyone used to say that the younger brother, Gyanendra, was the clever one, just as sharp and intelligent as his father.

Rumours were rife about the involvement of family members in the massacre that night and this public perception posed a big challenge for King Gyanendra. As far as my understanding of the events that night goes, Crown Prince Dipendra vented his rage against his mother because of her refusal to allow him to marry the girl of his choice. All other conspiracy theories are futile attempts to cast unnecessary mystery over the events of 1 June 2001.

But the ADCs on duty at the Palace that night must bear a lot of the blame. After hearing gunshots, why didn't they storm in? Wasn't their job the protection of the royal family? Why did they pretend not to notice anything amiss even when the Crown Prince, dressed in combat fatigues, walked into the party carrying so many guns?

Brigadiers/full colonels are always on duty at the Palace. There were at least 10 people, including the ADCs and military police, outside the hall where the royal family was gathered. Furthermore, what kind of security arrangement would allow anyone, regardless of who they were, to take weapons like that into the room?

While the country was still in mourning, the Army faced a slew of questions regarding what happened in the Palace that night. The uniform of the military stationed at the Palace was the same as that of the Army, so it was understandable when the Army Chief was questioned. Formally, these two forces may look like one but actually they are two separate entities. In fact, the Army Chief has no say in relation to the Palace's security forces, including in their training, transfers and promotions which are handled by the Military Secretariat or the ADC department. As Chief Prajwalla succinctly put it, "We will do whatever the Palace orders."

The royal massacre changed the course of Nepal's history. Thirteen days later, I received my shiny new badge of rank as a major general, a gift that I owe to King Birendra.

My life changed in the most unexpected ways after King Mahendra brought me to Kathmandu and nurtured me with his love and generosity. But climbing up the ladder and fighting against all odds to reach the two-star general mark wasn't easy for a boy from the boondocks, especially when the Army's leadership and HQ were bent on sabotaging my career.

King Birendra, the person who had ensured justice for me during a time of crisis, was no longer with us. But the reminder of that justice was pinned on my shoulders now: the two-star general's badge.

The Holeri Episode

In the winter of 2000, the then Home Minister, Govinda Raj Joshi, had to resign after being dragged into a controversy involving the Army. Earlier, IGP Achyut Kharel was sidelined after the Maoist attack on Dunai in Dolpa.

The guerrillas walked all the way from Panchkatiya in Jajarkot to Dunai, Rukumkot and Naumule over a period of a few months in preparation for the attack. The government was still caught off-guard and it would still not give the responsibility to the Army to contain the insurgency. That summer, the Army itself was surrounded by the Maoists at Holeri in Rolpa. Prime Minister Girija Prasad Koirala wasn't satisfied with the Army's role and his relations with the Army got so bad that he ultimately resigned in July 2001.

What really happened behind the scenes leading to the resignation of a powerful Prime Minister is an intricate story. A patrol of around 22 soldiers were marching through Holeri during a heavy thunderstorm. The Maoists took this opportunity to show their strength and surrounded the soldiers. The Army patrol could have easily decimated the lightly armed Maoists with their heavy weapons but the Maoists used women, children and elderly folk as human shields, preventing the soldiers from using their automatic weapons.

A helicopter sent to evacuate the soldiers came under fire itself from the Maoists on the ground. Co-pilot Binayak Bahadur Singh, son of General Kedar Bahadur Singh, was injured. The Army was still trapped but kept the news secret so as not to affect the morale of soldiers elsewhere in the country.

Soon after, the media started erroneously reporting that the Army had surrounded the Maoists. We didn't deny the reports and perhaps the Home Ministry was sent the same information through the Defence Ministry. However, the Army brass definitely didn't lie to the King about what was unfolding in the hills of Holeri in mid-western Nepal.

What I couldn't understand was why the Prime Minister wasn't told the truth about what happened. Maybe the Army was still driven by the notion that informing the King was enough. Whatever the case, this created a misunderstanding on the Prime Minister's part because he was not correctly informed.

The Home Ministry issued a statement quoting the Defence Ministry as saying the Maoists were surrounded by an Army unit. Based on the same statement, the media reported that the Army was ready to confront the Maoists. I still don't know the source of this misinformation about Holeri and the few things I have been able to dig up were only after becoming the Chief and watching a video of the incident.

I watched it because Girija*babu* a few years later demanded to know the "true story" of Holeri. In 2001, the Prime Minister was convinced that the Maoists and the Army were getting closer and sidelining him. His party, Nepali Congress, probably had the impression that the King was behind this. Holeri haunted Girija*babu* until the end of his days. He must have thought the Army had betrayed him and, after Holeri, actually started trusting the Maoists more than the Army.

I was convinced that the Army would never betray the country, the people and the democratic process. My conclusion was that the Army wanted to be mobilised in accordance with the law to retaliate in case it was attacked in Holeri, Dunai or anywhere else. The Palace and Home Ministry were not in favour of mobilising the Army, so we had to take a hands-off approach. Like his brother, King Gyanendra also didn't want to mobilise the Army. Since he was crowned King under such controversial circumstances, and it had only been a month since the massacre, his own confidence level wasn't very high.

The conspiracy theories were themselves contradictory. The Army was accused of not wanting democracy to succeed which was why it wasn't being deployed against the Maoists while, on the other hand, the political parties felt that democracy would be jeopardised if the Army were to be deployed.

The Chief's statement about the Army being mobilised "only if all the political parties agree to it" became controversial. Chief Prajwalla's stance was valid. The Army didn't want to get caught up in the political bickering over military mobilisation, since its main responsibility was to follow the law and uphold the constitution. The Army was criticised in the House of Representatives and the National Assembly for Prajwalla's supposedly political statement. It was only when the Army Chief clarified his stand before Parliament that the storm simmered down. The Army wanted political consensus.

After Koirala's resignation following the Holeri episode, Congress leader, Sher Bahadur Deuba, became Prime Minister. And for the first time, the Army's suggestions were implemented, albeit only partially. Deuba trusted the Army.

The Dang Attack

I was just getting started on my exercises one morning in November 2001 when the tenant at my house asked, "General, how were the Army's Dang barracks ransacked?"

I was shocked.

I didn't know anything about the overnight attack in Dang, so I gave him an ambiguous reply and slipped away. I thought about the soldiers, JCOs and others and a chill went down my spine.

The attack on the Ghorahi base in Dang on 23 November 2001 was a great political, military and psychological setback. The raid was the Maoists' first strike against the Army and it killed 14 soldiers, including a major, as well as seven police. More than three dozen people were injured. Seven Maoists were killed but the rebels made off with many heavy weapons, including 81mm mortars, rocket launchers, SLRs and lots of ammunition.

Chief of Army Staff Prajwalla was on a foreign visit at the time. The acting Army Chief Durganath Aryal might have called for a meeting with the concerned department heads, but I wasn't summoned. The disarray within the Army leadership at that time was frustrating. Our soldiers became martyrs, the Maoists captured sophisticated weapons and paraded them in a victory rally, but all the Army did in response was to hold meetings. Nowhere in the world would an Army sit on its hands when it was attacked like that. We were still waiting for "constitutional" orders to go in hot pursuit and bring back our looted weapons.

The Army's inability to act even when its barracks were looted would affect us into the future. Whose orders did we need to shoot the Maoists who attacked us, killed our people, looted everything and fled?

Back then I was at the Security Council Secretariat at Singha Darbar and the Army brass rarely called me for meetings. Still, I felt that if the Army had taken immediate steps the Maoists wouldn't have been able to flee so easily to Rukum and Rolpa with such powerful weapons. It took three days for the government to make the decision to deploy the Army on 26 November and by then the Maoists had already spread through several districts with their huge haul from Dang. Mobilising the Army after giving the Maoists three days to run away and hide the weapons was nothing but gross negligence.

After Dang, the Army formally entered the conflict.

I was taken to the new King to pay my respect after my promotion. It was customary for newly-appointed generals.

"When *dai* was alive your name was listed for the National Security Council, so you will be posted there," he told me.

The Constitution of Nepal 1990 had provision for a National Security Council and a Secretariat tasked with formulating national security policy. After the 1989 People's Movement, national security was not a priority and guarding our national boundaries was seen as its main task. All that changed after the Dang attack.

A state of emergency was declared on 26 November 2001 and the Army was mobilised. It was only then that the proposals from HQ were given priority. Prime Minister Sher Bahadur Deuba was positive about the Army's proposal to set up a Security Council Secretariat. The Defence Secretary was appointed coordinator and I was selected as co-coordinator.

The issue of a Security Council Secretariat had been raised as early as 1995 during Sher Bahadur Deuba's first term as Prime Minister. King Birendra wanted the Security Council to be active so Chief of Army Staff Dharmapal tried to take the matter forward. However, it took concrete shape in 2001 only. Deuba was a great help to the Council right from its inception.

We were given space in the Parliament Secretariat's garden for our office. What had looked like a dumping ground was transformed completely in just a few weeks. Everyone was surprised to see how well we managed the space among the huge buildings at Singha Darbar. The Danish Ambassador once joked with me: "General, I never knew there to be such a well-maintained place within this complex, and that includes the restroom."

Although the Prime Minister was the Council's chair and the Defence Minister and the Army Chief served as members, they would be present only for formal decisions. The Defence Secretary, who was the coordinator, couldn't give his attention to the Secretariat full-time, so I was usually the officiating officer in my position as co-coordinator. Since I enjoy new and challenging tasks, being part of the Security Council was a good opportunity for me to benefit from new experiences.

We started bringing in the best people from the security forces and the civil service to form a team examining both our internal and external security challenges. With the help of experts from various fields, we prepared a draft of the core national policy and national security policy, and prepared to take it to Parliament through the Cabinet to get it endorsed. Senior advocate Ganesh Raj Sharma and others suggested that we shouldn't be in a hurry because the fact that the draft was prepared by the Army might raise hackles. So we held off, waiting for the right time to present our draft to the Parliament.

At the same time, in the political scene bickering within the Congress party was rife, something which was beyond our understanding or area of responsibility. Deuba wanted to extend the state of emergency, which required Parliament's approval, but disunity within his party meant the chances were slim.

Deuba then dissolved Parliament and our task remained incomplete. But it was easy working with him. He clearly saw our role as valuable and used to send foreign visitors to the Security Council Secretariat to be briefed by us about the Maoists.

Security policy wasn't just a military affair. It had to take into account many different aspects, like maintaining our relationships with our two giant neighbours while, at the same time, upholding our sovereignty, protecting the national interests, making the most of our abundant water resources, formulating education policies that would help to produce globally competitive human resources, reduce trade deficits and develop industries. All decisions made by the judiciary, legislature and executive should have been driven by national interest, and the Secretariat's job was to monitor them all.

"Mr Deuba, don't talk to terrorists. You don't negotiate with them, don't compromise," US President George Bush said sternly, shaking hands with Deuba, "You just find them, fix them and finish them off."

I was present during the PM's US visit when President Bush had assured Deuba that the US was "ready to support Nepal in every way to fight terrorism".

After a short briefing about Nepal's contemporary political situation in the Oval Office at the White House, President Bush repeated his message: "Don't ever compromise with terrorists."

Prakash Sharan Mahat, Madhu Raman Acharya, Jaya Pratap Rana and others were also present during the meeting. Prime Minister Deuba informed President Bush about two rounds of formal talks which had been attempted with the Maoists. Both the talks faltered midway after which the Maoists pulled out and resumed their terrorist activities. After hearing us out, Bush made his stand clear: "Terrorists everywhere are against humanity. Our struggle is against the enemies of freedom."

After the Oval Office, the PM's team called on Secretary of State, General Colin Powell, whom I had met in Kathmandu during his visit. He asked why an army composed of so many famous Gurkha fighters couldn't defeat and wipe out those "rag-tag Maoists". Foreign Secretary Madhu Raman said that the insurgents were also Gurkhas. The Prime Minister looked around and saw me behind him. "My general will explain," he said and I was called to the front by the Secretary. As a result of my short briefing, Secretary Powell fully grasped the situation and Foreign Secretary Madhu Raman told me later that this was a turning point in the discussions. During the same meeting, the US committed to providing the Nepalese Army with weapons, ammunition and other military support. PM Deuba shared a great rapport with Julia Chang Bloch, former US Ambassador to Nepal, and she had briefed him on how to approach Bush and what issues to raise.

While the President had made a verbal commitment, the onus for implementing it rested with the officials working under him. We needed to be proactive to ensure followup, so I asked the PM's permission to discuss the issue with the concerned officials in the Pentagon.

He agreed so I asked the Defence Attaché at our Embassy to arrange a meeting with an officer from the Pentagon's South Asia desk and a working lunch was put in place.

"These are the things that were discussed with your Commander-in-Chief that need to be implemented as soon as possible," I said to the relevant official. I also briefed him about Nepal's security situation.

"You are leading the global fight against terrorism. I hope your President's promises will be fulfilled soon," I said.

We were able to discuss a lot of issues during our one-and-half hour meeting.

There had been a lot of wrangling over my selection as a member of the team accompanying the Prime Minister on his visit to the US. The Chief didn't want to send me and would have preferred to send DMO Pradip Pratap Bam Malla. But the PM was determined to have me on the team. He said, "Katawal has been doing good work at the National Security Council, so he should be with us."

The Chief had come to meet the Prime Minister and I was summoned to the PMO. The Chief started shouting at me right there in the waiting room.

"Trying to overstep the mark, are you?" he said. "Trying to curry favour with the Prime Minister?"

I couldn't grasp what he was on about and stared at him blankly.

"Are you the one who decides who will and who won't accompany the Prime Minister to the US?" the Chief shouted, his eyes and face burning, "Have you been buttering up the Prime Minister to get him to take you along?"

I answered back: "I will go along with whatever the chair of the National Security Council decides. I have not influenced anyone."

The PM was the head of the NSC but, given my role as day-to-day co-coordinator, I was his main contact point in the organisation. As a result, I had more meetings at Singha Darbar than I did at HQ which is probably why the Chief suspected I had been using those meetings to butter up the Prime Minister. Furthermore, a lot of people had been complaining to the

Chief that I had turned the NSC into an entity which was more civilian than military.

The Chief wasn't finished. "You won't go on the visit," he said firmly, "Someone from HQ has to go."

In reality, I didn't know until that point that I had even been selected for the US trip. Lobbying the PM to take me along was just not in my nature. The Chief was peeved because he had gone to great lengths to recommend someone else from HQ for the trip.

"I've already got the King to endorse Katawal's name for the trip," the PM told the Chief, "That chapter is now closed."

"Okay, sir," Prajwalla said.

I was a bit disheartened after finding out about this tug-of-war and also a little nervous because I had already been accused of being a Congress supporter in 1990 and there I was with my name being linked to a Congress Prime Minister. This would provide lots of ammunition for my enemies.

At the NSC, I got to brief the PM daily and he must have been impressed by my performance. Although I was put on the list of the Prime Minister's entourage for the US visit, my name wasn't initially included for meetings with President Bush and the UN Secretary-General. I learnt later that an official from the Ministry of Foreign Affairs had removed my name. I didn't want to miss out on the opportunity to meet Mr Bush and was determined to make the most of any opportunity that came my way.

The PM's wife, Arzu Deuba, found out how anxious I was about the situation. "Given the topics to be discussed, his knowledge of the subjects and his negotiating skills, it would be best to include General Katawal," she suggested to the PM.

"The General will come everywhere with me," the Prime Minister said, and that was that. After the programme in Washington, we went to New York. It was just a few months after 9/11. Security was tight and even the nail cutters in my briefcase were removed at the x-ray and destroyed in front of me.

There was a dinner at the Nepali Permanent Mission to the UN that evening. Everyone from the PM's team to the MPs and the staff of the mission attended. Deuba was upbeat after his meeting with President Bush and equally happy about my positive meeting with the Pentagon official.

Everyone except me raised their glasses in a toast.

"General, you can at least take a peg," the PM said amiably.

"Thank you, sir," I said, "But I'm planning not to drink throughout this trip."

He offered me a drink again. It put me on the spot. I could neither decline without giving offence nor feel comfortable drinking.

"Let's make your visit a success. Then we can enjoy our drinks in Kathmandu," I said.

During dinner, we began planning our meeting with Kofi Annan, the UN Secretary-General, my name having been reinstated to the list of attendees.

I was seated in the back row during the meeting with Annan. After the formal greetings, the PM said, "My general will brief you." I then took a few minutes to talk about the Maoist situation and other national security issues in Nepal.

Our delegation stopped in the UK after completing the US tour and Deuba was happy to be meeting British Prime Minister Tony Blair. They talked about their collective fight against international terrorism and Deuba briefed Blair on the Maoist threat.

The BBC wanted to interview Deuba. He took some time discussing the issues with his team and preparing for the interview. I thought he performed quite well.

That same evening, Deuba summoned me to his suite. I went in civilian dress.

"Please take a seat, General," Arzu ma'am said.

"How are you managing expenses?" the Prime Minister asked.

I understood what he was hinting at and immediately replied, "I have enough. Thank you, sir."

I wasn't surprised that he asked me about money. There were a few MPs in the team and I had seen him handing out dollars to them once in a while.

During our long trip I had several opportunities to talk to the PM. We didn't waste time talking about home and family or discussing movies and poetry. Even our informal chats used to be centred on the situation back home and security operations. I was able to clarify a lot of things about the Army for the PM. Deuba was a supporter of the Army, the monarchy and the democratic system.

After returning from the US, one day I received an invitation to Baluwatar from Arzu ma'am. I arrived there about 7 pm. I didn't know who else was invited that evening and was excited.

The PM hadn't arrived yet. I was taken directly to a private room upstairs instead of the waiting room. He reached Baluwatar a little while later and I was surprised to discover I was the only one invited that evening. So it was just the three of us, the PM, his wife and me.

A bottle of Chivas Regal was brought out. We drank, nibbled on finger-food and chatted for four hours but the Prime Minister wanted to keep on talking. I must have given him the impression that I was just another drunkard general.

4 October

Pyar Jung Thapa had taken over as the Chief of Army Staff. He was a gentleman who avoided controversies. He was a descendant of the Thapa family who were influential courtiers and this refined upbringing was reflected in his values. Carrying out orders from the Palace was always his top priority. He had known me well since my Nagarkot days.

After returning from my Europe and US trip, I began working with more zeal at the NSC. According to the then constitutional provisions, fresh elections had to take place within six months of Parliament being dissolved. Some of the ministers in the government had already been hinting since August that elections couldn't take place for security reasons. The Army's position was that elections had to take place, even if they were conducted in several phases. King Gyayendra agreed.

Some people in the PM's inner circle might have suggested to him that he could push back the elections and prolong his time in power. So towards mid-September, the PM and his team were convinced that the election couldn't be held as scheduled.

According to Chief Pyar Jung, both the King and the Army wanted elections to be held. The Constitution hadn't been drafted to account for a situation without elected representatives for more than six months, which would have created a constitutional void.

As it turned out, events unfolded exactly as we feared. The Prime Minister was on a collision course with the King about whether to postpone the elections or not. On 4 October 2002, the King removed the PM, citing Article 127 of the Constitution, and this sacking of a pro-monarchy Prime Minister ended up backfiring on the King himself. We had heard that the King sought the agreement of several key leaders, including Girija Prasad Koirala and Madhav Kumar Nepal, before taking that step. The fact that the leaders of the Congress party and the UML were silent about the royal move of 4 October for a whole week proved those rumours weren't without foundation.

After removing Deuba, King Gyanendra appointed Lokendra Bahadur Chand as PM. We had received information that the key leaders of the Congress party and the UML had agreed to Chand being PM but the situation changed dramatically after the new government was formed. The UML and Congress leaders who hadn't moved beyond minor protests over the royal move in the first week, suddenly became sharply critical. When Chand was sworn in as PM, it became clear to the political leaders that the King's move was "unconstitutional and reactionary".

Chand's affable nature might have been one reason for his appointment and I must say it was easy working under him at the NSC. After General Pyar Jung took over as COAS, working at the Secretariat had also become a lot easier for me. Soon I was also being called in for PSO meetings at HQ. With the Chief's permission, I went on frequent visits across Nepal. He never barred me from using Army helicopters and other resources. I used to travel from Mechi in the east to Mahakali in the west to review the security situation and prepare reports. I also had the opportunity for a weekly briefing session with the Chief.

Prime Minister Chand took the NSC Secretariat's advice very seriously. The NSC Secretariat analysed and synthesised all information to be included in any report which was sent to the PMO, the Palace, the Home Minister and the chief of the security forces.

We were trying to turn the Secretariat into an advisory body similar to the National Security Council set up in Britain in 1935. The council in Britain would brief the Cabinet of Ministers every week. Even the US had a similar body called the National Security Agency, which was created after World War II, although it was the President who made the final decision on the NSA's recommendations.

The Secretariat had an analysis group, intelligence group and others, which worked on papers on various assigned issues. The Secretariat then prepared reports after analysing these papers which were then used to brief the PM and other ministers. These activities lifted the profile of the NSC and no one regretted working there.

PM Chand gave me the opportunity to brief the whole Cabinet on security issues. "Now I will take 26 ½ minutes of your life," I would begin. And the briefing would last exactly 26½ minutes. Dr Upendra Devkota was Health Minister in the Chand government and always joked about me being "Mr Twenty-six-and-a-half minutes."

One day, I was on my way to the Army's Staff College in Tokha. Labour and Transport Minister Kamal Chaulagain called, "What have you done, General, drawing boundaries to put us in a difficult spot?"

"What's the matter, Minister?" I asked.

My relationship with him, a Communist politician from my neighbouring district, was known to all.

He said "It's been agreed that the security forces will stay within eight kilometres of their barracks during the next round of talks." He sounded worried.

The dialogue team formed during the Chand government included Deputy Prime Minister Badri Mandal and Ministers Narayan Singh Pun, Ramesh Nath Pandey and Chaulagain. The Maoists had sent Baburam Bhattarai, Ram Bahadur Thapa, Dev Gurung and Matrika Yadav.

"You're on the team. Didn't you protest?" I asked, "You're a member of the dialogue team, Mr Minister. Why didn't you raise the issue with me earlier?"

"The other members of the team didn't want me to have a say because the Cabinet, the Palace and the Army have already agreed to it," he said.

This information was disseminated during a joint press conference held by the dialogue teams from both sides. None of the members of the government dialogue team had said a word when they were told about the agreement to restrict the security forces to within eight kilometres of the district headquarters. Instead, they had all silently accented to the decision.

It didn't matter who approved the agreement. I was utterly upset that the security forces, including the Army, should have been locked into an agreement like that.

I was so stressed that I couldn't even complete the class I was teaching at the Staff College. Instead, I headed straight to HQ from Tokha and went to meet the Chief directly. Luckily, he was free.

"The Army is being confined like cattle in a pen within an eight kilometre radius," I said, "This cannot be allowed to happen."

"I don't know what's going on," the Chief said, also surprised, "How can an agreement like this have been made?"

The mature and gentle-natured Chief wasn't as furious as I was

"The Army should not accept this decision," I said. "It's demeaning." He just listened while I ranted and raved.

"Unlike the others, at least the Colonel should have understood everything," the Chief said about Narayan Singh Pun.

The FM stations were broadcasting the news about the eight kilometre agreement over and over again. The public who were tortured, abducted, slaughtered and robbed by the Maoists must have cursed the Army when they heard the news. I was outraged and started plotting a strategy to reverse this agreement. I decided to meet the PM and managed to get an appointment immediately.

I was just an ordinary general. But the dialogue team's ineptitude was so intolerable that I didn't care about protocol anymore. "What kind of agreement has the team gone and made? It needs to be suspended immediately," I told PM Chand as soon as I met him.

He listened intently but said nothing. "All the ministers should be summoned and directed not to do this again, sir," I said.

The dialogue team's coordinator, Badri Mandal, was also there and I shouted into his face: "Who gave you the right to restrict the security forces to within eight kilometres?"

"I don't know anything, General," he said meekly.

"Aren't you ashamed to say that you, as the coordinator, know nothing about this?" I was fuming.

"Really, General, I know nothing about it," he replied sheepishly.

Just then, Ramesh Nath Pandey and Narayan Singh Pun walked in. "Are all of you trying to imprison the national army?" I asked, "Why were you all so silent when Baburam talked about the eight kilometre limit during the press conference?" I asked.

Mandal was quiet but Pun said, "This is a political matter. I understand it because I'm an expert on conflict."

"And who gave you the title 'expert on conflict'? You're just a pilot," I said, "Take back the agreement to restrict the security forces to within an eight kilometre radius."

The discussion was starting to get heated.

"General, you might get into trouble if you start yelling at Cabinet ministers like this in my presence," Chand said in his calm and cool voice.

I took leave of the Prime Minister and went to my office. Mandal called me in the evening.

"You were rather rude to me this afternoon, General. I didn't know anything about the matter," he said, "Because they said the Army and the Palace had agreed, I didn't want to create a scene, so I was silent about it."

"Sorry, Minister," I apologised, "I argued with you and the other ministers because I was extremely concerned at the way the Army's movements were being restricted."

He told me that the Prime Minister had no idea about the eight kilometre clause either. Chand was a true patriot and a dignified, softly-spoken gentleman. People around him must have taken advantage of this. Members of the dialogue team were shrewd personalities chosen by the Palace and they were behind the agreement.

As it turned out, it helped that I went around venting my ire at the ministers and got into heated discussions with them. The Chief also raised this issue with the King that evening.

"Chief, I don't know anything about this." The King was also apparently surprised.

The next day, Ramesh Nath Pandey refuted the statement on the BBC Nepali Service saying "there has been no agreement on restricting the movements of the Army".

My attempts to not have the eight kilometre agreement implemented actually helped. However, they couldn't save the Chand government which fell after the whole incident was made public.

This was followed by the King calling for candidates to submit their "bids" for the post of Prime Minister. Everyone from the UML's Madhav Kumar Nepal to street showman, Laxman Singh Khadka, applied. People lined up outside the west gate of the Palace to submit their applications, a spectacle which demeaned and dishonoured the position of Prime Minister.

Finally, Surya Bahadur Thapa became Prime Minister. I thought he would do a good job because he had held the position before, had plenty of experience and was an adept political player.

As always I was prepared to brief the incoming Prime Minister about national security issues but the setting for the briefings wasn't arranged as it was during the Deuba and Chand governments.

A lot of people had told me that Prime Minister Thapa preferred reading the briefings of the police, Army and bureaucracy from files. So we were all geared up to make our briefings accurate and interesting and ensure that the Secretariat was just as efficient as before.

According to our analysis, the governments after Deuba's were faced with more challenges because of the protests by Congress, UML and other parties following the 4 October royal move. These protests intensified after Thapa's appointment.

Someone told me that the Prime Minister read all the files at home every evening. After finding this out, we changed our briefing style. We started printing our reports in larger fonts and began working on handing the briefing report directly to him. Requesting the Prime Minister's Secretariat to arrange a meeting would take forever. We had to get the reports directly into his hands.

I knew that Prime Minister Thapa was the person in his office with the most regular habits, so I devised a plan to brief him about the reports in such a way that his time wouldn't be wasted. I got the Army security at Baluwatar to inform me as soon as the PM left his residence. That way I could be at the Prime Minister's garage near Singha Darbar's main building before he arrived. The PM duly arrived, I saluted him and he instantly recognised me.

His brothers, Nagendra and Bhogendra, were my friends from school and college, so I had met him before. I had even stayed at Thapa Niwas in Biratnagar. Furthermore, I was stationed in his home district Dhankuta.

He was very fond of me and the Thapa family used to give me their famous white honey, which they also sent to the Palace. As soon as I met him at the garage, I informed the PM about the NSC, my responsibilities and the Secretariat's daily briefings.

After that, I began briefing him in the same way every day. He used to be at his office by 8 or 9 am and, on days when the Cabinet was meeting, he would be there by 7 am. I would tell him the key points and hand him the briefing paper. He would usually stand and listen to me there in the garage. However, when he had to hurry, I would brief him as he walked to his office. I used to wait for him at the garage in the evenings as well and brief him in the same way.

This went on for a few days, after which the Prime Minister must have felt uncomfortable. So he started calling me to come to his office. Now I finally had the opportunity to meet him regularly as I had in the past with Deuba and Chand. He also started including me in meetings with the Chief and other ministers.

The security challenges were increasing and my meetings with the PM became more frequent. He used to call me to join him when he had meetings with Foreign Minister Bhekh Bahadur Thapa.

"Tell me what's happening," Bhekh Bahadur Thapa would say. I was first introduced to him in Hong Kong when he was Nepal's Ambassador to the US. He had to once sleep in the kitchen because my residence was overflowing with guests at the time. He took it in his stride, which increased my respect for him.

Another round of peace talks began during Surya Bahadur Thapa's tenure as well. Baburam Bhattarai and Krishna Bahadur Mahara represented the Maoists while Prakash Chandra Lohani and Kamal Thapa were on the government's team. The PM gave the Secretariat responsibility for making the internal preparations for the talks. The dialogue committee secretariat's informal role was also assumed by the Security Council Secretariat.

The talks with the Maoists had elements of both security and politics so the Secretariat brought in experts in the relevant fields and provided the dialogue committee with input.

Despite several rounds of talks between the government and the rebels, nothing was achieved. The Maoists made the Constituent Assembly their main agenda, which the government didn't accept. The Maoists tried playing around with the government and were successful to some extent.

During the talks at Hapure in Dang, the Maoists walked out midway, issuing a statement, and their leaders soon went underground.

The Maoists' tyrannical behaviour was becoming more excessive with each passing month. The police, Army and APF were working in their own ways to tackle the worsening situation. Their objective was the same but their efforts were fragmented. As a result, security operations couldn't be effective. The Maoists were gaining from the state security forces' lack of coordination and the NSC Secretariat saw the need to remedy this.

We brought in the concept of a unified command which was approved by the PM, the Palace and the other relevant bodies. The Army assumed overall command of all the security forces. The unified command's objective was to properly train the police and provide them with the weapons to fight the Maoists. Spending more time with one another, eating, sleeping and sharing space would also unite the Army and the police. Although there were some complaints that the Army's training was too rigorous, that the food wasn't good enough and that the police were being pushed to the frontlines during operations, police on the ground felt a lot safer operating under the unified command. But from what we heard some of their bosses weren't so happy.

The police knew the villages and the terrain well. The Army felt that the Maoists could be contained by formulating a plan based on that knowledge. However, despite being part of the unified command, the shortcomings within the police force couldn't be fixed. The transfer system within the police was completely different from the system in the Army. Some police were stationed in conflict zones for as long as six years, while others kept being shuffled from one safe district to another. Despite all our efforts, the unified command wasn't able to contain the Maoist uprising and we should accept that we didn't achieve what we set out to do.

The Army was criticised for not being able to win a decisive victory against the Maoists. However, those who criticise the Army need to understand that Nepal wasn't facing a war between different ethnic groups. Neither were the Maoists separatists. So the Army's only goal was to give a chance to those people who had become Maoists out of fear, false hope, greed or coercion to mend their ways. We wanted to wean them away from the insurgency. The unified command's aim was the same: to disarm them, bring them to the negotiating table and address their valid demands.

We were to be on the defensive and we would go on the offensive only if the Maoists attacked us. But the Maoists continued to take advantage of that position.

During my tenure at the Security Council, I understood the importance of information. It is indeed true that information is knowledge and knowledge is power. The influential media were supporting the protests against the royal move and were generally against the King. Although the King, the government and the Army were trying to do our best, the media was biased against us.

We understood the role of the media in shaping the opinions of human rights activists, party cadres and the general public. So we started brainstorming at the NSC with a view to establishing a media house whose editorial policy would always support the constitutional monarchy as well as the democratic process. According to our estimates, it would take around Rs 160 million to start a newspaper, TV station and FM station to counter the negative propaganda. We would break even in five or six years.

The proposal was sent to the Palace. Some of the "hardcore patriots" around the Palace must have opposed the proposal because we didn't receive any feedback. Later, we found out there was no budget for it. I started thinking of alternative ways to implement the proposal. If money was the problem, a loan could be managed from the Army's Welfare Fund. Since the King was its trustee, getting a loan shouldn't have been very difficult. But even that proposal was shot down and the whole thing fizzled out.

The Palace was trying to move forward in its own way. The protests against the royal move of 4 October were still in full swing. Girija*babu*, the leader of the protests, was trying to meet the King and wanted someone to pass on the message. I was informed about this through contacts at the NSC. I wanted to help but how could I meet the mormain leader of the street protests without permission from my superior, especially with my reputation for being pro-Congress? I asked the Chief and he said it wouldn't be a good idea.

Eight

Mission Kotwada

In 2000, the government created Regional Administrative Offices to handle security at the regional level in the face of the widening Maoist conflict. While the police had their existing regional structures, the Army didn't have something similar. The Army had announced the formation of regional commands in its 10-year plan but, with the rapid rise of the Maoists, it had had to create three divisions within two years. Regional structure formations, headed by two-star generals, were then put into place.

I was stationed in the Mid-Western Division HQ which was in the heartland of the Maoist conflict. The division commanded both the mid and far-western regions and I was the fourth commander to be stationed there.

"The King's visit is coming up," COAS Pyar Jung Thapa said, "His Majesty has commanded that you be sent to the Mid-Western Division HQ."

After a few days, General Gajendra Bahadur Limbu, the Military Secretary, arranged for me to meet the King at Nagarjun Palace. I listed the issues I wanted to discuss including foreign affairs, the conflict, of course, and other matters. I briefed the King accordingly and also mentioned that our relations with the international community were faltering.

His Majesty was taking notes himself as I spoke.

"The conflict is getting intense," he said, "I will be visiting the mid-west soon, so make arrangements in Nepalganj accordingly."

I then asked the Chief about our operation's objective.

"To bring misguided Nepalis back to the negotiating table," the Chief said, "The King simply wants to disarm them for negotiations, not to kill our own brothers."

I respected the King's and the Chief's faith in me and was determined not to let them down. Since I thrive in challenging situations, this was an opportunity for me.

Before leaving for Nepalganj, I went to meet PM Thapa with the Chief. We entered the meeting of the Cabinet of Ministers.

"Sir, it's time for Katawal to leave for Nepalganj," the Chief said.

"You did exceedingly well at the NSC. I hope you'll do the same there too. All the best," the PM said, "I'll be there during His Majesty's visit."

His Majesty's mid-western visit was scheduled to begin a few days after I reached Nepalganj. Soon the various teams associated with the King's visit began pouring in. His first stop would be at Nepalganj for four days after which he would travel to Surkhet.

Rastriya Prajatantra Party leader, Pratibha Rana, Chief Secretary, Pashupati Bhakta Maharjan, Military Secretary, Gajendra Limbu and President of the World Hindu Federation and advisor to the King, Bharat Keshari Simha, were all seated around the fireplace with the King, Queen and other VIPs. COAS Pyar Jung Thapa was also there.

Bharat Keshari recited a few verses from the Gita. Those verses glorified the King as the only Hindu king in the world, king only of Hindus as well as their protector.

I couldn't agree with that and had to speak up. I wanted to ensure that the King got a broader perspective.

"Sir, even I have few things to say," I asked the Chief's permission.

"Sure, go ahead," the Chief said.

I then asked for His Majesty's permission. "Your Majesty, even I would like to say something."

The King gestured for me to go ahead.

"Your Majesty, everyone here is senior to me," I said, "But, unlike what General Bharat Keshari has said, I feel you are more than just a Hindu king. I think it would be better to say you are the leader of Hindus everywhere and King of the people of Nepal."

The King didn't look upset and, instead, seemed keen on hearing me out.

"Your Majesty, you are the King and guardian of the people of Nepal first, and then a Hindu king," I said, "Otherwise why would Nepal's Buddhists, Muslims and Christians have faith in the monarchy? Whom else would they consider to be their king? If Your Majesty is only a king to Hindus, then people of other religions will have to search for their own king."

I went on to recite a Sanskrit verse to convince the King of my argument.

"Our scriptures say that a man with a generous heart counts people from all the over the earth as his brothers and sisters,"

I said, "So, as everyone's guardian, it may not be wise to lean only towards one particular religion, Your Majesty."

It looked like the King was thinking over what I had said. Then he chuckled and said, "Why are you telling me? Tell Bharat!"

Since the King seemed okay with my argument, there was no point arguing with General Bharat Keshari. I didn't say anything. The King turned to General Bharat Keshari and said, "Bharat, answer him."

"Your Majesty, I meant to say the same thing," General Bharat Keshari replied.

Later during the conflict, King Gyanendra travelled mostly to the mid and far-western regions. On one occasion, he was scheduled to visit Kalikot when I received information that the Maoists were planning to attack him. If that wasn't possible, they had plans to foil the visit.

Since the forces were working on the ground under the unified command, we had information flow from various sources. Based on this information, we were planning an operation in Kalikot and we had intelligence that thousands of Maoists had taken control of Kalikot's Kotwada airport which was still under construction.

I was shocked when I heard about this, especially when another reliable source told us the Maoists gathered at Kotwada were using civilians as human shields. I immediately decided to send in troops to flush them out.

Troops of Number Four Brigade, under the command of the deputy brigade commander, were deployed for Mission

Kotwada. The airfield was across the Karnali River from Manma, Kalikot's district headquarters, which the King was supposed to visit.

We were informed that our troops had set up camp on a high ridge above the banks of the Karnali. The Maoists, who were perched on the hill top, had been attacking them, not just with bullets but with stones and tree trunks. Unverified reports said the Maoists even had heavy artillery and had set up a training centre at the airfield.

We could have attacked them from the air and cleared the area in just a few minutes. But we were mindful of the need to avoid civilian casualties. The troops under the deputy brigade commander couldn't move forward from their base for days while all the while they were being bombarded by the Maoists.

The King, who had by then arrived at Surkhet barracks, found out that the troops were trapped near Kotwada.

"I'll visit Kalikot later. Let's leave it for now," His Majesty commanded.

I knew there would be a huge uproar if the King couldn't proceed to the district headquarters of the area I was in charge of. Nothing could have been more humiliating than that. It would be a victory for the Maoists and boost their morale. I was determined to clear the path to Kotwada for the King's visit by any means possible.

I explained the situation to the Chief. "Tell the King about it," he said, without giving me clear direction as to whether or not to proceed.

Maybe the Chief was upset that I was included in the trip to Surkhet. He had wanted me to stay back at the Divisional

HQ in Nepalganj. Since the King was staying in the brigade HQ under my command, my enthusiasm should've been understandable. Furthermore, Uma had also accompanied me, with permission from the Palace, which ticked off the Chief. He might have felt that the King would notice me favourably during the trip.

The way I was treated in Surkhet, it was clear that the Chief was, in fact, upset about my presence there. Despite being the commander of Mid-Western Division I was given a very basic room in an uncomfortable area.

The Chief probably didn't give me a clear direction because he assumed I'd get the credit if I spearheaded a successful operation to clear Kotwada. Otherwise, it was the Chief who should have informed the King that I would be heading the operation. Next morning, I asked the King about launching an operation to relieve the troops.

"Ask your Chief. Why are you asking me?" he said, "It's a military operation."

I couldn't move ahead since there was no concrete decision from either the Chief or the King. The King's scheduled date for the Kalikot visit was inching closer. It would be humiliating if reports about postponement of the visit cited security reasons. I became even more disconcerted.

The Chief left for Kathmandu because the next day was Ghode Jatra. It was decided that the Crown Prince would preside over the Ghode Jatra celebrations since the King was tied up with his mid-western visit.

On the day of Ghode Jatra, I waited to meet the King during his morning walk.

"Your Majesty, I'm leaving for Kotwada. The Chief has ordered me to go," I lied.

"Okay, then go," the King said, "Take care."

I saluted him and left straight away.

After that, I immediately called the Chief. I told him I was leaving for Kotwada with the troops.

"Did you get the King's permission?" he asked.

"His Majesty has commanded me to go," I said.

"Okay, then go," the Chief ordered.

Both of them gave their permission only because the King thought it was the Chief's order and the Chief thought it was the King's. After that I left for Kotwada with Number Four Brigade commander, Anil Jung Thapa. A helicopter dropped us on the banks of the Karnali where some soldiers had come to receive us.

They asked for our rucksacks. "We carry our own bags," I said. "There's no reason you should carry anything."

We started the uphill march along the steep and treacherous trail about 3 pm. Both Anil and I had our rucksacks on our backs. Even a single misstep could have cost us dearly. We could see the blue Karnali flowing far below us.

"A lieutenant went missing after he fell from this trail a few days ago," Anil said.

We reached the security base. The troops were scattered but I knew that seeing their divisional and brigade commanders would boost their faltering morale.

The sun was almost down by the time we arrived. We could clearly see the Maoists moving around in Kotwada above us. Maybe they, too, found out about our arrival through binoculars because they started firing as soon as we got there. The bullets were raining down from Kotwada.

They were firing only to scare us because they were too far away to do any real damage. We could see that all of them were seated on the edge of the air strip and there weren't as many as I had thought. Nonetheless, we still had to return fire to intimidate them. My 56-year-old body felt a little drained but I was cautious to not let the others know it.

"Follow me," I said.

We moved about 100 feet, searching for a safe spot.

"Ready," I alerted the troops, "Everybody, take cover."

There were about two platoons there. I didn't see Anil because he was behind a tree.

"Hey, Anil, why are you scared?" I teased him.

"I'm not hiding, sir, I'm just taking cover," he said.

"You're also hiding," he yelled. He was right. I had also taken cover behind a tree.

In situations like this, we instinctively seek safety and look for cover but there was one policeman who was confidently firing shots from the SLR right out in the open.

Others too were still firing to scare off the Maoists. The firefight sounded like full-scale war.

"Hey, brother, why are you acting so foolishly? Don't you need to take cover?" I asked the policeman. The Maoists could have switched to long-range rifles at any moment.

"Sir, had he been fortunate, he would have been assigned to the airport or Thankot," his friend said.

"I have no connections. That's why I've been slogging it out on the frontline for almost seven years," the policeman replied.

"That's why you need to be more careful, lad," I said.

"No need to worry, sir. Their bullets won't touch me and, even if they do, they can't pierce my chest," he said confidently, "Anyway, the Maoists always miss their target."

My respect for the police increased after seeing such a brave *sipahi* as he was. The firing went on for about half an hour, which is a long time, but they showed no signs of leaving the airstrip. So, unwillingly, I had to resort to more force.

"Get the 81mm mortar ready," I told Anil.

We fired smoke bombs which provided direction and cover. It helped us estimate the distance to the target, based on which we hurled three high-explosive mortar bombs. Despite knowing the target, we fired sideways because I feared for the civilians who could've been forcibly pushed into the trench they'd dug up there.

But even then the Maoists didn't break up. They knew that we didn't want to cause causalities and were trying to take advantage of it. I ordered the 120mm mortar from Manma to open up but even that didn't seem very effective.

It was becoming clear that scare tactics alone weren't working. We had no option but to use additional force. A helicopter with rocket launchers was ready in Manma. It flew above Kotwada and fired rockets from its pods. The pilot calculated the distance and released them with the touch of a button. Since these were expensive weapons, worth thousands of dollars, we didn't use them unless absolutely necessary.

Only after we fired the rockets, did the Maoists start running helter-skelter.

"Attack," I shouted to the troops.

We clambered uphill. "The Maoists can return. So stay put for some time," I ordered the pilot.

The helicopter continued to hover around Kotwada.

It was already 8 pm by then. It took us two hours to reach the air strip.

"Okay, take a good position," I ordered the soldiers. The commander started deploying his men.

Our forces took control of the helipad and the entire hill. We set up a post immediately and made all the necessary arrangements. Anil and I returned to Manma around midnight.

The next day we took some journalists, including Nepal Television's Rama Singh, to Kotwada. All of them had appropriate gear on, including bulletproof vests and helmets. We showed them the Maoists' toy-like cannon made of tin. Rama Singh interviewed me in the helicopter on the way back to Surkhet.

"Can the Maoists just walk around terrorising people?" I asked. "Can they create a state within a state? The security forces are capable of conducting operations against them anywhere in the country."

Anil added, "There is no place in the area under my command where our troops can't go."

"Congrats, Rookmangud," General Bharat Keshari said to me the next morning after I got back to Surkhet. "You gave a fantastic interview."

"You saw it then?"

I didn't have a TV in my room or the time to watch it so

I didn't even know that my interview in the helicopter had been aired.

"You have to point out the weak spots in my interview, sir," I said

"Well, I didn't get to see it," he said, "His Majesty told me what a fantastic interview you gave. He's highly impressed."

When all the VIPs of the visit team were gathered that night, the King had asked General Bharat Keshari if he'd watched my interview.

"No," he replied.

"Katawal spoke well," the King said.

The day after we cleared Kotwada, we sent an advance team from Manma, including the ADC, Principal Military Secretary and others without whose approval the visit couldn't go ahead.

After that there were no hassles in Kotwada and the King's visit concluded peacefully.

Thousands of people got to talk and raise issues directly with the King. The people there, like thousands of others in remote districts, only wanted peace. Even if we go to bed hungry, we at least want to sleep in peace, they said.

"I understand," the King would reply, "We'll look into it."

But meeting the people's demand for peace wasn't possible overnight. A collective initiative of the King, government, other state bodies and political parties was required to bring the Maoists into mainstream politics. In order to achieve it, everyone needed to work within a plan, policy and strategy with clear aims and objectives.

The people also demanded drinking water, roads, electricity, schools with teachers, hospitals with doctors, courts with judges, as well as forestry and agriculture offices. While the demands were clear and simple, fulfilling them wasn't so easy.

So the Maoists further stirred the people up, saying, "See. Your King doesn't keep his word."

In 2003, heavy snow around Hagulte in Dadeldhura blocked the highway which hampered transportation from Dhangadhi to Dadeldhura, Doti, Baitadi, Achham and other places further west.

The Maoists seized this opportunity and created further obstacles by blocking the roads with trees. So, even after the snow melted, the road remained closed. I ordered the Number Five Brigade to go on an operation there under the command of Brigadier Gaurav Shumsher Rana.

The Maoists were perched on top of Hagulte hill. Our troops set up base on the next hill and a firefight began. There were casualties on both sides. Hagulte is covered in such dense forest that it was dark underneath the trees. Our troop couldn't secure the highway. Gaurav called for reinforcements but even that didn't allow us to reopen the highway.

"This is humiliating, Gaurav. I'll go to Hagulte now," I said.

Gaurav would be accompanying me, so I flew from Nepalganj and picked him up at Dipayal.

"Would you like some breakfast, sir?" Gaurav offered.

"Not now. We'll have something to eat after capturing Hagulte," I said.

We stocked up on rations and ammunition at Dipayal. The

helicopter landed at our base camp and I gathered everyone and asked, "Who can give me Hagulte by tonight?"

There was complete silence for a while until Major Madhav Thapa from Dhangadhi finally stepped forward and said, "I will give you Hagulte by this evening, sir." I had asked them to clear Hagulte by tonight but Major Thapa went a step further and promised to clear it by evening.

"Well done," I patted him on the back.

Gaurav wished him luck too.

His troops were ready to march towards Hagulte.

We had two 120mm mortars at our base. The mortar team started building the base plate. The barrel was fitted and we fired around five shots towards Hagulte.

We were hungry by then. Gaurav had asked the troop to prepare food. We used tree trunks for chairs and tables, covered with immaculately clean white cloths. Even up there on the hilltop, the arrangements were on par with royal dining, complete with cutlery.

"Wow! Such high standards even here! How are things in the brigade then?" I joked with Gaurav.

Joking around is the only way to fight stress during operations like this. By the time our troops reached Hagulte that night, the Maoists had already left.

We decided to move forward from the Western Division HQ, pursuing development activities hand in hand with military action.

During the operation, I walked to Thawang in Rolpa which is called the "Maoist Base" because the insurgency began there. Some journalists were also there. My address to the soldiers in Thawang attracted a lot of interest.

I told them it was a myth that the Maoists controlled Nepal. "Where are the terrorists? Show them to Nepalese Army," I roared from Thawang. The speech was covered extensively in the media. Everyone could now see there was not a single place that the Army couldn't penetrate. The message disseminated through the media across the country was that Maoists had not been able to build base areas despite terrorising the people.

I stayed in Thawang with the journalists for three nights. It reminded me of my village in the eastern hills and people there were suffering at the hands of the Maoists.

During my stay there, I also wrote a song.

Rukum cried

Rolpa cried

And so did Rumjatar.

The next day I spoke in Thawang again, "There is no state within the state."

My sound bite made headlines in the national media and was featured prominently on the front page. After my address in Thawang, the cradle of the Maoist insurgency, the morale of the Maoists was severely bruised. As they couldn't fight me directly, they turned their attention to tormenting my family.

I rarely stayed at the divisional HQ because I was mostly out on operations and I used to call home only after returning from them. It had been a few days since I last talked to Uma and, in the meantime, someone had rung her and said, "Katawal is dead. Get a white sari ready.”

She panicked and called HQ. “The General is out on an operation. Don’t worry. No one can hurt him,” they assured her.

I called her after returning to Nepalganj. She sounded worried.

“Tell me what’s happened,” I said.

“I’m being bombarded with all kinds of calls and I haven’t heard a word from you,” she said.

“What calls?” I asked.

“Not one call from you and here I am getting threatening calls from people telling me to buy a white sari,” she said, her voice choking.

I almost broke down myself.

“Listen, do you think cowards who resort to terrorising a helpless woman on the phone could actually kill her husband?” I told her firmly. “Your husband is strong enough so that no one can even come close, let alone hurt me.”

That seemed to comfort her a bit.

Even the Chief was worried about my safety, “Rookmangud, it seems you go anywhere without hesitation. Don’t be so reckless. You need to be careful about your own safety,” he told me on the phone.

“Sir, I’m not alone. I’ve been with the soldiers here. Our lives are the same,” I replied.

But he wasn’t convinced.

“It’s not the same, Rookmangud. The death of a soldier and the death of a divisional commander are vastly different things. If anything happens to you, can you imagine what fodder that'll be for the terrorists' propaganda campaign?"

"Okay sir, please don't worry," I said, "I am cautious about these things and, besides, my staff are always here to restrain me if necessary."

Our intelligence network had expanded as a result of increased interaction with villagers during our development activities. I tried to visit as many schools and colleges as possible during the operation to talk to the students.

After our increased activities in the villages, the mid-western region, which was considered the Maoist heartland, was now largely under the control of the security forces. A lot of Maoist leaders were driven across the border, unable to withstand the pressure from the Army and the police. The Maoist propaganda machine went into full swing in an attempt to counter the reality of the situation.

Thawang wasn't spared their psywar tactics. They emptied the whole village and took the people to the jungle saying the Army was about to attack. After that, the Maoists burned down the newly-constructed health post. When the villagers returned, the Maoists showed them the remains of the post and put the blame on the Army.

The Maoists had shut down most schools and colleges in the region, saying the curriculum was not "revolutionary education". On the other hand, they also spread rumours about technical courses being taught in Thawang through medical and agriculture colleges.

The list of our development works in the mid-western region was extensive. We built a concrete bridge in Rukum, a reservoir in Liwang, improved the buildings with additional rooms on the Salyan Campus and worked on Dolpa's college. With the help of the King Mahendra Trust for Nature Conservation, we also built a bridge over the river in Dolpa. A building was added in Nepalganj's Mahendra Ratna Campus which was named Khaptad Kaksha.

In undertaking our development work, we coordinated with local bodies in the remote mountainous districts and the Tarai. After I inaugurated the reservoir, we put taps in all the households, including one in the house of the up and coming Maoist leader, Krishna Bahadur Mahara. Our feeling was that we couldn't deny fellow Nepalis access to drinking water even if they were misguided enough to be involved in terrorist activities.

I went around 24 districts, mobilising almost 27,000 members of the security forces. After I went to the mid-western region and the security forces came under the control of the unified command, they experienced fewer casualties in comparison with previous years.

As we were returning from Surkhet to the divisional HQ in Nepalganj, we heard reports that the Maoists had surround the Army post in Sonbarsa near the Indian border. There could be an attack at any time.

It was a rainy monsoon evening. I couldn't leave the soldiers in Sonbarsa in danger while I landed safely in Nepalganj. Since it was already dark, there was no option to send in extra forces.

I decided to join the soldiers in Sonbarsa myself. There were three security personnel and a major with me.

I ordered the pilot to turn the helicopter south. The Maoists would normally run off when a helicopter hovered over a post which had been surrounded by them. We usually didn't need to do more.

Captain Subhas Rai was the pilot, an honest and responsible officer whose father was a full colonel during the war in Burma and had won the *Military Cross (MC)*. He had been one of Uma's students and my son's senior at the Army College so I was close to him.

We flew into a massive storm with rain and hail. There was no way we could fly further. Subhas was just hovering, hoping the weather would improve.

"Sir, you're an only son?" Subhas began.

"Why do you ask?" I said.

"You're out this late flying in the rain," he said. "I don't have orders to fly at night."

"Soldiers are in danger and you'll simply wait for orders?" I said, "Do you think that's how your father won the MC in Burma?"

"It's not that I don't want to go, sir," he said, "I'm just informing you."

He steered the conversation back to family. "Do you have brothers?" he asked.

"Why are you trying to rattle me by bringing up the subject of my family now?" I said, "Duty first and then everything else."

The fear of death was evident in his tone and in his eyes.

"I'm not scared of dying," Subhas added, "My death won't matter much. I have two brothers."

The poor chap hadn't even turned 30. He was just as mischievous as I was in school and college and renowned for his pranks at the Bhaktapur-based Army School. I had heard that the school principal, Hemanta Rana, missed him when he graduated.

"Who will lead the students in stealing radishes and cucumbers in Bhaktapur now?" the principal apparently joked.

The rain and hail stopped and we flew on. Despite the poor weather conditions, Subhas landed the helicopter at Sonbarsa on a helipad lit up by fire to make it visible.

"I will lead the attack," I told the soldiers gathered there, "Where are the terrorists?"

With their divisional commander with them, the soldiers' morale soared. I instructed the unit and also shed light on the Maoists' tactics. I reminded the soldiers of their responsibilities and also asked about their rations, arms and position.

"Sir, you can go back. We'll take care of the Maoists," they all said.

Subhas then flew the helicopter back to Nepalganj.

"The General doesn't care about his life. He flies at night to fight battles," Subhas told Uma on the phone.

She called me.

"Please be more careful about your safety. Why do you have to fly to fight at night?"

I repeated my previous answer, "Don't worry. The terrorists don't dare to even touch me."

Subhas and others from the air service unit at the divisional HQ had performed exceedingly well. He was later killed during an MI 17 helicopter accident, one of thousands of soldiers who lost their lives in the insurgency. To this day, I get very emotional just thinking about him.

We were informed about Maoists' activity building up across the Babai River where they had captured a village and were harassing the locals. HQ gave us permission for a unified operation. We formed a force comprising a platoon from the Army, a company from the Armed Police Force and a team from the Nepali Police. The Deputy Inspectors General (DIGs) of APF and Nepal Police and I jointly took the decision to go for a unified operation.

Our colonel took over its command. The 400-plus strong troop, which also had two Deputy Superintendents of Police, was deployed in different groups. They were to be in constant touch with the divisional HQs' operations room. This was especially important should the troops be thwarted part-way through their mission, in which case a rescue mission would be needed.

During operations, we usually walk throughout the night and rest during the day. The troops became unreachable from the very first day. They couldn't be contacted despite several attempts, after which the operations officer informed me of the situation.

I hurriedly contacted the police and APF but they hadn't heard anything from the troops either. They were out of touch the whole night, after which I informed Army HQ. We spent that night in the control room. I asked the junior officers to take turns sleeping. There was no way I could sleep.

We couldn't trace them even through the Army, APF and police posts around Surkhet, Bardiya and Banke. I asked the Public Relations Officer to discretely check with journalists and other sources but even they were of no help.

It was a stressful night for everyone. The next morning a helicopter was sent out. It hovered over the dense forest but found nothing.

That same evening we received an unverified report from the APF that the troops had been attacked by Maoists and that some of them had taken shelter. We spent a second night in the operations room. Since I didn't go to sleep, the other senior officers also remained awake that night.

The APF couldn't bring in any more information. On the third day, some soldiers from the force started trickling in. The first lot arrived at the APF camp in Shamsherganj. We asked them what had happened.

They had arrived at the camp disguised as villagers. Some of them managed to sneak in their weapons while some had hidden them in the jungle. They said the Maoists fired blindly at them when they were about to cross the Babai River. This was only a scare tactic but it worked.

Since it was dark, the firing startled everyone and sent them scurrying for cover. When the troops became separated from each other, so did their weapons. The LMGs, live rounds, mortar bomb and barrel ended up being divided among the groups who dispersed in different directions after the firing. The ones trained in using the communications equipment and the ones carrying it were also separated. Furthermore, they lost their way in the jungle and returned disguised as civilians. Many of them arrived wearing only their underwear.

Less than one third of the troop arrived on the third day. Although we became hopeful after seeing them, we were still worried about the others. What if these were the only ones who survived? I spent a third night in the operations room.

But around 10 pm, all that sleep deprivation took its toll on me. I felt a throbbing pain in my head and felt like I was sweating profusely. Sharad Neupane was watching me.

"Let's not worry too much now. You should try and get some sleep," he insisted.

"How can I sleep when so many soldiers are still missing?" I said, "The ones that have returned are okay but what about the others?"

"What will happen, will happen. We can't do anything about it," Sharad said, "If you don't rest for a while, you'll make yourself ill."

I could neither go to bed nor sit up straight in the operations room.

It reminded me of our commando training in Madhya Pradesh in India and the ranger and special forces training in the US that involved a high degree of physical exertion, stress, strain and sleep deprivation. We were supposed to catch up on our sleep while walking and could rest for only two hours in 36. Added to that was the heavy load on our backs. We would be so physically drained and dazed by lack of sleep that we wouldn't even realise if someone took food from our rucksacks.

But this episode was a lot more nerve-wracking than training which was largely only physically taxing. I was mentally stressed now thinking about the troops, their families, the security forces as a whole and the country's honour.

"We're talking about 300 people here," I told Sharad, "I can't possibly sleep."

The usually sedate Sharad jokingly said, "Just down two pegs of Black Label and some juicy barbecue. Sleep will come running to you."

He was in my first batch at Nagarkot so we also shared a friendly teacher-student relationship.

Although the troops continued trickling in, they didn't know anything about the others who were still missing. We were still as worried as we had been on the first day when all 400 had gone missing.

By the end of the fourth day everyone had arrived back, having used various tactics to make it back in one piece. It was the misjudgement of the commander that had led to this. Luckily, the security forces escaped a major loss of life.

I didn't need the whisky after all. Nothing works better for sound sleep than a relaxed body and mind.

1 September

More than six months had passed since the talks between the Maoists and the Surya Bahadur Thapa-led government had faltered. The Nepali Congress, UML, Nepal Workers and Peasants Party, Jana Morcha and Sadbhawana Party had joined forces for a five-party alliance to lead demonstrations in the street, while the Sher Bahadur Deuba-led Nepali Congress-Democratic was also creating a stir. CP Mainali's CPN ML also took to the streets to protest. These latter two parties weren't included in the five-party alliance at that time.

Surya Bahadur Thapa resigned because he couldn't contain the situation on the streets or in the jungle. The Palace might have asked for his resignation. The King then began searching for another Prime Minister. According to my understanding, Deuba was the most appropriate candidate for the post. Given his faith in the monarchy, the democratic system and the security forces, I thought he fitted the bill.

I called him from Nepalganj.

"How's everything, sir?" I asked.

"I've been called to the Palace this evening," he said. He didn't try to hide anything.

"You have to take on the responsibility now," I said.

Back then the country needed an accommodating person like him. It was very easy working with him because he trusted the security forces. It wasn't long before he became Prime Minister. I congratulated him from Nepalganj.

"You have to help, General," he said, "All of us need to work together to bring the terrorists into the mainstream."

In the evening of 31 August 2004, the news broke about the brutal killing of 12 Nepali workers in Iraq. I happened to be in Nepalganj that day. It was heartbreaking to hear what had happened in Iraq.

The reports about the killings of Nepalis by the terrorists, who accused Nepal of siding with the US, spread across the country. Television channel Al Jazeera even aired footage of the killings. After seeing the clips the outrage of the common people was understandable.

Nepalganj had a volatile history as far as religion was concerned and had witnessed conflict between Hindus and Muslims in the past. So I was cautious about not letting communal riots flare up in Nepalganj after the Iraq episode.

"His Majesty is worried about riots in Nepalganj. Remain alert," COAS Pyar Jung told me on the phone. "Coordinate with everyone and ensure there's no violence, as the King has commanded."

I immediately called the regional administrator, CDO, DIG, police, APF and Intelligence SSP. The CDO was to decide on a venue for a meeting since the Army taking the initiative wouldn't have been appropriate.

We gathered at the CDO's office. It wasn't possible for the regional administrator to come all the way from Surkhet on such short notice. We decided to take measures to ensure the security situation was on high alert. The security forces were mobilised extensively, with 24-hour security deployed around the mosques.

The police guarded all the mosques and Muslim areas. The Army would back up this force dressed as civilians. Nepalganj didn't witness any violence because of all these precautionary measures. The then CDO Dilli Raj Joshi and DIG Keshav Baral played important roles to ensure peace during that time.

On the other hand, Kathmandu was engulfed in flames, vandalism and attacks on 1 September. It looked like there was no government to contain the anarchy on the streets. The mosque adjacent to the Valley DIG's office was ransacked.

The massacre in Iraq and the people's outburst back home were used as the rationale to stage protests aimed at disrupting religious harmony.

Migrant recruitment offices and media houses including *Space Time Daily* and *Channel Nepal* were vandalised. *Kantipur* was also targeted. Had the Army not been mobilised quickly, the Kantipur complex would probably have been burnt down. While smoke rose from burning tyres all across Kathmandu, the government simply watched the mayhem unfold.

I remembered everyone including the King had been worried about violence in Nepalganj, the Chief who alerted me, the Prime Minister, Ministers and the security chiefs.

An emergency meeting of the Cabinet of Ministers had been convened on the evening of 31 August. It condemned the killings and I assumed that the meeting had also discussed probable reactions and precautionary measures to deal with the situation. What unfolded the next day was far worse than I had imagined.

I called the chief of the Valley Divisional Command, Major General Dilip Karki. Based on analysis of the security situation he had suggested a curfew. The meeting at the Home Ministry Secretariat went on until 7 pm after which the Army suggested to PM Deuba and the concerned ministries that a curfew be imposed the next morning. But Karki was astonished when the curfew wasn't imposed.

We took initiatives to ensure that the flames engulfing Kathmandu wouldn't spread elsewhere. In Nepalganj, we gathered representatives from all religions and political parties, as well as intellectuals, business community leaders and other distinguished locals. The meeting concluded that the violence in Kathmandu might spread throughout the country. So we organised a mass peace and solidarity rally on 2 September to disseminate the message of harmony.

The media spread Nepalganj's solidarity message across the country. Hindus and Muslims embracing each other and coming together for the rally helped disseminate the message of peace and brotherhood. This wouldn't have been possible without the support of Muslim leaders in Nepalganj. Member of the National Assembly, Iqbal Iraqi, and others also played an important role.

The chiefs of the four security forces – the Army, Nepal Police, APF and the National Investigation Department (intelligence service) – met the King on 1 September or the day after.

The King apparently asked them all, "How could all this destruction take place in the capital?"

Not one of them could provide an explanation.

According to the Army Chief, the King was very worried and asked, "What were you doing when anarchy disrupted centuries of religious harmony?"

After no one replied, he looked towards the IGP who was forced to give an answer: "Your Majesty, we couldn't do anything because the Minister didn't give us orders in time."

The others were simply staring at each other. The King was disappointed and furious in the face of his trusted security chiefs' helplessness.

In my view, the incident of 1 September was no different from the royal massacre or the attack in Dang. All the security forces were established with the objective that they could be immediately mobilised to safeguard the country and its people.

Why should the people pay for a security force that didn't do anything to protect the people? They couldn't even stop an arson attack or a mosque right in front of the DIG office from being ransacked. The police, Army, AFP and the intelligence service all failed miserably to fulfil their primary duty.

One doesn't stand by and wait for orders when people's lives and property and cultural heritage are being destroyed right in front of one's eyes.

Nine

The Royal Move of 1 February

"I need to see you urgently," Keshar Bahadur Bista called me around 10:30 pm one night in December 2004.

He was the son of famous sociologist, Dor Bahadur Bista, and had also served as Education Minister during the Panchayat years. Following the stampede in the Dasharath Stadium on 12 March 1988, which killed scores of people, he resigned from his post taking moral responsibility.

I invited him over to my house and he arrived around 11 pm with his son. Only a single vehicle could fit in my garage, so I parked mine outside and asked him to bring his car in.

"The Maoist leaders want to meet you," he said, "They believe you could communicate effectively with the King."

"I won't meet them without the Chief's permission," I said.

The top brass of the security forces were sneaking out to the Palace for meetings every evening. Something was cooking because even during the Panchayat years the Army Chief met the King only once a week. There were rumours about talks to bring the Maoists into the mainstream. Even the Maoists seemed to be keen on holding talks with the Palace. People also used to come to me almost every day with messages from Maoist leaders Krishna Bahadur Mahara and Ram Bahadur Thapa. I sent those messages straight to the Chief since I wasn't authorised to deal with them. As far as I know, all those alleged meetings in Dhorpatan between Maoist Chairman Pushpa Kamal Dahal and King Gyanendra were only rumours.

The grey clouds building up over Nepal's political scene were getting darker. I was a three-star general in the Army and the third man down in the military hierarchy. The second man down was another three-star, Lieutenant-General CB Gurung, who looked after operations, training and intelligence matters. I was in charge of peacekeeping, the Welfare Trust and nature conservation.

As the two of us were essentially second and third ranked in the Army, we were in line for the job of Army Chief and didn't want to upset the Chief at any cost. I feared that being reported to the Palace could ruin my chances. So, despite my risk-taking nature, I learnt to step back unless absolutely necessary.

A political storm was brewing in the country but there was no way I could ask the Chief what was going on.

Senior officers usually stay back at HQ until the Chief leaves for Shashi Bhawan. So, on the chilly evening of 31 January 2005, all of us were still at the office waiting for the Chief to return from the Palace

He came back around 8:30 that night and called all the PSOs. Just then the Indian Ambassador called. "I don't know anything about it...no, nothing like that," we overheard the Chief saying. It looked like the Indian Ambassador had got wind that something was brewing.

Although the Chief repeatedly assured the Ambassador that nothing was planned, his demeanour changed, suggesting that he did actually know that something was afoot. After hanging up, the Chief turned to us with a stern face.

"His Majesty will be addressing the nation tomorrow at 10 am, so get here early and remain on standby everyone," he instructed us.

It was clear from the Chief's order that this wasn't just any royal address. Something was definitely cooking. The next morning, I reached the office even before the thick Kathmandu fog had lifted. I sat in my office waiting for the King's address.

The live telecast began. King Gyanendra announced that he had dissolved the Sher Bahadur Deuba government under Article 127 of the Constitution. He said he was taking over leadership of the Council of Ministers and, by the time the royal address was over, all mobile phone networks and landlines went dead. There was a complete communication blackout.

King Gyanendra, who ascended the throne after the royal massacre in 2001, had now thrown down the gauntlet. Nepalis for the most part welcomed the move, giving him the benefit of the doubt, hoping this might help bring the raging Maoist insurgency to an end. A lot of them considered him to be just as sharp as his father Mahendra and someone who could manage the Maoists, restore peace and control corruption. I must say, I thought the same thing.

An informal meeting of PSOs was called on the second day of the King's direct rule. "If the King is able to restore peace then it will be good for the country and the monarchy," I said, "The government must look into corruption and inflation and ensure the smooth flow of daily necessities, but the restrictions on the FM radio stations and the media could be counter-productive."

I was aware that we could tame the media and bring journalists onto our side but the crackdown could turn public opinion against us. I talked about it to the Chief in private as well. The next day, industrialist Ravi Bhakta Shrestha invited me to a party. I asked the Chief for permission to go.

"Who's Ravi Bhakta?" he asked.

"He's a businessman," I said, "His family has been pro-monarchy since his father Indra Bhakta's days. He was Consul-General in Lhasa during the Panchayat years."

"Go then," he ordered.

"I understand it's going to be an important gathering. What's our line?" I asked.

"You know what to say," he said. "Report back what happens there."

The gathering was at Ravi Bhakta Shrestha's residence in Sanepa. A lot of ambassadors, including the American, British, Indian and several others from European and ASEAN countries were there, as well as a sprinkling of locals.

Since it was only a few days after 1 February, everyone was talking about what the King had done. The focus suddenly shifted to me when I walked in. British Ambassador Keith Bloomfield and American Ambassador Jim Moriarty wanted to know about the King's move. I wholeheartedly supported it. It was my professional *dharma* to do so. Furthermore, meeting the three most influential ambassadors in the same place was rare. So I made the most of it.

"The King was compelled to take this step to disarm the Maoists, bring them into the mainstream and restore peace. He wants to hold elections within three years and then hand over power to the political parties," I tried to explain. "I hope you understand why he had to do it. The sole objective of the royal move is to strengthen the faltering democratic institutions and then hand over power to an elected government."

They bombarded me with questions. I tried answering them as clearly as I could.

"The Army is not interested in power," I said "And all we want is for the King's move to be successful and to strengthen democracy."

The other diplomats gathered around to follow our discussion which went on for about 30 minutes. I asked for everyone's support, saying, "Since the fundamental aim of this move is to strengthen democracy and bring the terrorists to the negotiating table, each one of you should support and help us."

The ambassadors' official and unofficial positions in relation to the King's move were starkly different. They told me they were obliged to officially call the King's move "a setback to democracy" but unofficially they told me: "If peace can be restored by bringing the Maoists into the democratic process then the King should be allowed to do so. This will also be a major lesson for the political leaders. We think this is the best solution at the moment to pull Nepal out of the present political crisis."

I usually don't stay for drinks and food at such parties. But, as I was preparing to leave, Dr Tulsi Giri, the powerful minister from the Panchayat years, walked in. I hadn't seen him for 27 years since I met him in Dhankuta.

There were rumours that Giri had arrived in Nepal on the eve of 1 February and was staying at the Yak and Yeti Hotel. I said hello to him without mentioning our meeting in Dhankuta and then headed home. He probably didn't remember me.

On my way back, I thought of all the things the ambassadors had said. The three influential ambassadors weren't negative about the royal move after all. If the King wanted to set things straight, this was an opportunity for him.

The next day I asked for an appointment to report to the Chief about the previous night and was summoned at 1:30 pm. The Chief ordered tea as soon as I entered the room. I summarised the discussion with the ambassadors. "Congratulations," the Chief said with a smile, "His Majesty has asked me to thank you."

"Why, sir?" I asked in surprise.

"The ambassadors were apparently impressed by your explanation about the present situation," said the Chief. I was surprised that the Chief had already been informed by the Palace about my conversation with the ambassadors the previous night, so I didn't really need to brief him about it.

Soon after, Ravi Bhakta became the Minister for Tourism.

CB Gurung retired a month after the royal move and I was transferred to the position of Chief of General Staff (CGS). I was the "second man" in the Army now. The responsibilities of the CGS are far more important than those of a CoS. The office of the Director General of Military Operations (DGMO), the office of the Director General of Military

Training (DGMT), the Directorate of Military Intelligence (DMI), budget division and other important divisions fall under the CGS. But this was only a formality really since these divisions took direct orders from the Army Chief and reported to him.

While all this was happening, I had been defending the royal move personally and at the institutional level. But as days went by, I started having my doubts. When players break the rules and fight each other during a match, it's the referee's duty to bring things back on track and penalise them. But if the referee steps into the fray, the game can't go on. No one objected when the King took the step to bring the political parties into line but now it seemed he was concentrating power in his own hands and removing everyone who didn't agree with him. He excluded the Congress and UML from his Cabinet of Ministers and selected former office bearers from the Panchayat regime. Furthermore, there were no signs of improved governance.

King Gyanendra appointed himself Chair of the Council of Ministers and roped in Tulsi Giri and Kirtinidhi Bista as Vice Chairs. Sharad Chandra Shah, who was formerly associated with the Panchayat regime, was apparently influencing the Palace. The people's trust in Gyanendra was evaporating quickly because he had brought in discredited old personalities from the past. The Palace should have understood that the new generation wouldn't accept them.

The crackdown on the media, which included sending soldiers into newsrooms to censor newspapers, ultimately backfired. The security forces' censorship of the media sent the message out all over the world that this was essentially a grab for power.

In the 45 years since 1960, the speed and spread of communication technologies had made the world smaller. When King Mahendra dissolved Parliament and took over in 1960, the White House only found out about it the next day. The people in Dolpa learnt that King Mahendra had "made himself the Prime Minister" eight months later. But the news of his son's move spread instantaneously despite the mobile, internet and phone lines being cut. If only someone had advised the King not to cut the telephone lines and the mobile network or censor the media, things wouldn't have been so messy. Although I was in no position to talk to the King myself, I raised this issue several times at PSO meetings. There were a lot of other generals who also believed that the freedom of the mass media should not be restricted.

"If the restrictions on media aren't lifted, the King's position will weaken," I said.

It wasn't long before the censorship of the media was lifted. After that, there was no stopping the aggressive media backlash against the royal takeover.

Just when things were going from bad to worse, UML's senior leader Madhav Kumar Nepal's house was raided. His phones and computers were taken away. It was the UML's faith in the monarchy that resulted in them joining the Deuba's government in 2004, leaving behind the five-party alliance's campaign of agitation. I don't think it was the King's order to treat a pro-monarchy leader like Nepal in such a way. Nepal's arrest sent shockwaves through Kathmandu-based embassies which, till then, had been in a wait and watch mode.

Less than a month after the royal takeover, seven government secretaries were dumped to a reserve pool.

People who had served the monarchy were being punished, triggering fear and suspicion among government officials. Their faith in the monarchy was crumbling fast. Even the common people started losing hope when they saw no change in governance, administration, justice, development work and in their daily lives. The international community joined hands against the King's takeover. The frustration wasn't just limited to people outside the Palace – even the two Vice Chairs and ministers appointed by the King shared similar concerns. They complained that their voices were being drowned out by those of the security chiefs, especially the Army Chief, who were being given more importance by the King.

The ministers would come to meet the Chief regularly at HQ. "We couldn't meet the King or talk to him," they used to say. Radha Krishna Mainali often came to me with such complaints. Even the likes of Niksha Shumsher who had been appointed for being a loyal supporter of the Palace were treated the same way.

"The King is surrounded only by non-political people who are close to him, so we aren't even counted," they used to say.

"Only the Chief can meet the King from the Army, so talk to him," was my standard reply.

But what surprised me the most was seeing Home Minister Dan Bahadur Shahi struggling to meet the King.

The conflict was at its peak back then and, constitutionally, the Home Minister was responsible for all security matters. The Palace must have trusted him enough to appoint him Home Minister but even he was frustrated with the way things were going. "I was made minister just to fill a vacant chair," he once said.

It was strange how the Home Minister couldn't meet the King for weeks, while the security chiefs (police, APF, Army and intelligence) met him almost every day. We used to meet regularly at the Central Security Committee where I represented the Army. "If His Majesty thinks everything can be done through the IGPs, then why was I appointed Home Minister?" Shahi would ask.

There were several other ministers who wanted to quit as well but didn't have the courage. Not just ministers but even senior Vice Chairman of the Council, Dr Tulsi Giri, had grievances. "The King doesn't listen to us," he said.

Dr Giri invited me for dinner one evening along with the American and British Ambassadors and other VIPs. It was disheartening to see him pouring out his grievances to the ambassadors of foreign countries. He was the senior Vice-Chair of the royal council, the King's second man, but I saw how helpless he was.

"If your voice isn't being heard why don't you just resign?" I asked him bluntly.

Dr Giri didn't reply.

"Your King is a liar," British Ambassador Bloomfield told me one day.

I could not accept such things being said about our Head of State and Supreme Commander. I shot back: "How could you even say that about my King?"

"He's not fit to be King," the Ambassador said even more tersely.

We exchanged opinions for a while but I couldn't convince him. None of the ambassadors were for an active monarchy and, therefore, they were not welcome at the Palace. But the people surrounding King Gyanendra, and those who were using his power for their own ends, didn't warn the King that he was losing international support. At a time when he should have been showing some flexibility, the King had become more rigid. Girija Prasad Koirala and Madhav Kumar Nepal were also tired of waiting for dialogue with a sneering Narayanhiti Palace, despite several attempts.

I tried to convince the Chief several times to take the message to the King that he should meet with Congress and the UML, which still had popular support. He never replied.

The King was in Itahari during his eastern regional visit, accompanied by the Chief, the Principal Military Secretary and others. When the Principal Military Secretariat hosted a dinner for Her Majesty Queen Komal's birthday, the Chief called me from Itahari and asked me to represent him. Gajendra Limbu, the Principal Military Secretary, also had come from Itahari to host the party. It was usually the Army Chief who raised a toast to the Queen on her birthday.

I was the chief guest and all of us, including officers and other guests, were gathered for the dinner. Soon drinks were being served. I seized the opportunity to talk privately to Gajendra in the billiards room.

"Gajju, you people are always with the King," I said, "Please tell him that the parties and the Maoists have already joined forces. The country can't run this way. It'll sweep away the monarchy."

"Tell him what?" he snapped.

"To hand over the reins of government to the political parties," I said, "Otherwise the monarchy will be in jeopardy."

He was furious with me.

"I had heard a lot about you and now I finally know firsthand," he said, "How can a person in your position even think of withdrawing support for the King during such difficult times?"

He had misunderstood what I was trying to say.

I sensed that if he spread the word about what I had tried to suggest it could land me in trouble. I didn't want him to misinterpret what I had said, so I tried steering the conversation onto something else. "I didn't mean it that way. I'm sorry."

Although I was able to reassure Gajendra that day, it was clear that I wasn't in the Palace's good books. It wasn't long before I got a call from King Gyanendra's ADC, Binoj Basnyat. "Hey, Katawal, don't try acting too smart. Do what you're told and mind your own business." He said this was an instruction to me from the King.

I was surprised to suddenly receive such a blunt message from the Palace. I later found out that people around me had tried to complain to the Palace about me through the Chief. But I couldn't believe that a sensible man such as the Chief could feed those complaints upwards. Some of the generals and officials close to the Palace knew I had tried convincing the Chief to get the support of the political parties. Someone from among them must have complained to the King.

The truth was that I wasn't siding with the parties. I was only trying to protect the monarchy, the Nepali people and the Nepalese Army. I was worried that if there was too much pressure on the parties they would get closer to the Maoists which would then be detrimental to the monarchy. If anything were to happen to the monarchy, a symbol of national unity, the country would plunge further into instability. But it was clear that the Palace misunderstood me and instead tagged me as a rebel who refused to follow the Chief's orders.

There were two options open to me. I could simply do my job by following the Chief's orders and staying mum or I could send my frank suggestions and analysis of current affairs to the Palace without disobeying the Chief's orders.

As the Chief of General Staff, it was my duty to send analysis of the political situation based on available information. We based our judgments on discussions with politicians, diplomats, journalists, economists and others. This information was then condensed into a single page and sent to the West Gate on a weekly basis to go to the King through the ADCs on duty. The report had suggestions regarding the royal council, the relevance of local elections, which were being boycotted by the parties, and bridging the gap with the international community. I kept tabs on whether or not it reached the ADCs who then informed me about when it was presented to the King. I didn't tell the Chief anything about it.

We had meetings with the heads of the security forces twice a week. The Chief Secretary, Home Secretary and other secretaries were called when needed. Since the four security chiefs used to meet the King regularly, I always told them, "If His Majesty fails to act wisely, it won't be long before the monarchy is swept away. I assume that all of you have been telling this truth to the King?"

These meetings always discussed how the political parties shouldn't be sidelined. But the Palace continued doing exactly that. It either meant that the security heads weren't conveying what was discussed in the meetings or they couldn't convince the King.

One day I vented my ire at them: "Are you all really conveying everything to His Majesty or are you misleading him?"

But even the security chiefs had their own grievances. They met the King daily but blamed the Palace secretaries and the King's relatives for misleading him. They were equally concerned about the future of the monarchy.

I was overwhelmed just thinking about the serious consequences of the decisions being made by the Palace. If I had direct contact with the Palace or met the King regularly, I would have told him everything a long time ago.

I even tried talking to the King during a party at the Palace after Kamal Thapa was appointed Home Minister. The political parties had just boycotted the municipal elections called by the government, further distancing the King from both of them and the Maoists.

King Gyanendra was sitting alone at the bar and I seized the chance to talk to him.

"Your Majesty, may I have a word with you please?" I went near him to seek his permission.

He inched closer to me, out of earshot of the bartender.

"Keeping the political parties at arm's length won't do the monarchy any good. What do you intend to do, Your Majesty?' I asked.

"I'm not going to tell you that now," he said abruptly and turned away.

I tried asking and saying as much as my status allowed me. Maybe he didn't have the patience to hear anything more from me, and I was clearly not in a place to say more than that.

The root of the problem, in fact, lay in our military structure. Although the Palace's Military Secretariat formally works without interfering with HQ and the Army Chief, it exerted unnecessary pressure on the Army. The Secretary used his power unconstitutionally, just because of his proximity to the Palace. So when it came to Palace affairs, the Principal Military Secretary had more influence than the Army Chief.

After the downfall of the Panchayat regime, the Secretariat's influence had diminished overall but not vis-à-vis the Army. Unlike in the Panchayat years, the police, Army and intelligence service no longer had to go through the Secretariat to meet and talk to the King. But since the King was the Supreme Commander of the Army, all the important decisions still had to be sent to the Palace for approval. The Military Secretary continued to capitalise on this opportunity to exert control over the Army by trying to blur the lines between the King and the Secretariat. I always sensed how wary the Army Chiefs felt about the Secretariat, though no one dared raise the issue openly.

The unofficial power centre of the Army was, therefore, the Principal Military Secretariat. It was interested in promotions, transfers and appointments in the higher ranks and also about large contracts in the Army. There were few Army Chiefs who could tell it like it was to the King. The helplessness I saw among higher ranking Army officers following the 1

February royal move was just a continuation of the Secretariat's influence.

The situation was now going from bad to worse. After appointing unpopular faces like Senate Shrestha and Jagat Gauchan, the Palace made it clear that it didn't want to compromise with the parties no matter what the cost. The King's stubbornness was inviting disaster. I was also getting restless since neither my requests to my senior nor the suggestions being sent to the Palace were being acted on.

I was now in search of a person who could be relied on to convey my message to the King. After thinking it through, I remembered Prabhu Shumsher Rana, a close friend of King Gyanendra. I had known Rana as a selfless and relaxed person since my Hong Kong days. I thought I could trust him as my confidant.

I called him early one morning and he asked me to meet him at 9:30 am. I told him how all the suggestions which I had passed on through the Army Chief and ADCs at the Palace following the royal takeover had been ignored. I was in a difficult position since the Palace thought I supported the parties while the parties thought of me as being close to the Palace. It was an hour-long and emotional conversation during which I sometimes teared up.

"*Prabhu Rājā*, you have to make the King understand the message that Katawal has been trying to convey," I said, "Please make him understand that I am telling him all this only because I care about the monarchy."

He looked serious after hearing me out.

"Okay. I will arrange a meeting," he assured me.

It was more than I had expected. Sure enough, that same week I received an invitation for dinner at Prabhu Shumsher's residence. AIG Krishna Basnet, Finance Minister Madhukar Shumsher Rana and Lawa *Rājā* (titular King of Salyan who was like Gyanendra's court jester) were also invited. We were all talking very informally.

"His Majesty is waiting," Prabhu Shumsher said, directing me towards a room inside, "Please go in."

I had a whisky in one hand because I didn't know what to do with it.

"What about the drink?" I asked.

"You can take it along," he said.

I entered the room with the whisky and saluted the King. He motioned towards a chair and asked me to sit. He seemed to be in a good mood. "Your Majesty, can I say something?" I came straight to the point.

"Go ahead," he said.

"Your Majesty, the monarchy and the country are in a difficult situation," I said very frankly, "It will be better if you hand over power to leaders who believe in democracy."

All I heard was a feeble, "Um, yeah." After that he placed his own whisky down on a table and walked out of the room without saying anything more.

I was taken aback.

We all went in for dinner. The King and the Queen had theirs in a separate room. Everyone queued up to see the King off around midnight. It looked like the King was going to drive back himself.

I stood at attention and saluted him. The King didn't even look at me.

The Maoists attacked Butwal, so we flew there the next day. The loss of life and property was overwhelming and it was because of the weakness of the security forces.

We were scheduled to go to the Palace after returning from Butwal. This time, the seconds in command from all the security forces were also called to go to the meeting along with their chiefs. My counterparts from the police, intelligence service and APF had already arrived when I got there. Lawa Raja, Prabhu Shumsher and General Bharat Keshari were also present.

"What happened in Butwal?" the King asked.

"I sent Katawal there. He'll report to Your Majesty," COAS Pyar Jung turned towards me.

"Your Majesty, it was the security forces' weakness and negligence that led to so much destruction there," I said.

"I hope you will take care of it, Chief," the King said.

The whisky was already being served by then.

Suddenly, General Bharat Keshari piped up. Usually, once he got started, he went on for a bit and others never got the chance to get a word in edgewise.

"We were able to contain anti-national elements – meaning insurgents – in 1961," he said, cursing the Army and the police, "What the hell are you people doing now?"

I was furious. But since the Chief didn't say a word it wasn't wise for me to speak up. All of them, including the chiefs of the APF, police and the intelligence service, kept quiet.

This encouraged General Bharat Keshari to go on, "In Malaysia, the communists were pulverised and what have you done here?"

His words were an insult to our soldiers who had died on the frontline. Their families were still mourning their losses, while some bigwig was criticising them over whisky at the Palace.

"This is a huge let down for His Majesty," he said, trying to curry favour with the King.

I couldn't stand it any longer, so I asked the Chief, loud enough for the King to hear, for permission to speak. The Chief, in turn, gestured towards the King to ask for his consent.

"Your Majesty, can I make a point?" I asked.

"Go ahead," the King said.

"In Malaysia, the general's decision was the final word," I said as all eyes turned to me. "They didn't have Ian Martin, ambassadors, the UN, journalists, NGOs and INGOs there. They didn't have political parties to deal with. Democratic norms meant nothing to the British Army. Furthermore, they had plenty of arms, ammunition and resources backing them up. They didn't have to abide by human rights laws."

I was just getting warmed up.

"Is the world still how it was in 1961, General?" I said, "The government and the security forces are under the scrutiny of the whole world now. We'll gain nothing if we still have a sixties mentality. How can you even talk to the King about such backward times? It's easy to ramble on and on over drinks in air conditioned rooms, General. The soldiers in the trenches in Rukum and Rolpa know what it means to fight. Can the present day terrorists even be compared to the few hundred 'anti-national elements' who had nothing but sticks, spears and unsophisticated guns in 1961?"

The whole room went quiet as I continued speaking. I had known General Bharat Keshari since my lieutenant days and had learned a lot from him including the importance of physical fitness. But I had to confront him because what he said was so intolerable.

The King then put his whisky glass down on the table and, just like at our last meeting at Prabhu Shumsher's home, got up and went to another room. ADC Binoj followed him.

Everyone stood up after the King left. The atmosphere suddenly felt ominous. I didn't know what to do, so I headed to the restroom. Someone grabbed me from behind. It was Prabhu Shumsher and IGP Shyam Bhakta Thapa, both extremely sensible people.

"Finally, someone dared to speak out in front of the King," they said, "That was amazing."

But this infuriated me even more.

"The monarchy is about to be swept away and none of you say a word to the King, so what's the point of flattering me now?" I snapped at them.

When I became the second man in the Army hierarchy, I once invited all security chiefs (except COAS), Defence Secretary Upreti, Sudip Pathak of the National Human Rights Commission, Sagar Timilsina, Principal Secretary to HM with their spouses for dinner at my house in Koteshwor. After a couple of drinks, I told Secretary Timilsina, "Sir, the institution of the monarchy is under threat. You should all encourage the King to transfer power to democratic forces, otherwise it may be too late." Pathak supported the idea. But the Secretary said, "We have taken a forward looking step and there's no question of turning back now. General, how could you say that?" The conversation then took a different turn.

"I'm coming to see you, General," Chief Secretary Lokman Singh Karki told me on the phone. He would always meet me when he came to HQ and I used to ask him to meet the Chief as well.

"Please come," I said. We had a long discussion.

"His Majesty has summoned me this evening. What should I tell him?" It seemed he wanted to pick my brains.

"Can you speak the truth?" I asked.

"Why not?" he said, "I'm a Chhetri's son. It's my *dharma*. Anything for the monarchy and the country."

"Then tell the King that everything will be in tatters. If this situation continues, the monarchy won't survive. The only way to protect the monarchy is to hand over power to democratic forces as soon as possible."

"Okay. I'll tell the King," Lokman said. He called me around midnight and woke me up.

"What's the matter?" I asked.

"I just finished half bottle of whisky, despite the doctor telling me to stay away from it," he said.

"Why? What happened?"

"I said everything to the King that you suggested. It didn't go well. The King was agitated. I don't know what will happen now. I've lost my job for sure. What if I'm imprisoned?"

"No need to be afraid," I assured him, "What you did was exactly what any patriot and monarchist would have done faced with the current situation."

So, it was only Lokman who had the guts to tell King Gyanendra about the situation in the country as it really was.

The next evening, the King summoned Lokman again. He feared being arrested for what he had said but nothing like that happened. "His Majesty was very friendly today. He even asked about my family," Lokman briefed me later that evening.

The uncertainty was like the calm before a storm. The gap between the King and the parties grew even wider. It looked like the King, who had tried sidelining the parties, would himself be isolated. At a time when he was being cornered by the parties and the international community, he took another step that backfired badly.

During the SAARC Summit in Bangladesh, Nepal proposed to grant China observer status in the regional cooperation body. If King Gyanendra was trying to make a mark by including China in SAARC, he should have sounded out the other member countries first. Sri Lanka, Pakistan, the Maldives and some other members also wanted to have China in SAARC but King Gyanendra now had to bear the repercussions from India which was miffed. So India also pushed its proposal seeking observer status for Afghanistan.

Both countries were granted observer status but the monarchy had to pay a huge price for that outcome. Less than two weeks after the SAARC Summit, the seven-party alliance and the Maoists signed a 12-point agreement in New Delhi. The King was now totally isolated. Even the security forces were cornered, the supply of arms and ammunition was cut. India, the US and the UK withdrew their support.

The royal massacre shook the foundations of Nepal's monarchy and the 12-point agreement was another powerful jolt. Since it was an important political happening, the agreement was reviewed at the PSO meeting at HQ. "End of absolute monarchy" was one of the points in the agreement, which we interpreted as establishing constitutional monarchy. When I checked with some of the Congress and UML leaders who had signed the agreement, their explanation was no different. The Army understood that the 12-point agreement's objectives were constitutional monarchy, bringing the Maoists into the peace process and restoring democracy. Maybe that's why the Army leadership didn't reject it outright.

Some hardcore supporters of the monarchy and a few ministers were egging the military on to declare the UML and Congress terrorists after the Delhi agreement. But the military leadership didn't pay any attention to them.

The People's Movement of 2006

Since the King chose to walk alone, there were now three power centres in Nepal: the Maoists, the democratic forces and the Palace. When the parties and Maoists joined forces, it was a threat to the third point in the triangle. Furthermore, it didn't help the Palace that the international community was now on the side of the political parties. Following the 12-point agreement in New Delhi, the Maoists were on the streets of Kathmandu waving the flags of Congress and the UML. The parties formally began the People's Movement on 6 April 2006 and the very next night the Maoists simultaneously attacked Butwal, Kapilvastu's district headquarters Taulihawa and other places.

They had used full force to attack Butwal and Taulihawa and our military commanders were radioing for reinforcements and helicopters all night. But we could only send one and the fact that we couldn't help the brave soldiers on the frontlines haunts me to this day. If only we could have sent two or three helicopters to Butwal and Taulihawa that night, things would have been a lot different: fewer casualties and the ability to evacuate the injured. The Maoists could have been surrounded and captured.

We weren't able to send more helicopters that night because we only had one with us. The King was in Pokhara and during his stay there he expressed the desire to go to Mustang. The helicopters had to be on standby for the royal tour and hundreds of soldiers had to be ferried there for his security. Entertainers had to be flown in by helicopter for the amusement of the royal guests.

The King had absolutely no idea how difficult it was for the Army to arrange visits to remote areas during the height of the conflict and those who knew how difficult it was didn't have the courage to tell him. Maybe the security chiefs were only concerned about currying favour with the King and were afraid to be bearers of news that might upset him.

The King's Pokhara visit didn't achieve much and not many people went to meet him. Since it was curfew days, even unimportant visitors ended up being treated like VIPs just because they showed up to meet the King. The divisional commander and others used to call me to share their grievances.

"The Chief is there. Tell him about it," I told them.

Not just the visitors but the journalists who were flown from Kathmandu were useless. They belonged to those papers with a circulation of less than 500 which printed slander for anyone who was willing to pay for it. There was no lack of such sycophantic journalists in royal circles. Influential media houses and leading journalists were against the royal takeover and the Palace had to rely on incompetent and inconsequential journalists whose writings had no effect to counter the opposition.

It was our misfortune that the journalists whom the King should have listened to weren't allowed anywhere near him by his courtiers. He only got to meet editors who would tell him what he wanted to hear.

"Your Majesty, the people no longer trust the parties," is what they would tell the King. "They welcome your active role with open arms."

These journalists also tried pleasing everyone at the Palace from the Secretary, Chief and generals down to the majors. I told Binoj and Tika there was no point living in the bubble created by those journalists. But my warnings were not heeded.

With the People's Movement gaining momentum in April 2006, the meetings of the Central Security Coordination Committee became more frequent. But nothing of consequence was ever discussed there. We strongly opposed imposing curfews, since they would only exacerbate the people's anger and lead to hardship. Valley commander Dipak Bikram Rana and DGMO Kiran Shumsher Thapa were also not in favour of curfews but our decisions at the Committee to tighten security without curfews were always reversed by people higher up.

Even Home Minister Kamal Thapa was tired of the way things were going. He wouldn't even be told about curfews before they were announced.

During the People's Movement, the UML General Secretary Madhav Kumar Nepal's house was raided and his TV, mobile phones, computers were reportedly taken away. They even cut off his telephone line. I found out that he was being taken back and forth between Kakani and Balaju. This was no way to treat a former Deputy Prime Minister and this further agitated the pro-democracy activists.

The People's Movement was getting stronger with each passing day. The Army and King Gyanendra had been against using excessive force against demonstrators from the very beginning. The King had told COAS Pyar Jung that he didn't want to be a King who spilled the blood of his people.

Therefore, I believe it was the King, the Army and the security forces which minimised the casualties and damage during the People's Movement. We even coordinated with the pro-democracy leaders to provide them with routes around areas where we had a presence to minimise the chances of direct confrontation. So, despite curfews, we didn't stop protestors and we made sure the Chief had a good understanding of the situation along with Madhav Nepal and other leaders from the agitating parties.

On 21 April, the King addressed the people and called on the political parties to form a government. But the parties didn't budge from their demand that the House of Representatives be reinstated. It was clear that the King had to step down.

The next day, the crowds on the streets of Kathmandu had swelled to unprecedented numbers. The King's exit was now a certainty. What remained to be decided was how he would leave and to whom he would hand power. By then, there was already a feeling of triumph among the protestors and the Maoists, as if they had defeated the state security forces.

Two days after the King's address on 23 April, the Maoists attacked the Sindhupalchok HQ in Chautara. They used the hospital as a shield to attack the Army base, police, administration, prison and telecommunications system. The attack on Chautara was against the spirit of the 12-point agreement between the Maoists and the parties, and it looked a lot like the Maoist attack on Rumjatar in November 2002 in which young children were drugged and pushed into the line of fire.

When the Chief and I reached Rumjatar after that attack, two guerrillas we had captured were still unconscious. They were teenagers who had been drugged before the fight. That was how the Maoists were fighting: pushing young boys and girls to the frontlines, taking advantage of poverty, illiteracy and unemployment. The next day we found hundreds of syringes in millet field in Rumjatar.

The attack on Chautara was no different and was obviously intended to send a message to the Palace, the Congress and the UML. King Gyanendra then agreed to read live on TV a declaration prepared by Nepali Congress President Girija

Prasad Koirala and Madhav Nepal. On 24 April 2006, the King stepped down and his direct rule ended.

Now it was only the Army that the Maoists needed to take care of. They knew very well that the Army was the only disciplined, coordinated and united institution in the country. They wanted to put the Army in its place as they saw it and under their control in order to complete their mission of taking over the state. They would go to any lengths to accomplish that.

This was evident from what CPN-Maoist Chairman Pushpa Kamal Dahal aka "Prachanda" said during his first public appearance after emerging from hiding. "Since the Sugauli Treaty, this Army hasn't fought any war. It's done nothing except rape women and kill the people of Nepal," he said.

So, the Army was nothing more than rapists, murderers and a burden to the nation. Those sentiments might have been expected from the leader of a rebel group but what hurt us the most was the silence of the Prime Minister and other senior political leaders when they heard these words. While the leaders were trying to build a new relationship with the Maoists, the Army, which had been mobilised for the protection of the people of Nepal, was being openly dishonoured and humiliated. They may have been secretly pleased because bashing the Army was a way to get back at the King.

Everyone forgot that the soldiers were just following the orders of the government to fight for the good of the country. I thought of all the soldiers who had given up their families and homes to do their duty and was infuriated at the way they were being treated.

I was in no position to react immediately myself but neither could I simply keep quiet. I asked the Chief to immediately refute Prachanda's statement but he wanted the political leadership to take the first step. That was unlikely to happen since the political parties had finally brought the Maoists into a fragile peace process.

We met the PM, party leaders and several Ministers and expressed our outrage at the statement by the Maoist leader. The Chief was also under pressure from the PSOs to refute the statement. Under his orders, I went around trying to convince several party leaders to take our side. They would nod their heads and agree with us behind closed doors but didn't dare utter a word in public.

A week later, Deputy Prime Minister and Foreign Minister KP Sharma Oli returned to Nepal and, with the Chief's permission, I went to meet him at Sheetal Niwas and told him everything. He was receptive and assured me he would speak out.

The next day, during an interview with the BBC Nepali Service, he refuted Prachanda's statement in his trademark razor-sharp style and did his best to protect the national army's dignity. Finally after six days, with Oli's political backing, HQ formally issued a statement refuting Prachanda's allegations. But some ministers like Mahantha Thakur and Krishna Prasad Sitaula weren't happy with the Army's stand and tried to appease the Maoists.

I had lobbied strongly for action to be taken to refute Prachanda's statement and ministers who now considered the Maoists as all-powerful had informed them about me. That essentially marked the beginning of the rift between the Maoist leadership and me. Some of the ministers even thought that I had been bought by the Palace and told the Maoists so.

A central level Maoist leader even told me: "We were negative about your work since your Nepalganj days and now that you lobbied against our Comrade Chairman, you are top of the party's blacklist."

The Army was also on the watch list of the international community. Unless a state fails, outside entities aren't allowed to enter the country. But even during King Gyanendra's rule, the Office of the High Commissioner for Human Rights (OHCHR) was unnecessarily allowed to set up an office in Nepal. As per the Paris Principles regarding human rights, OHCHR's entry in Nepal wasn't required at that time. After all, we had a Human Rights Commission as per the 1990 constitution.

Since the Royal Palace had sidelined the parties at that time, no one opposed it when OHCHR came in. Foreign Minister Ramesh Nath Pandey had actually been tricked into signing the Geneva Conventions two months after the King's direct rule started.

We had tried to prevent this since we feared that Pandey may be interrogated in Geneva over "human rights violations by the security forces". We knew that activists in Nepal had exaggerated the security forces' actions and wanted to bring it up in Geneva. After informing the Chief about it, I suggested we send a capable officer to Geneva.

"I agree but how can we possibly send one?" he asked.

"Let me talk to the minister to see if the government delegation can include someone from the Army," I said.

I was with the Chief at a programme in Chhauni and immediately called Minister Pandey. He was convinced, so we decided to send Major Anup Jung Thapa whose work had been appreciated by all. The Army would also benefit from his report from Geneva.

On 15 March 2005, OHCHR set up shop in Nepal. Its chief was British national, Ian Martin. His responsibility was to monitor the human rights situation and report on it to UN headquarters but Martin was soon moving beyond his terms of reference to target the King and the Army. He didn't miss a single opportunity to condemn the government. Except for throwing stones, Ian Martin did everything that the agitators on the streets were doing, while hiding behind the UN's blue flag. The Army strongly objected to his behaviour. The political parties, civil society and the media enjoyed OHCHR portraying the King as the enemy of democracy and the Army was always dragged into it.

After the People's Movement, OHCHR celebrated the victory with just as much fervour as the activists in the streets. OHCHR benefited from the Nepali mindset that a white man can do no wrong. The UN's High Commissioner for Human Rights, Louise Arbour, visited Nepal twice and strongly criticised the King's crackdown on democracy while not uttering one word about human rights violations by the Maoists. OHCHR was obviously biased and its only job was to degrade Nepal to make itself relevant.

When the Maoists stepped into the open political arena, Martin and other members of the international community were blatantly biased towards them. They danced and mingled with them at the combatant camps. It was clear that some diplomats from the UK, Switzerland, Denmark and Norway also had a soft spot for the Maoists. Like Martin, they all fell for the belief that the Maoists were the only "progressive" party. The Maoists took full advantage of this.

Emboldened by the international community's support, the Maoists started a drive to downsize the Army. Prachanda openly said that there was no need for more than 10,000 soldiers in the Army. He accused everyone above the rank of colonel of being monarchists and publicly said that all of us should be fired. The other political parties also went along with this line, calling for "democratisation" of the Army. Civil society sways whichever way the wind blows, the media which is attracted by popular slogans and other professionals also joined in the call to "democratise" and downsize the Army.

This continuous attack on the Army was becoming intolerable to me. I requested the Chief to counter the accusations and raised the issue in a PSO meeting. The Chief and I met PM Girija Prasad Koirala and I was given the chance to speak.

"Why is the Army the only villain here?" I asked Girija*babu*.

"What do you mean?" he questioned.

"Did the Maoists defeat the Army?" I asked.

"No."

"Then why is the Army being incessantly attacked? It seems the Congress, UML and others are all for destroying the Army as a solution to all the problems of this country," I told him, "The Maoists haven't given up violence yet, they still have their weapons. If you downsize the Army to become popular, who'll gain and who'll lose? That's for you to mull over."

The PM listened attentively. He seemed to be convinced by my argument.

"Why are the parties bent on weakening the Army, while the Maoists don't even have to hand over their weapons?" I went on. "If the Army is downsized in the present situation, democracy, the democratic process and the parties will bear the brunt of it. A lot of leaders from the Congress and UML are enjoying the Army's humiliation. My only suggestion to you is that if this institution unravels, so will you."

The PM must have taken this seriously because after that there was no more talk of downsizing the Army.

Safe landing on 29 May

The People's Movement. had restored the House of Representatives and preparations for its first sitting were underway. Proposals about abolishing the monarchy, amending laws about succession to the throne and provision to have females become the Head of State if the monarchy were to remain were being floated.

The Congress, UML and other parties were referring to this proclamation as "Nepal's Magna Carta" and excitedly working on the declaration. We were following events closely. Valley Division Commander Dipak Bikram Rana kept tabs on all the security measures for the first meeting of the House of Representatives on 29 May. The battalion at Singha Darbar which was under his command was on alert.

"The DGMO office has ordered us to surround Singha

Darbar," Dipak reported to me that afternoon. The Director General of Military Operations is technically under the Chief of General Staff and gives orders about mobilising troops. I had been at HQ all day but didn't know anything about it.

The battalion at Singha Darbar, which falls under the Valley Division Command, had apparently received direct orders from the Royal Palace. Dipak felt that following the orders could have grave repercussions for the Army, so he correctly reported it directly to me. We had known each other since our Dhankuta and Nepalganj days and had a close relationship.

"If we do anything right now, it will bring dishonour to the Army," Dipak said.

Colonel Sahadev Khadka, battalion commander at Singha Darbar, had received a call from the Military Secretariat at the Palace that morning. The orders were to "vandalise the mikes, surround Singha Darbar and do everything possible to foil the meeting".

After getting such orders, Khadka had immediately informed the brigadier and division commanders. Dipak felt that the Palace's moves would backfire.

"Don't do anything now. Just carry on with your regular duties," he ordered Sahadev.

After that, Dipak summoned Number One Brigade commander Ram Krishna Adhikari and said, "Just stick to my orders." He met Adhikari to ensure that Sahadev wouldn't get conflicting orders from him and the brigade commander.

The DGMO office had called Dipak again to ask what was happening. He sensed that HQ, the Palace or the Military

Secretariat were planning a coup. So, he clearly told the officials at HQ and the Principal Military Secretariat in the Palace, "If you want us to carry out your orders, we need them in writing."

The first meeting of the House of Representative used to be addressed by the King. So, the Army had managed the security accordingly. Gajendra Limbu, Principal Military Secretary at the Palace, called with the same question again, "What's happening at Singha Darbar?"

"Nothing more than what happens on other days. We'll need written orders to do more," Dipak replied.

It now became clear to me that the Army was being pushed by the Palace to do its bidding. Gajendra talking directly to the division commander, the calls from the Chief's most trusted DGMO officer, the Palace following up with the colonel at Singha Darbar were all signs pointing towards a looming crisis. The Palace wanted the Army to foil the meeting that day but no one had the courage to step forward and actually give the order. So, I met the Chief and told him everything that I knew.

"The Army shouldn't go against the people and the government's constitutional orders," I told him clearly.

"Well, I don't know anything about it," the Chief sounded indecisive. The other generals started pouring into the Chief's office and all of them were against any attempt to foil the meeting of the House of Representatives. The Army leadership was no longer confused.

It was Dipak's astuteness which averted a crisis that day. The meeting of the House of Representatives concluded peacefully. The country became a republic. And although neither the pro-democracy movement on the streets nor the 12-point agreement had called for a secular Nepal, the Parliament decided to make the country secular, federal and a republic.

Rayamajhi Commission

The Rayamajhi Commission was formed with the sole intention of taking revenge against Army, the police and civil servants that had performed their duties in accordance with the state's constitutionally valid orders. The Commission started by summoning the Chief and other Army officers.

The Army was mobilised during the People's Movement only after the local administration sought our help. We were there only as a backup force. Despite the Commission knowing this, it seemed Army officers were summoned just to be taunted.

COAS Pyar Jung was hesitant to even give them a statement. He had asked the PM's permission to leave for western Nepal on the day he was summoned to appear before the Commission. I didn't know anything about it.

"Where's the Chief?" I asked the DGMO.

"He left for the west," he said.

The next day, I received a letter from the Commission. I couldn't take any decision without asking the Chief, so I called him.

"It's up to you to decide if you want to go," he said hesitantly.

Since I didn't get a clear reply from the Chief, I went directly to see the PM's Defence Advisor, Ramesh Jung Thapa. He also called the Defence Secretary.

"How can I appear before the Commission ahead of the Chief?" I asked them.

"This is a powerful Commission, even above the Constitution. It would be better to go," Defence Secretary Bishnu Datta Upreti suggested.

"It won't look good if I go when the Chief himself hasn't," I repeated.

The Defence Advisor took my side and called the Commission. Defence Secretary Upreti then sent a letter to the Commission stating, "The Chief isn't in town, so how can the second man appear ahead of the Chief?"

When the Chief returned two days later, I told him, "The Army leadership needs to face the Commission and tell everything squarely."

This issue was discussed in the PSO's meeting. All the generals suggested that the Chief should go to the Commission and finally he did. We didn't know what transpired there. We didn't ask and he didn't think it was necessary to tell us.

The Commission called me the day after and I asked the Chief what I should do. "Go after the letter of summons arrives," he said.

"If I follow you to the Commission, they might start calling everyone else too," I said, "What will happen to the Army's morale if everyone is called in? What significance will the chain of command hold then?"

But the Chief was in no mood to listen. I went to the Commission the next day. There were Maoists disguised as journalists who asked me provocative questions and tried to put the Army down.

Ram Prasad Shrestha and Harihar Birahi took down my statement, which lasted almost four hours. I then requested them to allow me to have my say before the Commission's Chairman, Krishna Jung Rayamajhi.

"Imprisoning people isn't the Army's policy. Everyone here is aware of the Army's chain of command. I don't see any point, lining us up here since you've already talked to the Chief."

"If the Chief had told us this yesterday, it would have been easy for us make that decision," Rayamajhi said, "He asked us to talk to others about a lot issues, so we had to call you."

From the next day onwards, Army officers queued outside the Commission which was prepared to make scapegoats of soldiers and government officials who had simply followed sanctioned orders.

Everyone vented their ire at the security forces. The Commission finally blamed a select few people in the APF, the police and the intelligence service but couldn't find anyone in the Army to grill.

Ten

An Amazing Three Years

COAS Pyar Jung Thapa's four year tenure was ending in three months. Based on all the criteria, including seniority, qualifications, experience and long-established practice of the Army, I was the sole contender to be the next Army Chief. The other three-star general was my junior.

But conspiracies were being hatched by my detractors to prevent me from getting the top job. I was accused of being a monarchist. Efforts were underway to extend Pyar Jung's tenure for another year. The Maoist leadership was firmly against my promotion. It was reported that even some influential leaders in the government were in favour of extending Thapa's tenure or dumping me to promote my junior as the next Chief.

If Thapa's tenure was extended for a year, I would retire in November 2006 and Lt General Balananda Sharma would also retire the following January. There were rumours that Kul Bahadur Khadka's name was being floated for the Chief's post after Sharma and I were dumped. I found out that some people from the PM's family and a few influential Congress leaders were also scheming to kick me out.

Around the same time, Kul Bahadur was suddenly brought to the Valley Division Command from the Far West. He was made the striker in this game to extend the Chief's tenure. The

PM's close aides thought Khadka was a hardcore republican and a Congress supporter.

My enemies had again raked up the issue of my age and taken it to Girija*babu* to prove my ineligibility. This issue, which had already been resolved twice in the past, was being raised at yet another crucial juncture in my career. My opponents wanted to entangle me in an age controversy to pave the way for Thapa's extension or the promotion of my junior. A case was filed in the court accusing me of lying about my age.

People even went around saying that I was King Mahendra's adopted son, raised by Her Majesty Queen Ratna and treated like a brother by Gyanendra. They argued that if Katawal was made Chief, it would pave the way for a return to monarchy.

Another implausible allegation was that I had masterminded the royal move of 1 February 2005. Others spread rumours that King Mahendra had even consulted me, still a school boy in Pharping, about his "coup" in 1960. People trying to foil my chance to be Army Chief also pointed out that I was in charge of the Army's operations during the 2006 People's Movement.

These rumours were being fanned not just by my domestic opponents but also some international ones. I learnt that some officials at OHCHR had also lobbied against me. But I wasn't going to go around appeasing people just to get the Chief's post.

It was around this time that PM Girija Prasad Koirala was visiting New Delhi where the appointment of the next Army Chief came up in discussions. Home Minister Krishna Prasad Sitaula and the PM's daughter, Sujata Koirala, were against my promotion to the top job. Shekhar Koirala and journalist, Kanak Mani Dixit, were also present during these discussions in New Delhi where only a few took my side.

The PM was advised to bring in CB Gurung instead, since I was considered too controversial. It was also argued that this would send out a message of change and the establishment of a new order.

"CB has already retired so how would that be possible?" someone asked.

"Well, arrangements can be made to bring him back," was the reply.

The embers of the People's Movement were still glowing. Being tagged as an associate of the King or the Palace was still a black mark, just as the label "anti-national element" was during the Panchayat years. My opponents were, therefore, campaigning fiercely against me, so much so that plans to extend the Chief's tenure or bring in Balananda Sharma or push both of us aside and give a "double promotion" to either Govinda Gurung or Kul Bahadur Khadka were being floated.

But the government feared a backlash from the rank and file if the decision went against the Army's rules of promotion. Most politicians knew I was popular with the soldiers.

Some businessmen, journalists, government officials and stalwarts of civil society whom I count as friends, came to me, worried about the Army's structure, institutional values and traditions being tampered with. An editor of a major daily was persistent that I "keep fighting and not give up." He was worried that political meddling could turn the Army into a "sister organisation of the political parties."

"You need to be running around lobbying to become the Chief. This is Nepal, the job won't just land in your lap," others advised me.

The race for the top job was getting tighter by the day. A businessman came to see me at my residence. "It's about the Army now, so you have to do something. We are ready to help," he said.

"I'm the only person in line to be the next Chief, so it will happen by the rules," I tried explaining.

"Everyone is lobbying hard for the top job. Furthermore, the Prime Minister, Ministers and some other senior leaders don't favour you. How can you become the Chief with this laid-back attitude?" he pushed me.

"I believe my professionalism counts for something," I said, "I've done nothing wrong and nothing to the people of Nepal that can stop me becoming Chief."

I gave the same answer to everyone. Since I was the most senior, the rules, law and practice meant I was the sole contender for the post. So why should I go around kowtowing to people to make me Chief?

My rationale didn't convince my businessman friend, however. He had heard that other candidates were offering money as part of their lobbying efforts and hinted that I might do the same.

"Thank you," I said, "I'd rather retire with pride than resort to such tactics."

It was Saturday so I was at home that morning. The sentry came running in to inform me that Sujata Koirala was at the gate. Why would the PM's daughter be coming to see me?

"Maybe she's lost her way. Give her directions," I told him.

"No, she says she's here to see you."

I stepped out of the door just as she was coming through the gate.

"*Namaste*, General."

"*Namaste*, Sujata *jee*."

"So good to finally meet you in person," I said.

"I was passing by so I came here to introduce myself, without even asking for your time," Sujata said.

I invited her to stay for lunch.

I was impressed by her unpretentiousness at that first meeting. On Saturdays we eat *dāl, bhāt gundruk, masyaurā* and *bhatmās,* simple food with no fanfare and she seemed to relish the meal.

"So why are you here?" I asked her.

"I had heard about you, so I dropped by to say hello," she repeated, beating around the bush.

Maybe the PM had sent her to snoop. Later, when I had heated discussions with the PM, I told him: "I never kowtowed to you to become Chief."

"Didn't Sujata come to your place?" he said with a smile.

The Chief is customarily on leave about a month before retiring. But COAS Pyar Jung wasn't on leave yet and there were rumours that his tenure would be extended by a year. I went to the Chief to find out what was really happening.

"There's talk about your tenure being extended," I told him, "If that's the case, I'll resign now."

"If tenure is extended, it won't be just mine. I'll ensure a one-year extension for all," the Chief said, "It won't affect your promotion to the top."

Balananda Shrama and Kul Bahadur Khadka were still lobbying hard for the top job. Reports started trickling in about friction between the political parties over the selection of the Chief.

Khadka's in-law, the late Bishnu Pratap Shah's wife, had a late night meeting with the PM's advisor, Ramesh Jung Thapa.

"For the sake of your friend, you have to make *samdhi jyu* the Chief," she reportedly told him, "We're ready to help."

In July 2006, the Chief took me to Baluwatar. "The Palace asked me to take you along," he said.

After a week, I was again asked to accompany the Chief to Baluwatar under orders from the PM. Since the Chief was getting orders to have me around him most of the time, he became suspicious that I was spying on him.

Everyone was sceptical about me. Not just the Chief, even Baluwatar used to think that I was spying for the Palace. And as for the Palace, well, to them I was always a political party supporter.

So, the Chief and I went to meet the PM but, before we could start talking, the PM asked me to leave the room.

COAS Pyar Jung returned after almost an hour, looking crestfallen. I returned to HQ with him. Later that afternoon, I got a call from the Chief's office and by the time I went around at 4 pm all the other PSOs were already gathered there.

"The orders are to hand over responsibility to General Katawal who will be the Acting Chief from tomorrow. I won't be coming to the office anymore," the Chief announced.

Handing over the Army leadership is a major milestone. Despite knowing each other since my lieutenant days, the Chief didn't look very happy when he made the announcement. Earlier, we used to have a ceremony where the Chief and the Acting Chief would exchange files and best wishes to mark the occasion, but not this time.

The other generals congratulated me. The decision to send the Chief on leave and make me the acting Chief further cemented my chances of getting the top job.

The Thapa family was upset with me since the Chief's daughter's wedding which was being planned long before the Baluwatar meeting. Finance Minister Dr Ram Sharan Mahat used to repeatedly talk about it and the general feeling was that it had been "extravagant". The media even noted that all the generals were present at the party, except the number two man. Someone told the Thapa family that I had planted those wedding stories in the papers. Uma got a call from Shashi Bhawan, the Chief's residence, a few days after the wedding.

"Drop by in the evening for a cup of tea and bring the General along," the Chief's wife said. I assumed the Chief's tenure was going to be extended after all or that he would be made Field Marshal.

We reached Shashi Bhawan on time. It was just us, the Chief and his wife. I was surprised how unfriendly they were that evening.

"Okay, we'll take our leave now," I joined my palms to say *namaste* and stood up.

Suddenly, the Chief's wife started spewing venom at us. "I hope the person who planted the nonsense reports about our daughter's wedding doesn't live to see tomorrow and rots in hell forever," she fumed.

We were taken aback. They had fed us well just so they could vent their ire on us? The Chief sat quietly in a corner, looking dejected. I was furious but didn't want to quarrel with a woman.

"You're right. I also hope the person who did it gets punished," I added and left.

During all the internal and external lobbying for the position of Army Chief, senior Congress leader, Bal Bahadur Rai, whom we knew as MP as he was elected as the Member of Parliament from Okhaldhunga in the 1959 general elections, had written to PM Koirala in my support. I learned about it only after his death.

Rai had written: "Let's just stick to established tradition and law for the Chief's appointment. Even in the Indian Army, appointments have never been affected by politics."

Following the House of Representatives' decision to oust the King, the PM was the officiating Head of State. And he knew very well that the political leadership couldn't withstand the Army if it defied interference over the Chief's appointment.

On 11 September 2006, PM Koirala pinned the Army Chief's insignia of rank on my shoulders.

When I became Chief, the public's perception of the Army was not very positive. It was still considered to be the private army of a despotic royal family. So many people would have been wondering why have an army at all? People who were against institutionalising the democratic process were the most vehement opponents of the Army.

Yet the rule of law cannot be established if the Army is weak. People with muscle power wanted to rule so they were bad-mouthing the Army publicly and naïve people just followed the herd. There were arguments that the Army only served the royal family and, since Nepal was too small to fight India or China, we didn't really need it at all.

It's true that Nepal's military cannot be compared to that of India or China. But if military strength were to be the deciding factor in the very existence of countries and democratic institutions, then only powerful countries like US, Russia, China and India should have armies.

Gone are the days when armies were mobilised only to fight neighbours. Nowadays the strength of the Army lies in deterrence and it is indispensible for a country's internal security. Modern political scientists consider the Army to be the very foundation of democratic processes. It is imperative for stability and peace in a country. Just look at India to see how imperative the Army's presence in Jammu Kashmir, Punjab, Jharkhand and the North-East is. Even in Nepal, the group that opted for an armed struggle to install a communist totalitarian government was ultimately forced into the political mainstream because of the Army.

The Nepalese Army has helped spread the country's name and fame throughout the world. Burma's democratic leader, Aung San Suu Kyi, US President Barrack Obama and even the UN Secretary-General have praised the Nepalese Army's respect for civilian authority.

There were plenty of leaders in the past who thought the Army wasn't necessary but they also extolled the Army's role in international peacekeeping operations. It has become a major point in Nepal's favour when our Prime Ministers and Foreign Ministers meet UN officials.

So when I moved to Shashi Bhawan, I tried to dispel negative notions about the Army and to demystify the military. I invited people from all walks of life – politicians, lawyers, doctors, professors, government officials, journalists, businessmen, students and workers – to Shashi Bhawan every evening to discuss and address their concerns. It was an undeclared Shashi Bhawan Public Relations Campaign that helped raise the Army's profile and gain respect for it.

I kept on impressing upon foreign and Nepali people across the board that the Nepalese Army would act as the bedrock on which democratic institutions could a take a firm hold and the rules of law and objective civilian supremacy could be established just like in any other democracy. It is the only stabilising institution in Nepal, as well as the oldest Army in the region.

After the People's Movement in 2006, the country was on the verge of anarchy. There was competition between radical ideologies. After the King was ousted following the proclamation on 18 May, the Army became an easy target for everyone. The argument of those opposed to the Army was that guns and freedom couldn't go hand in hand, especially because the Army only supported tyrants and weakened democracy.

But I tried reasoning with them, citing examples of countries like the UK, USA and India where powerful armies had strengthened the democratic process. "The Army plays an important role in ensuring peace, good governance and people's fundamental rights," I'd remind them.

The Nepalese Army had always followed the government's constitutionally-valid orders and respected the people's aspirations, and would continue to do so.

During the rehearsals for Fulpati (the seventh day of Dasain) during my first year as Chief, I received a letter from the Defence Ministry saying that this time guns and cannons wouldn't be fired during the celebrations at Tundikhel. The letter was signed by Secretary Bishnu Datta Upreti.

I raised the issue with some ministers but got no clear reply. Senior Maoist leaders were apparently pressuring the PM not to allow the Army to use weapons, even for a festival. I decided to send a fitting reply through Defence Ministry channels. The PM's Defence Advisor summoned Secretary Upreti who informed him there were orders not to allow the King to worship at Hanuman Dhoka as well.

"The tradition that has continued since Prithvi Narayan Shah's time will continue," I replied tersely, "Cannons and guns will be fired on Fulpati. The King will also worship at Hanuman Dhoka as he always has. Who told you to issue arbitrary orders?" I shouted.

"I'm only passing on instructions from the very top," Upreti said meekly.

I don't know to whom the Defence Secretary and advisor passed on my fulminations but there were no barriers for the Army after that. The programme from Fulpati to Nawami went ahead as it had for centuries. Even suspended King Gyanendra went to worship at Hanuman Dhoka.

The following year there was another notice during Shivaratri not to celebrate the festival because the country was now secular. It was the Maoists again. This time I met the Prime Minister directly.

"Who says we can't celebrate Shivaratri, sir?" I asked.

"The country is secular now," he replied, "How can the festival of one particular religion be a celebration for the national army?"

"The Army has always been secular. It's just that our special celebration day coincides with Shivaratri," I explained.

"Really? The Army has been secular?" he said, pretending to be surprised.

"We have people of all religions in the Army who are free to celebrate their festivals and observe religious traditions according to their own beliefs," I explained.

The Army had not been divided along communal lines since King Prithvi Narayan's time. Obviously, this was something new for the PM. "Muslims from Banaras were recruited into the Army to make bullets, arms and ammunition during Prithvi Narayan's time," I continued, "The Army respects Bouddhanath stupa and the mosques around Ghantaghar as much as Pashupatinath."

The PM was convinced and gave orders that the tradition was to be followed. It was a step-by-step battle to protect the Army's traditions.

The Army Chief had always been invited to the ceremony when ambassadors presented their credentials to the Head of State. This tradition started during the Rana regime and remained intact throughout the changes from democracy to the Panchayat era to multiparty democracy. After I became Army Chief, ambassadors from two countries presented their credentials but I wasn't invited to either ceremony and only watched on TV.

This was a blatant insult to the Army.

"You've started excluding us from programmes that we were always part of. This situation needs to be rectified immediately," I told the PM.

"Why?" he asked.

"This will send a negative message about the Army and its faith in democracy," I said, "It will only benefit authoritarianism."

He then asked his aide to order the Chief Secretary and Foreign Affairs Secretary to never leave the Army Chief out of future credentials ceremonies.

General Pawan Bahadur Panday recently reminded me about the Norwegian Ambassador who had come to see me as soon as I took over the Army's leadership. He went on and on about how the Maoists were the true democratic force, the representatives of people power who fought for individual freedom and universal justice, and how the Nepalese Army had to go all out to support them. I then asked Pawan, who was at the meeting as my Military Assistant, to open the door and show the Ambassador out. The diplomatic community's eyes were opened only after watching the Shaktikhor secret video in which the Maoists' tactics and strategies to establish a one-party communist dictatorial regime in Nepal were revealed.

Although the Maoists had entered the peace process, their parallel rule was still thriving. They had been underground for a long time but only a few months after they emerged from the mountains, the Home Ministry was powerless before them. The rebels had dared to call the national army rapists and murderers at the PM's residence, in the presence of former PMs and Home Ministers.

Had this struggle taken place in any of the larger democracies, one could imagine the global impact it would have had. Think of a military taking a constitutional stand against a one-party, leftist dictatorship trying to impose an ideology that had existed for 73 years but been rejected by the global community because it had failed to deliver. The mass media would have gone wild with constant global coverage of the struggle. I'm sure it would have been perceived as a major event in world history.

The former rebels had portrayed the Nepalese Army in a negative light as rapists and murderers and tagged them a private army. People forgot the historical contributions the Army had made during the national unification campaign and in the world wars. People also forgot the continuous and large contribution it had been making to global peace and stability which had been rightly praised by the international community.

Nepal's political leaders feared risking their reputations by speaking up for the Army and, instead, bashing the military became routine. Under those circumstances, keeping the Army's morale high was a challenge for me, especially after the Rayamajhi Commission went around looking for scapegoats.

Generals, colonels and other officers who were under the Army Chief's command were called to appear before the Rayamajhi Commission. Taking their cue from this, a number of other organisations began summoning soldiers for questioning as well.

I raised this issue with the Prime Minister.

"Whenever and wherever the Army is summoned, I and only I will go – no one else," I said, "How will my subordinates be expected to fulfil their duties if they have to make the rounds of various courts and offices?"

After that no one had to line up outside courts and offices. Experts from the Army's legal and human rights departments gave statements on my behalf, taking the burden off ordinary soldiers.

I sent letters to everyone in our bases across the country, hoping to lift their flagging morale. The main objective was to ensure that the Army remained a cohesive and strong unit, unaffected by the rubbish going on around it. I wanted to assure the troops that their Chief was always on their side.

Despite claiming to have entered the peace process, the Maoists continued in their old ways, including looting and abducting people. They were playing a two-faced game, while the Home Ministry was reduced to a mere spectator, watching as the Maoists carried on their excesses right under its nose.

We didn't want anyone in the Army to worry about the security of their family, land or property in these circumstances. So, HQ issued a circular stating that if serving or retired soldiers of any rank or their families were extorted, abducted or subjected to coercion, then the nearest Army base would immediately take action on their behalf.

Some of the criticism of the Army concerned alleged discrimination in the kitchen and mess. So we decided that everyone would dine in the soldiers' mess once a week. I had always eaten with the soldiers since my lieutenant days anyway, so for me it was nothing new.

This didn't just put an end to the rumours but actually helped improve the quality of food and sanitation in the soldiers' mess. We began this practice in HQ with the support of all the generals and it soon became widespread.

Throughout my military career, I have always tried to improve the units I commanded. When I was the Adjutant General in 2001, I entrusted cooking duties to a Dalit soldier for HQ's Dasain feast. Most appreciated it, although there were always those who accused me of doing things just to make myself popular.

Since the Dalit community was the most oppressed in Nepali society, I was aware how important it was to lift their self-esteem. So I always interacted with Dalit soldiers during my visits to the districts. Even after becoming the Chief, I continued visiting Dalit soldiers' families across the country, sharing food with them under their roofs.

My faith in the monarchy hadn't diminished even despite the institution being sidelined. So, as always, I wanted to receive *tikā* from the now suspended King during my first Dasain as Army Chief. I had planned to receive *tikā* from the King in the morning and then celebrate Dasain with soldiers in far-flung units and sub-units, and I informed PM Koirala of my intentions.

I called ADC Binoj on Nawami. "*Tikā* for the public will start after 2 pm," he told me.

I told him about my plans to spend Dasain with the boys on duty.

"If I could receive *tikā* a bit earlier with the ADCs and Palace staff, I could then move on to the barracks," I explained.

"I'll get back to you," Binoj said.

Since soldiers couldn't go home for Dasain, I wanted to be there for them during the celebrations.

"It won't be possible in the morning," Binoj told me later

on the phone, "You've been asked to come after 2 pm along with the others."

I had been accused of spying for the Palace and was loathed by those who called me Gyanendra's brother but, in actual fact, the Palace couldn't stand me at all. The Army Chief receiving *tikā* from the suspended King would have created quite a stir but I was willing to face the criticism and go ahead with it. Those who thought I was the adopted son of Mahendra and Ratna would have been astounded to learn that I had never been allowed to speak to Her Majesty Queen Ratna even once in all those years.

Keeping up with the Nepalese Army's tradition of honouring the monarchy, I paid my respects to them at Dasain. This tradition was enshrined in the institutional culture of the Army and had remained intact despite changes in regime, administration and politics. The Army's reverence for the monarchy wasn't just limited to Dasain, of course. The Army had also always sent gifts to the King and Queen on their birthdays, a practice which continued throughout my tenure as Chief. I believe in change but with continuity.

After becoming Chief, I spent all three Dasains away from home, travelling from Chyangthapu in the east to Darchula in the west to celebrate Dasain with ordinary soldiers. Dancing and rejoicing with the soldiers under the leaky barracks roofs was more enjoyable to me than revelling with friends and family in Shashi Bhawan. This was only possible because of the support of Uma and our family.

"It's just three *Dasain*s anyway," Uma used to say, making it easy for me. "It's a small price to pay for the happiness of hundreds of soldiers." As the Army Chief, I needed to be in touch with people at all levels, regardless of their ideology, class or faith.

One day, the editor of a weekly magazine told me that Maoist Chairman Prachanda wanted to meet me. Before I could reply, he explained, "He's the leader of the third power and personal contact with you is necessary."

I had been meeting everyone, so the Maoist Chairman should be no exception.

"Invite him to dinner on my behalf," I told the journalist.

He was hesitant. "Maybe it should be discreet, at a private place somewhere other than your residence," he said

"The Army Chief won't meet secretly with a Maoist leader. Shashi Bhawan is open to all," I replied, "Privacy will be maintained there."

The editor called me a few days later with the news that Prachanda had accepted my invitation.

I gave security at the gate the registration number of the vehicle to be let in. Just the two of them, Prachanda and the editor, arrived in that vehicle. It was difficult to recognise Prachanda who was wearing a hat.

I had arranged the meeting in a secluded room on the ground floor of Shashi Bhawan. The journalist's job was only to organise the meeting so he was taken to a separate room for dinner.

We made a toast that night, marking the start of our formal relationship. Our first few meetings went well. Giving up arms might have changed him for the better, I thought.

But from our fourth meeting onwards, I could sense Prachanda playing sly games in an attempt to force the Army to dance to his tune. His behaviour and the activities of other Maoist leaders gave me reason to doubt his sincerity, yet I continued to meet him. My motive was to try to understand the Maoists' strategy, disarm and demobilise them and bring them into the democratic process.

We used to discuss a lot of issues and almost always had differences of opinion. Yet, despite our differing outlooks and interpretation of trends, we became regular visitors at each other's houses.

After our first meeting, Prachanda's son, Prakash, started driving him to Shashi Bhawan. Our families met for dinner on several occasions. Prachanda was probably the only guest to have frequented Shashi Bhawan so many times.

He was very easy to talk to. "We have fantastic chemistry," were always his parting words.

Several other Maoist leaders also visited me at Shashi Bhawan. They slipped in surreptitiously and didn't want others to know about our meetings. Only the seniors spoke while all the others listened and maybe that's just how the communist leaders were. Krishna Bahadur Mahara, Netra Bikram Chnad and Hitman Shakya came in the same group to meet me several times. Since Netra Bikram Chand hadn't appeared in public yet, Mahara did all the talking. Others in their group listened respectfully when he spoke.

Mohan Baidya also dropped by sometimes with his own comrades, including Ram Bahadur Thapa. Baidya *jee* spoke less but it was always from his heart and never with even a hint of deceit. Baburam Bhattarai and Hisila came to Shashi Bhawan only twice.

Although the Maoists came in different groups, they always put forward the same the party line. "This country won't move forward unless the Army and the Maoists work together as a single strong unit," they used to say.

Like the Maoists, other communist leaders also preferred meeting in the evenings or over dinners rather than in broad daylight. UML leader Bharat Mohan Adhikari was an exception because he preferred to meet in the afternoon. I also frequently met other UML leaders, including Amrit Kumar Bohara, Bishnu Poudel, Rajendra Pandey, Surendra Pandey, Ghanashyam Bhusal and Yogesh Bhattarai. We exchanged information and their insightful analyses were always useful to me.

Although Congress leaders also had their own factions, they were never discreet about their meetings like the communists. Bijay Kumar Gachchhadar and Sharat Singh Bhandari were always together. Upendra Yadav used to drop by separately sometimes.

I tried to meet as many Maoist and Madhesi leaders as possible since the problems in the Tarai were the most pressing in the country after the Maoist insurgency.

Although the Maoists had been welcomed into the mainstream, they hadn't really won the war. In fact, they had come to the negotiating table only because they couldn't defeat the Army. Contrary to what they said outside, they hadn't been able to establish "a state within a state" or hold any part of the country for any length of time. The Maoists came to the negotiating table only after understanding that political power didn't come from the barrel of a gun after all. In fact, their leaders publicly admitted that they agreed to the ceasefire because a military victory wasn't possible. They publicly declared that as long as there was a Nepalese Army they could not win a military victory, so they had no alternative but to negotiate. Thus the security forces accomplished the mission which had been entrusted to them. The aim was not to kill the Maoists but to force them to the negotiating table. The security forces had been able to break the Maoists' will to fight and win a military victory, however, the politicians failed miserably to capitalise on it.

The Maoists had capitulated and given up their armed struggle under pressure, yet they were treated like the victors. And they took advantage of that. They cajoled or coerced people to their side and hounded those who refused. The weakness of the state apparatus gave the Maoists the upper hand to continue with their excesses. This special treatment went to their heads and they considered themselves to be the country's dominant force.

We regularly briefed the PM about the Maoists' strategy and their long-term objectives. But the parties never listened because they were too busy trying to win the Maoists over. The Maoists went on to receive a red carpet welcome at Singha Darbar, where they came in carrying guns. Maoists were seen as a force that could wipe out the UML, so they received an equal standing in the Interim Parliament. After the King was removed, they cleverly used the presidency as bait on several agreements to restrict the Army as part of their overall goal. Even when UNMIN joined forces against the Army, not one among the democratic leaders chose to speak out about it. The Maoists' hardcore guerrillas were outside the cantonments and active through the YCL, while new "fighters" were recruited to fill the camps in an attempt to inflate the numbers before UNMIN's verification.

The Army kept the PM, Defence Minister, political leaders and members of the government negotiating team informed of all these developments. "The Maoists have recruited new cadres and corrupted UNMIN's verification process," we informed the government. "The real guerrillas are in the YCL and holding on to their weapons."

I also regularly updated the international community, civil society and the media. In the end, UNMIN verified about 19,000 Maoist combatants comprising mostly new recruits. They staged a show of handing over their unusable rusted weapons, which were kept locked up in containers inside the camps. So, they ended up guarding and having the keys to their own weapons.

"Where else in the world has a UN mission given one side in a conflict such an upper hand?" I asked many people.

I never got an answer to this question from Ian Martin.

"General, talk to your politicians," he used to brush me off, "We're only implementing what your leaders have agreed to."

The Maoists didn't hand over even a quarter of the weapons they had looted from the security forces, including modern weaponry. They successfully promoted the idea that the monarchy had been the main enemy of the nation with the Army as its minion. In the name of turning Nepal into a republic, decisions were made that ultimately benefited only the Maoists.

Home Minister Krishna Prasad Sitaula was enraged when the Army told him the Constituent Assembly elections couldn't be fair because of the leniency of the government's approach in disarming the Maoists.

"Are you trying to sabotage the peace process, Chief?" Sitaula asked angrily. He was juggling conflicting responsibilities. As Peace Minister he was trying to be flexible with the rebels while as Home Minister he was responsible for national security. And it wasn't just Sitaula. Other leaders of Congress and the UML were vying to take the credit for the success of the peace process.

It was only when the Shaktikhor video, made secretly in one of the Maoist camps, was made public that Nepali politicians, media houses, professionals, lawyers, diplomats and the international community became aware of the Maoists' real strategy and future designs to establish a one-party communist dictatorship. The tables had turned then and the Maoist leadership's true colours were exposed.

In the video, Prachanda claimed to have 7000 combatants, despite our estimate that the number was actually 5000-5500. Furthermore, he revealed that the number had been inflated after the Comprehensive Peace Agreement (CPA) to 35,000 with new recruitment which went against the spirit of the CPA. Eventually, the UN Mission certified the Maoists' strength at about 19,000. Thus Prachanda had deceived everybody, including the UN Mission led by Ian Martin. Dahal bragged about being able to cheat everybody.

Senior leaders of the main parties were driven by their own interests, either aiming for the presidency or even aspiring to win the Nobel Peace Prize. Therefore, only the security forces respected the spirit of the peace process and, while there were several attempts to restrict the security forces, the Maoists were free to do as they pleased.

The government went all out to project itself as republican by representing the Army as pro-monarchy. It began churning out one decision after another regarding the Army while keeping HQ completely in the dark.

For example, on 15 December 2006, the Cabinet passed a decision to withdraw the appointments of the military attachés in Nepal's embassies in Bangladesh and Pakistan, meaning Full Colonels Raj Rana and Bijay Moktan would have to return from their duties in Bangladesh and Pakistan respectively less than a year into their appointments. HQ wasn't informed of this even though it was our personnel who were being recalled. DMI General Pawan Bahadur Pandey found about it only when he was informed by the attachés themselves.

Rana called me from Bangladesh. "I was sent here on the basis of a government decision for a three year posting, as set out in my letter of appointment," he said "I've made arrangements accordingly at home and enrolled my children in school here. Now I'm being called back after only one year."

Moktan was in a similar fix.

"What to do, sir?" he asked.

"Don't return unless I order you to," I told them both on the phone. Needless to say, this was very upsetting. How could the Cabinet make such a decision without even informing us?

"A lot of decisions made during the King's rule have been overturned, maybe this one too. How about asking the Defence Ministry about it?" Chief Secretary Bhoj Raj Ghimire suggested.

"Oh, really? How did that happen?" the Defence Secretary said to me, trying to dodge the question.

Deputy Prime Minister and Foreign Affairs Minister KP Sharma Oli also said he didn't know anything about the decision.

"Can these appointments be cancelled simply because they were made during the King's rule?" I asked them.

The same Cabinet meeting that had appointed military attachés during the King's reign had also named police to be posted to the Delhi embassy and other positions. However, because Sitaula was Home Minister those postings were left intact. Everyone feared being tagged as politically regressive, which mean they didn't dare speak out in the Cabinet in favour of the Army.

As the Prime Minister was looking after the Defence Ministry, I informed him about the recalls. The administration and political leadership didn't consult me but we were told a final decision about the attachés would be made "soon". But the Cabinet of Ministers remained undecided even after two months, during which time the military attachés didn't receive their salaries and used to be insulted by their civilian colleagues.

"We have bills to pay. How can we continue hanging on?" the colonels would ask. The attaché in Bangladesh couldn't even use the phone in the mission for official work.

"They didn't even allow them to fax a letter to HQ," DMI told me. I wasn't prepared to stand by and see our officers humiliated in that way. The Army had already written to the Cabinet asking it to review its decision but, in order to make things easier for the attachés, I got the Defence Secretary and Chief Secretary to write letter to the embassies.

"There has been a request to the Cabinet to revise its decision to terminate the military attachés' appointments. Until the final decision is made, they will continue to perform their duties," the embassies were told. Conditions for the officers improved slightly after that.

This was only a temporary reprieve, however, as the uncertainty carried on for a year while the Cabinet dithered. So, in a crisp September morning in 2007, I went to meet the Prime Minister at his residence. "What is it?" the PM asked through an oxygen mask.

"What's going on with the government, sir?" I said, showing my impatience. "There's a limit to what anyone can put up with."

"What happened, Chief?" he asked.

"It's been months since the military attachés in Bangladesh and Pakistan were advised that their positions were being scrapped. Despite your repeated assurances, there has still been no clear decision on their futures," I said.

"Even if there is no decision, I won't call them back before their stipulated tenure ends. I will talk to Pakistan and Bangladesh and ask them to make arrangements for our attachés," I added.

"Isn't it against diplomatic norms to ask a foreign government to take care of our diplomats?" he stated.

I maintained that those military attachés had to complete their tenure. There and then the PM called the Secretary at the Ministry of Foreign Affairs and berated him about the situation. The Secretary blamed insufficient funds from the Finance Ministry. I called up Finance Minister Ram Sharan Mahat.

"Plenty of funding has been allocated for Foreign Affairs. Who says it's not enough for two attachés?" Mahat asked.

"Don't worry. A decision will be made within a week," the PM assured me.

After that, a decision was finally made by Cabinet to keep the attachés' positions intact until the end of their tenure but only after the Army leadership had made its position clear.

I was a bit rude to the Defence Minister and asked him why he was treating Army staff so unfairly. But I still couldn't find out who was behind the decision and why.

Soon after, I invited Indian Ambassador Rakesh Sood and his Defence Attaché for dinner.

"You want the Indian Army's support in everything but you make decisions which put the Indian Army in a difficult position," Sood said over dinner.

"What do you mean?" I asked, puzzled.

"You pressed for the overturning of the Cabinet's decision to call back the military attachés in Pakistan and Bangladesh," he said.

"Well, that's an internal matter for Nepal. You don't need to concern yourself with it," I replied tersely. "It will be best if you maintain your distance on this, Your Excellency."

"I understand very well the threats that Bangladesh and Pakistan pose to India," Sood said.

"Prove to me that our military attachés have in any way hindered India's security interests and we won't just call them back, they'll face court martial," I said, "Otherwise this is none of your business."

The Defence Attaché came to see me the next day.

"It was unfortunate what happened between you and the Ambassador last night," he said, "I knew nothing about the attachés in Bangladesh and Pakistan. As far as I know it's not on the Indian Army's agenda."

"So should I talk to General Kapoor (Indian Army Chief) then?" I asked.

"Sir, I don't think that'll be necessary. From what I know, the Indian Army didn't raise the issue. Had it concerned the Indian Army, our Chief would have talked to you directly."

The next decision of the Girija Prasad Koirala government was to remove *Prithvi Jayanti* from the public holiday list. Since several ministers from Congress and UML were bent on projecting themselves as revolutionaries, the government decided to stop celebrating the anniversary of the birth of Nepal's founding king and unifier of the nation, Prithvi Narayan Shah. Maybe the Home Ministry's decision to do so was also part of the Maoists' grand design. I was furious about the decision and went to meet PM Koirala.

"How can Prithvi Jayanti be removed? This cannot happen," I said. "The Cabinet's decision is already out in the public domain. Your ministers have already spoken about it on TV."

"Oh really?" he said, feigning ignorance. "We'll need to immediately rectify that decision then."

But that didn't happened. So I continued pestering the PM about it.

"From next year onwards, Prithvi Jayanti will be celebrated as National Unity Day," he said, making another empty promise. The calendar for the next year came out only a few months later, and sure enough, Prithvi Jayanti wasn't a holiday. It was disheartening to see that the most powerful Prime Minister in Nepal's history since Janga Bahadur Rana couldn't keep his word.

But I wasn't about to give up.

"I don't know," he said and avoided the issue.

Although successive governments showed no initiative to reinstate Prithvi Jayanti as an official public holiday, it was still celebrated at the local level. Rastriya Prajatantra Party-Nepal marked the day with celebrations and later, when Madhav

Nepal became the PM, he attended programmes marking Prithvi Jayanti.

Overnight, prints of a lifesize portrait of Prithvi Narayan Shah were put up in the public halls in all Army HQs. Mandatory orders were passed to all formations, units, sub-units and every post to keep this image on display. Even the paintings and photos of other former royals weren't removed from my official residence and Army HQs while I was the Chief. I strongly believe that a nation's history is the foundation stone for its future.

Also in 2006, we received a letter from the government instructing us to remove pictures of the King and Queen from our offices. This followed the spree of removing the word "royal" from the names of institutions and even changing the names of streets and towns.

"Don't remove Prithvi Narayan Shah's portrait under any circumstances," I instructed all units, even though I knew I could face serious consequences as a result. I strongly believe that a nation's history cannot and should not be erased, and especially not Prithvi Narayan Shah who is still considered a hero by many Nepalis for giving us a united and sovereign country. I salute him as the architect of modern Nepal.

Former British, French and Portuguese colonies continue to safeguard the monuments, inscriptions and names from their colonial periods and here Prithvi Narayan Shah was being portrayed as a villain. Ironically, the statue of Juddha Shumsher towering over the city's major thoroughfare wasn't a headache for the government.

A UML heavyweight fiercely opposed my refusal to follow the government's orders. When he had come for dinner at

Shashi Bhawan, he was seated right below portraits of Prithvi Narayan and other royals. I had also deliberately put a full-length portrait of Prithvi Narayan Shah in the VIP meeting room.

It soon became a fad for the government to change the names of highways, municipalities, colleges and schools that were named after the King, Queen or other members of the royal family. There were instructions to remove any of their slogans and quotes that had adorned the walls of government offices and public spaces.

But as a patriotic soldier, I couldn't give orders to remove Prithvi Narayan Shah's portraits or his respected words. I instructed that everything should remain the same in the halls at HQ and the other formations as well.

The Cabinet of Ministers used to be invited to HQ for briefings. The Maoist government was also invited, so I organised a programme at the Army Officers' Club. I didn't think it was fitting to invite them to HQ or any other barracks until they disavowed their armed struggle completely to enter the democratic process. My stand was that they must first disarm and dismantle the camps.

The club premises were adorned with full-length portraits of Prithvi Narayan Shah and Bhanubhakta Acharya. After inspecting the hall, Kul Bahadur Khadka feared that the Prime Minister and the Maoist ministers might be put off by the arrangements.

"Maybe these portraits need to be removed," he said.

The ADC informed me about it and I told him that, if anyone objected, he should tell them it was the Chief's orders to keep the portraits there.

The PM, Prachanda and members of the Cabinet were briefed in the hall and there were no objections. Later, during Madhav Nepal's government, Bidya Bhandari became the first woman to ever become Defence Minister. I assumed it would be easy working with such a sensible leader. One day, she came to HQ and I took her to the VIP room.

"Why are there so many pictures of Prithvi Narayan everywhere?" she said looking around the walls, "I see them even during the Army's TV programmes."

"Just give me a moment to explain," I said.

Since Chhatra Man Singh Gurung would soon replace me, I called him in too to listen to my explanation.

"Prithvi Narayan's portraits adorn the walls here because he was the architect of Nepal and this Army," I said, "I'll be leaving soon, Madam Minister, but even General Chhatra Man won't dare to remove them. We don't believe in erasing a nation's history."

I then sought permission from the Defence Minister to ask her a question.

"I don't know about your home but your party office is adorned with pictures of Marx, Lenin, Mao and Stalin. What have they done for Nepal and Nepalis to be venerated in that way?"

The Defence Minister nodded. "I also respect Prithvi Narayan Shah and his contribution," she said. Because of ideology, foreign communist leaders' portraits were hanging in the UML's office but she willingly accepted that Prithvi Narayan was the founder of modern Nepal and the Nepalese Army.

Bidya Bhandari was a die-hard supporter of the Army's constitutional stand. Despite her differences with Madhav Kumar Nepal, the new PM, she stood like a rock behind the Army. It was unfortunate that I would be hanging up my uniform quite soon. As it turned out, the Army didn't work with her for long and failed to take full advantage of her positive attitude. I was naturally disappointed.

After Prachanda was forced to leave Baluwatar, the PM's residence, and Singha Darbar, the PM's office, Madhav Kumar Nepal from UML was chosen as the new PM. The very next day he had about six hours of meetings with the Maoist leadership at the Godavari Resort. The day after that he sent three emissaries asking for my resignation, fearing that the Maoists wouldn't let him function as PM otherwise or let him sleep in peace. The emissaries were pleading for my resignation and one can guess the answer they were supposed to take back to the new Prime Minister.

The vacant post of the three-star general rightfully belonged to Chhatra Man who was the senior-most two-star general, so he was in line for the top job.

This was a chance to create history and have an Army Chief from an ethnic minority. Since I had also trained him in his cadet days, I was more than excited to have Chhatra Man as the three-star general and pave the way for him to become Chief. No one from an ethnic minority had ever headed the Nepalese Army in its modern history. I was the first person outside the establishment Rana-Shah family to become the Chief, and it was Chhatra Man's turn after me to set a precedent.

Around the same time, rumours about Chhatra Man lying about his age started buzzing in the Army. Even the PM, officials from the Defence Ministry and the Cabinet began informally enquiring about his age. Chhatra Man was worried.

I found that these rumours were fuelled by the Maoists. They used Kul Bahadur as a pawn to try to block Chhatra Man's promotion and it was Kul Bahadur who had filed a complaint at the Military Secretariat about Gurung's age. It must have been him who took the matter to Baluwatar as well.

He had also brought papers regarding Chhatra Man's age from the Examination Control Office in Sanothimi. We even received an official letter alleging that Chhatra Man was older than the age stated in his documents. It was disheartening to see Kul Bahadur still up to his old tricks, especially because he and Gurung had been friends in college and even shared accommodation before being recruited as cadets.

I was not prepared to let this opportunity to make a general from an ethnic minority the Chief of the Nepalese Army slip by.

"Certify only what's on the official roll," I instructed the Military Secretariat, "Don't register the letter that was just brought in."

But the conspiracy against Chhatra Man continued.

"This old guy has lied about his age," Kul Bahadur told me one day.

The second man's recommendation was also required to promote Chhatra Man to a three-star general.

"I'm not signing it," Kul Bahadur said.

"It doesn't matter if you don't. I'll do it by myself," I retorted.

The Maoists' clout in the coalition government led by Girija Prasad Koirala was way above their actual strength. But even after joining the government and a year into the peace process, they refused to give up their old ways.

The date for the Constituent Assembly election was announced as 22 November 2007, after having been postponed from the earlier date of 7 June 2007. There was growing disillusionment about the political parties and the government after the election was postponed. But the Maoists were still making excuses to try to avoid going to the polls.

In September, the Maoists suddenly resigned from the government. Irrespective of what led to their resignation, it was clear that their sole objective was to postpone the election until the situation was more favourable for them.

Holding the polls became uncertain after the Maoists left the government. The PM was tired of the constant harassment and pressure from the Maoists. The security situation had become bleak while the Maoists continued with their excesses, looting and abducting people. They had the license to do whatever they liked and their parallel government was still alive and kicking. The situation in the Tarai was equally volatile with several armed outfits still active in the region.

Less than a week after the Maoists left the government, I was called to Baluwatar. Girija*babu* looked frail and was struggling with his asthma. His Defence Advisor wasn't present that day and he made his dissatisfaction with the political stalemate and the peace process clear.

"The Maoists betrayed us," Girija*babu* said, wheezing, "And there's no basis to trust the King either."

Even a person of his stature who was leading the

government and peace process couldn't conceal his frustration. Even his body language gave away his feelings. The officiating Head of State looked dejected and anxious about the future. Finally he told me, "The country needs to be saved. The Army is free to do anything it deems fit."

Both of us were silent for a while.

"Get ready to manage the anarchy. You have my full support," he said emotionally, "Even our neighbours don't support me. Now only the Army can save this country."

It wasn't possible for me to give Girija*babu* an immediate reply.

"I'll let you know by tomorrow. I need some time to think it over," I said.

The Congress was under increasing pressure to give in to the demand to turn Nepal into a republic but Girija Prasad favoured some form of titular monarchy.

I pondered over Girija*babu*'s request and began thinking about what the Army needed to do if it had to really take over. I also analysed the possible consequences, evaluating army rule in Pakistan, Bangladesh, Burma and even as far away as African and Latin American countries. Bangladesh's Chief Moim's words were ringing in my ears. Everyone had urged him to take over but when the same people couldn't milk his government, they turned against him.

During his visit to Nepal, Moim had told me, "The situation is getting ripe for you to be asked to take over. I was in a similar position and I went ahead and took the step. After six months, I was desperate to hand over power to someone else. Don't ever make the mistake of dragging the Army into politics."

Given Nepal's economic, social and geo-political situation, it wasn't possible for the Army to take over, no matter how pure the intentions, I concluded. Just because Girija*babu* wanted the Army to step in, it wasn't going to be possible.

Girija*babu* was waiting for my reply at Baluwatar the next day.

"The Army cannot lead without the backing of the political parties," I replied.

He then came up with another alternative: an independent government backed by the Army.

"Should I approach Bishwanath Upadhyay to lead a civilian government then?" he proposed.

Upadhyay was one of the main architects of the 1990 Constitution. He was well-educated, honest and a strong supporter of democracy.

"If the Parliament appoints him as the Prime Minister, we'll support him wholeheartedly," I replied.

I was informed that Upadhyay then declined Girija*babu*'s offer to take the leadership, citing health reasons. I also went to meet him twice regarding the same matter but he didn't seem interested.

With the Maoists' excesses spiralling out of control, a lot of people came to me with the same request, "You have to step in and take over, Chief."

Businessmen, lawyers and journalists, even politburo and central level members of Congress, UML and Madhesi parties pushed me to act.

"The King made the move in February at the instigation of people like you. I'm not going to make the same mistake,"

I told them all bluntly. They said the country was headed towards anarchy. There was no rule of law and Nepal was on the verge of disintegrating.

"The Army can take over for a few years, hold free and fair elections and then hand power back to the parties," they would argue.

"It's easy saying that here but can you repeat these words in the media?" would be my reply, and they would shut up. "Once you get 50 or 60,000 people out on the street, demanding that the Army take control, then I'll act. If you can get thousands of people to vandalise Shashi Bhawan, chanting slogans to tell the Army to take over, and broadcast it on BBC and CNN, only then will I take over," I would say.

Even holy men from India would exhort me to take over to protect the Hindu religion. "*Veera bhogyā vasundharā* (The brave ones will rule the earth)," they told me, referring to a Sanskrit adage.

"I'm grateful you took the trouble to meet me, *swami jee* ," I told one such *guru,* "But the Chief of Staff of the Nepalese Army is a non-sectarian position."

Around the same time, the Constituent Assembly's National Interest Preservation Committee asked the Army for suggestions towards drafting the constitution. We prepared two volumes entitled Core National Policy and National Security Policy. A working group comprising Chhatra Man Singh, Gaurav Shumsher, Ananta Thebe and other generals contributed to the two reports.

The Committee summoned us soon after. We assumed it was only to submit those volumes, so my colleagues suggested I go alone. Nevertheless, I took all the generals who had worked on the reports and we went in our official *mayalpos* dress.

The atmosphere in the Committee was a lot different than we had expected. The 42 members looked like they were there to ambush the Army. It goes without saying that there were plenty of Maoists on the Committee.

When I saw cameras and journalists in droves around the room, I understood that this was a well-laid plan to trick the Army. I decided to make full use of this opportunity to set everything straight, if given a chance to speak.

I was seated next to the Committee Chairman, Amik Sherchan.

"We have submitted our suggestions. If anything needs to be clarified we can come back again," I said.

"Generals, we wish to interact with you today. Everyone is eager. We want to discuss the contents of these reports," Chairman Sherchan said.

The camera lenses were all aimed at me now. I was flooded with questions.

"One by one, please. I'll reply to all of you," I assured everyone. The Maoists bombarded me with nonsense queries and I fielded them all to the best of my ability. I presented the Army's position on fundamental issues of the constitution and also on holding a referendum on major issues like federalism, secularism, republicanism and others before the constitution was written. The Army has always had a consistent stand on those issues.

The question and answer session went on for almost two hours and I made the most of it.

"Are you an Army Chief, political leader, human rights activist, lawyer or judge? It's difficult to tell who you really are," Sherchan joked.

The Army's views provided plenty of fodder for the radical communists to criticise. But the Army wasn't concerned about any of that. We were there to present our argument in favour of a referendum on those issues and we accomplished our task. The new, hungry national media couldn't wait to break the hot news next day.

The CA members in the Parliament and CA committee members, mostly the Maoists, would always ask me when the Army would become an "inclusive institution". I tried explaining the Army's work and recruitment processes to them.

"Recruitment and promotion in the Army are governed by laws and criteria prepared by people's representatives like all of you here," I explained to the CA members, "The Nepalese Army accepts all Nepali citizens who are qualified to join. Give me an example of when qualified candidates have been rejected just because they are Dalit, Janajati or Madhesi," I asked. The entire Committee fell silent.

Among the CA members, there were plenty of new entrants into the Maoist fold, who had risen up the ranks in administration and security by sucking up to the Panchayat.

The recruitment process in armies around the world requires candidates to meet certain pre-requisites to qualify for enlistment. They are judged by their physical, mental and educational abilities to fulfil the criteria, not by the way they look. The Army cannot be divided in proportion to a country's ethnic composition anywhere in the world.

In fact, we claim that Army is more inclusive than other government bodies in Nepal. It has more Dalit and Janajati than anywhere else. Furthermore, Janajatis have higher representation among the Army's top brass than in other public sector bodies.

Madhesi leaders have always accused the Army of discriminating against them. Senior Madhesi leaders from the late Gajendra Narayan Singh to Mahantha Thakur, Upendra Yadav, Rajendra Mahato, Hridayesh Tripathi, Anil Jha and others of the present day still complain that the Army is not inclusive enough.

On that day, however, they seemed convinced by what I had to say. But they continued to publicly accuse the Army of discrimination for political reasons. I had started a campaign to ensure that more Madhesi youths were recruited and the openings were advertised through local media. We requested leaders from Madhes to closely follow the recruitment process and even made arrangements for them to travel, with food and accommodation provided, to the nearest barracks.

"If you feel any Madhesi candidate is being treated unfairly, tell me about it," I said.

I also requested the Public Service Commission to allow failed Madhesi candidates to sit the exams again. Despite the re-test, their results weren't encouraging. There was only so much the Army and the Madhesi leaders could do.

"We can take the horse to water but we can't make it drink," I explained to the leaders.

Even during my earlier stint in eastern region, I had noticed that Madhesi men weren't very keen on joining the Army. Gajendra Narayan Singh used to criticise us in every forum saying Madhesis weren't being recruited into the Army. I was in the Number Two Brigade which used to oversee the eastern region back then. COAS Dharmapal gave me instructions to ensure that Madhesi candidates were given high priority. I was convinced that we had to recruit as many qualified Madhesis as possible. To make things easier for Madhesi candidates, we began recruiting from Rajbiraj.

But we only received 250 applicants from the Madhesi community there. After the written, physical and medical tests only 67 were accepted for further training and most of them pulled out midway. So, it's not the Army's fault that there are comparatively few Madhesis in the military.

Even in India and Pakistan, the military forces are dominated by particular ethnic groups or come from particular states. In India, Punjabis and Marathis make up the largest number. Bihar and Uttar Pradesh are under-represented in proportion to their population. In Pakistan, Punjabis comprise the biggest component of the armed forces and it's not because the others are discriminated against.

The national army of any democratic country is never divided on ethnic or geographic lines. Joining the Army is entirely a personal choice, which then depends on how well the candidate fares in the entry tests. No matter how many times Madhesi leaders complain of discrimination against them, members of their community have a significant presence in the fields of medicine, engineering, forestry, agriculture, veterinary science, the judiciary, education and health. Even in the Army, it's our Madhesi colleagues who dominate in the technical areas.

After being postponed twice, the Constituent Assembly elections were now scheduled for 10 April 2008. The Prime Minister was bending over backwards to finally get the elections over and done with. After creating one nuisance after another to push the poll dates back, the Maoists had finally come around to agreeing to the April date. Since the situation seemed more favourable to them, they were back in government.

The Madhes uprising, immediately after the declaration of the Interim Constitution, had rocked the entire nation. On 28 February, PM Koirala and Madhesi leader, Mahantha Thakur, signed an agreement which among other things allowed the mass recruitment of Madhesis into the Nepalese Army.

The Army Act, formulated after the People's Movement, set criteria for recruitment into the Army. Koirala's agreement with Thakur violated this.

The next day, Koirala attended a Rastriya Sewa Dal's (NCC) programme with his Defence Advisor. During the programme, I made my strong opposition to the agreement on mass recruitment clear and informed those present that it was against the constitution, law, regulations and established norms. I intentionally voiced my opinion in a public place to get the message across to the media.

After the programme ended, I was surrounded by journalists

"The agreement isn't legitimate," I said, "Mass recruitment isn't accepted in any army anywhere around the world."

The press had more questions, so I directed them to the Directorate of Public Relations, saying it would elaborate on the Army's position. We took the stand we did because we understood that mass recruitment wouldn't be possible in any army. Had we been silent about the government's agreement to mass recruitment of Madhesis, the Army would have had to give in to Maoist integration later on.

The peace process now seemed to be all about tying the Army's hands. Nepal's so-called intellectuals parroted the Maoist line about how the Army should also be locked up in cantonments like the ex-guerrillas. It wasn't difficult to read the Maoists' intentions – to do as they pleased while confining the Army to barracks.

The leaders who signed the peace agreement forgot that the national army belongs to the country of Nepal and its people. The Maoists only had dummy combatants in the cantonments while the hardcore guerillas were walking about freely, disguised as YCL. Comrade Ian Martin and others ignored all this, while the Maoists continued to threaten, abduct and brutalise people.

It was only after the election that the Maoists and PM Koirala, who was also Presidnet of Nepali Congress, found common ground on the issue of army integration. The election should have been held only after army integration but the Congress and UML leaders feared that the Army would take the King's side and that would prevent Nepal being declared a republic. The Maoists cashed in on this fear.

The Maoists exploited the public apprehension about their combatants, weapons and the YCL when they went to the elections. In such a situation, the police alone could not ensure free and fair elections. The Army needed to be formally mobilised, as was the case in previous elections, but the Maoists prevented this from happening.

Since Home Minister Sitaula and the Maoists were joined at the hip, they agreed to recruit temporary police for election security and a lot of former guerillas signed up. This resulted in extensive interference and intimidation by Maoist cadres during the elections.

The Army briefed the Prime Minister about these abuses, who then informed the Home Minister. But all Minister Sitaula ever did was to fling the peace agreement in the Prime Minister's face.

Koirala had summoned me two days before the election.

"We still have time. Let's mobilise the Army," I said.

"The Maoists won't agree. It will result in the elections being postponed again," he said, "Everyone, including the UN, US, India and the EU, want these elections to go ahead."

"I'm only asking you to postpone the elections for another five months," I said, "If the Maoists can orchestrate the date being pushed back, why can't you?"

One thing was certain: the elections wouldn't be free and fair. All the other parties were unarmed while one party was allowed to go to the polls still carrying weapons.

According to an Army internal report, the Maoists were preparing to conduct massive cheating and fraud to ensure a comfortable victory. Their strategy was not to cause any bloodshed but to take control of polling booths and use subtle intimidation.

The Congress and UML were already on a high, predicting big wins for themselves. Several pre-poll surveys showed the UML as the top contender, while the Home Ministry's and PM's reports showed Congress in the lead. Some Congress leaders were already smug, concluding that the Maoist votes would cancel out those of the UML, making them – Congress – the big winners.

The Home Ministry's report concluded that Congress would win with a majority of at least 140 seats out of 240 constituencies. But I remained convinced that the Maoists would execute their well-planned strategy on polling day.

"We still have time. Let's postpone the elections," I said to the PM yet again.

"Our pollsters tell me that Congress will get at least 140 seats as a result of direct elections alone," Koirala said.

"It'll be a surprise if you get even 40 seats," I said.

"Why?" Girija*babu* asked, looking astonished.

"Armed Maoist guerillas are on standby all over the country," I said, reflecting the Army's findings, "Everyone, including dead people and those working abroad, will cast their votes. Just wait and watch how many places record a 100 per cent turnout."

Girija*babu* looked worried but didn't say a word.

"Nothing might happen in bigger towns but we have intelligence that, in the villages, the Maoists are targeting Congress and UML cadres to prevent them coming to the polling stations," I said, "The Maoists will then have their own cadres pose as UML and Congress representatives. Additionally, they're already threatening voters, saying they know who is and is not going to vote for them."

"That might not happen," Girija*babu* said, "Even the EU and India predict that Congress will win at least 118 seats."

I tried one last time: "Please postpone the elections on the basis that the time is still not right," I said. "There's still a chance if you do it."

"Even if the Maoists use some force, they can't produce a landslide," he said confidently.

"But the Maoists will get votes simply by threatening

people and, if intimidation alone doesn't work, they plan to use physical force," I said.

The PM refused to take my warnings seriously.

"Let the elections take place, Chief," Girija*babu* said, ending the discussion. "The Maoists have to be confined inside the democratic prison."

I also suggested that Koirala should take part in election campaigning just to keep an eye on the Maoists. I even offered him an Army helicopter to fly to all the five regions but he refused.

"I have to be neutral, so I won't go," he said.

"Don't go to ask people to vote for the Congress party," I said. "Just tell the people to vote fearlessly."

I even tried using other Congress leaders to convince Girija*babu* to do it. My suggestion was that he could go around the country, talking about democracy and free and fair elections, which would at least boost the faltering morale of the cadres of the non-Maoist parties.

"I'm still the Head of State. It's a question of ethics," he said, refusing again.

But his argument wasn't convincing. While, as Head of State, he could still preside over Congress and collect money for the party, when it came to delivering speeches for the sake of fair elections, it was suddenly a question of ethics. He was worried about the party's dwindling funds and had mentioned this to me many times.

It was obvious that he wanted to appear neutral, to pave the way to becoming the first President of the Republic of Nepal after the elections. He had his eyes set on that. The Maoist leadership was ceaselessly coaxing and convincing him to be the first president. This was also an opportunity for him to take revenge on King Gyanendra Shah.

The so-called royalists always accused me of not playing a part to save the monarchy. According to them, I owed my military career to the King who had brought a hillbilly like me to Kathmandu and I was supposed to repay my debt.

I didn't challenge the decision when the people's representatives declared Nepal a republic in the first sitting of the new Parliament. The monarchy was suspended before I became Army Chief; the political decision to overthrow the King had already been made. Had the Army taken a stand earlier, perhaps the monarchy in some form could have been saved.

I became Chief five months after the proclamation of a republic. As Army Chief, I had to follow the orders of an elected civilian government, not act on my own. When the Constituent Assembly abolished the monarchy, it was disheartening for me at a personal level but I had no choice but to accept it. The Nepalese Army was already being seen as a pro-royal military. If the Army had tried in any way to block the vote for a republic, it would have reinforced that belief. By accepting the CA's vote, we proved that we were a democratic military and not the King's private army.

We had a PSO meeting a few days before the first meeting of the Constituent Assembly. The officers decided unanimously that the Army shouldn't challenge the CA's decision to proclaim a republic. Everyone understood that times were changing and the Army had to accept it and move on accordingly. Gajendra Limbu was the only one in the meeting who was disheartened by the Army's silence on the subject.

"The Army can't do anything contrary to the people's mandate," I explained, "The Army will not resort to bloodshed to defend a King who has been rejected by the people."

Hardcore monarchists wanted us to disrupt the Constituent Assembly and even resort to violence to defend the monarchy. But I wasn't going to bow to that pressure.

It was public anger directed at King Gyanendra that led to such an ignominious end to Nepal's monarchy. We weren't happy about how the monarchy had been uprooted to pave the way for the Republic of Nepal. A referendum would have been the best way to decide it. I had spoken about this in several public fora, the Constituent Assembly and even in parliamentary committees.

Perhaps nobody put in as much effort as I did, in an official capacity, in trying to protect the monarchy before the 28 May vote. Given Nepal's geography and complex culture and society, we needed some form of symbolic monarchy, as a figurehead to be respected by everyone. Koirala and even Prachanda were receptive to my point of view.

The understanding of the Maoist leaders was that if the King's past mistakes and personal weaknesses could be addressed then people would be more receptive towards the institution.

There was a glimmer of hope that people could change their minds about Gyanendra if he could just change the common perception that he was a greedy King. I had some ideas about how Gyanendra could do this. He could start a charitable trust with a few hundred million rupees from his pocket, as well as the public assets of the late King Birendra and Queen Aishwarya. With the PM as the trust's chairman, King Gyanendra and his son, Paras, could declare that they wanted Nepal, Nepalis and its democratic process to prosper more than anything else. The money could be used to build orphanages, hospitals, universities and old age homes across the country. The people of Nepal would then welcome the monarchy with open arms.

This seemed like a simple and flawless plan. I told the King's ADCs, Bijay Kumar Khadka and Binoj Basnet, as much.

"Fantastic! We'll convey that message to the King," they assured me.

After that, I turned to trying to convince Girija*babu* to create an environment which would be conducive to the King to making the declaration. After much persuasion, he agreed that a ceremonial king was needed as a symbol for national unity. He declared it publicly from Biratnagar.

It had been two months since my proposal was conveyed to the King but I hadn't heard a word from the Palace. The PM called me to Baluwatar and looked angry.

"So, did you hear anything from the Palace?" he asked.

"You think that a businessman will really start a charity? Gyanendra is a shrewd businessman. His interest is money and he doesn't really care about the institution of the monarchy," Girija*babu* said, hopping mad.

The PM had been rebuffed and after that it was impossible for other parties to protect King Gyanendra and his throne.

Although the crown was slipping off Gyanendra's head, I

didn't give up trying to convince Girija*babu* one last time to retain the monarchy with a proposal for a "baby king".

King Gyanendra and his son, Crown Prince Paras, were hugely unpopular among Nepalis, so maybe, I thought, Gyanendra's grandson, Hridayendra, could be declared King. Parliament had already amended the law to allow female succession to the throne, so, theoretically, even the late King Birendra's granddaughters could become queens.

"No way," Girija*babu* said when he heard my idea.

But I didn't give up easily and persisted until he finally agreed.

"The Maoists might create a stir if I mention it here. I'll test the idea in Biratnagar first," the PM said. "You talk to the Palace."

I told the ADCs to convey the proposal to the Palace, explaining to the King that this was the last hope of saving the monarchy. After a few days, Girija*babu* did float the "baby king" trial balloon in a public speech in Biratnagar.

ADC, Brigadier General Bijaya Bikram Khadka, wanted an urgent meeting with me and I was hopeful that the Palace might be positive about the proposal. Saving the monarchy would benefit the country, democracy and Nepalis. Bijaya Bikram told me that it was the King's command not to raise the issue of the monarchy anymore.

Again, I got an earful from the PM because there was no response from Gyanendra. Even then, I gave it one last shot via Prabhakar Shumsher. He was not only related to the royal family but also was a good friend of Gyanendra. I invited him for dinner at Shashi Bhawan where we talked about the proposed trust and the "baby king" proposal for almost three hours.

"Please explain to His Majesty," I said, "He will be replaced by his grandson but he can still be the Regent. What difference does it really make?"

I also reminded him of how Gyanendra himself had ascended the throne temporarily as a three-year-old child.

"Chief, I can't tell him the way you want but I can tell him that we must have contingency plans in place," Prabhakar assured me.

He called two days later.

"So did you convey the message?" I asked, "What did he say?"

The King didn't really respond after hearing what Prabhakar had to say but because he had to send Prabhakar with some sort of reply he simply said, "Tell the General I have heard you."

The Palace wasn't willing to bend even a little, as if Gyanendra had no idea we – and he – were running out of options. Instead of embracing people's aspiration for change, it seemed the Palace wanted to turn the clock back. Anything beyond this from the Army would have invited major bloodshed and the Army may well have been disbanded. This is what the Maoist leadership was hoping for. And everybody was dancing to the Maoists' tune.

"Baby king? Over my dead body!" is apparently what Gyanendra told some people. Clearly Gyanendra didn't warm to the idea of his grandson ruling in his place. Having Hridayendra on the throne could also have paved the way for India to exert pressure through his mother, Himani.

The Nepalese Army was not in a position to do anything more for the monarchy. The Prime Minister had already rejected saving the monarchy as a priority. The Maoists cashed in on this opportunity to assure Girija*babu* that he would be the first president of the new republic after the monarchy was abolished. It was now futile for me to continue to lobby the PM with a view to saving the monarchy.

I had tried my best to rekindle the relationship between King Gyanendra and Girija*babu* when the latter was admitted to hospital.

"Please ask the King, Queen and Crown Prince to visit the hospital," I told the ADCs, "Their kindness will go down well with the people."

"Protocol won't allow it," was the Palace's reply.

"To hell with protocol! This is about basic human courtesy," I fumed.

If only the King agreed to do some public relations exercises, the monarchy could perhaps have been saved. Nepal's neighbours would have gone along with it. A certain section in the Palace was relying on Sujata Koirala to prevent the monarchy from being abolished but she didn't have the reach to accomplish that. Sujata did send me a message saying the monarchy had to be saved. But by then, it was too late.

King Gyanendra was listening to his relatives and high officials at the Palace who gave him unwise advice because they were only out to protect their own power and privileges.

As former Prime Minister Surya Bahadur Thapa said, the King's relatives and courtiers were always the shadowy "underground gang" wielding state power. We often joked about how the King was always managed by these powerful secretaries.

As Kings rarely spoke publicly, these people used their silence to make decisions on their behalf. They would front for the King, making statements and decisions which were not always coming from the King.

The Raj Parishad gained influence during Birendra's reign and reached the peak of its power during Gyanendra's rule. King Mahendra dealt very tactfully and intelligently with this faction in the Palace. His public relations advisors drew on alternative sources of information. The Palace doors were always open during that time to anyone who genuinely had the country's best interests at heart.

Birendra was humble to a fault. He had a liberal outlook, believed in democracy and was equally concerned about the welfare of the nation and the people. Perhaps it had something to do with his British education but he didn't have the shrewdness needed in a Nepali king. Maybe he thought Nepalis were just as aware about issues as the people in other constitutional monarchies.

They say that the Palace secretaries wielded more power than the Prime Minister and the Cabinet during Birendra's reign. People would line up to appease these secretaries and generals. Their influence extended even to the appointments of the Prime Minister, ministers and zonal commissioners.

During Gyanendra's direct rule, it started looking more and more like the country had slipped back into the Panchayat era. The King relied more on these all-powerful people behind the scenes than he did on the ministers he himself had handpicked. Eventually, it was this same "underground gang" at the Palace which led to the downfall of the monarchy.

Finally, it was time for the long-awaited first meeting of the Constitutional Assemby whose first order of business was to declare Nepal a republic. The rumour mills were abuzz about the Maoists taking extreme actions following the declaration. Even Kul Bahadur had been telling me about how the Maoists were planning to kick the King out from the Palace. "It will be difficult for you, sir", he used to say.

The Maoists were preparing to welcome the republic by parading inside the Palace on 28 May 2008.

"I will not allow the Maoists to parade inside the Palace. If anyone tries to forcibly enter the Palace, shoot them," I ordered.

A team led by Speaker Subhas Chandra Nembang was planning to hold a ceremony at Narayanhiti Palace after the formal declaration of the republic by the CA. The Maoist cadres were getting out of control a few days before the CA's first meeting. Immature leaders and cadres of other parties followed suit.

I sent BA Kumar Sharma of the legal division to meet the Speaker. Since Nembang was his classmate, I thought it would be easy for BA to get the message across effectively.

My message was that soldiers would guard the Palace and use their guns if they had to. But the Maoists and people from their sister organisations were still threatening to enter the Palace to forcibly remove Gyanendra. Youths affiliated with Congress and the UML were competing with the Maoists as to who could sound more revolutionary.

I sent the Army's message through various channels to Padma Ratna Tuladhar, Damannath Dhungana, Nilamber Acharya and others.

"The Army Chief and the Army will follow the constitutional decision made by Parliament," I told them, "But if the Maoists try to enter Narayanhiti, the soldiers will not stand idly by. They will do their duty."

I also informed Girija*babu* about the situation. We then installed cameras, parked armoured vehicles and set up security equipment around the Palace before the 28 May meeting.

These measures were enough to frighten the Maoist leaders and cadres and prevent them from marching to Naryanhiti. I had told the ministers that we wouldn't allow anyone past King Mahendra's statue on Darbarmarga, so the Home Ministry made arrangements accordingly. The police stopped and dispersed YCL cadres in front of the Sanskrit Hostel who were trying to create a nuisance in front of Tri-Chandra College.

Finally, it was time for King Gyanendra to vacate Narayanhiti and move to Nagarjun. Personally, I found it painful to watch him leave. The King and Queen put on brave faces, smiling and waving from their vehicle as they swept out of the Palace compound.

This event marked the end of the Shah dynasty and changed the course of Nepal's history. There was not a tinge of grief or sorrow on the King's face. I was surprised by his equanimity. His patience, his dignity, his capacity to endure the strain and stress of the situation were almost superhuman. The monarchy, symbol of national unity, as well as the prestige and pride, the glamour and glory of the dynasty had come to an unexpected end, and still he was smiling. Where were all these divine qualities when he was wearing the crown?

The state honoured him by sending him to Nagarjun Palace but there was a lot of wrangling over the decision. The Home Ministry was working on the transition from monarchy to republic and wanted to send the King and Queen to go to

Nirmal Niwas, their private residence.

"Nirmal Niwas won't do at all," I told the PM.

I had heated discussions about it with the PM after which the government allowed the former King to stay at Nagarjun Palace.

The decision also required Queen Mother Ratna and Tribhuvan's mistress, Sarala Devi Manadhar, to leave Narayanhiti Palace. Her Majesty Queen Ratna lived in Mahendra Manjil and Sarala Devi lived in the main Palace. Both of them were over eighty. According to the ADCs, Queen Ratna had a deep emotional bond with Mahendra Manjil since it held memories for her of King Mahendra.

Bishweswor Prasad Koirala had written that Prince Mahendra married Ratna against Tribhuvan's wishes, after which Mahendra Manjil was built. Although the building was within the Palace premises, her father, Hari Shumsher, apparently took care of all expenses.

I heard it was the Chief Secretary and other secretaries who were bent on evicting the two old women because the transition to a republic would be incomplete without it. I was determined that these two elderly ladies should not be forced out of Narayanhiti.

I asked the PM to make time to discuss it.

"The Queen Mother should be allowed to live in Mahendra Manjil," I said, "And where will Sarala go at her age?"

"Why?" the Prime Minister asked.

"How many more years do they have really?" I asked, "Furthermore, Her Majesty Queen Ratna has a special bond with Mahendra Manjil. You must have heard that from BP."

"If the former Queen is still allowed to live in the Palace, how will we really be a republic?" he said, wanting to close the chapter.

"Is your republic really so weak that it needs two old women to be ousted to gain strength?" I shot back.

"Fine then. Both of them will be allowed to stay in the Palace," the PM gave his word.

Girija*babu* was becoming impatient to be the first president of Nepal. The Maoists had tempted him with the idea of the presidency and had leaned on him to make a lot of concessions regarding the peace process.

"Only Girija*babu* will be Nepal's first president," Prachanda was always saying to sweet-talk him, "Your elder brother was the first Prime Minister from among the common people, your brother was the first elected Prime Minister and now you need to keep the tradition alive by becoming the first president."

But Prachanda double-crossed Girija*babu* after the Maoists emerged as the biggest winners in the 2008 elections. Since the number of seats held by the Maoists was more than that of the UML and Congress combined, Prachanda felt no obligation to keep his promise.

Finally, Girija*babu* got wind of the fact that Prachanda was stabbing him in the back. After the elections, the Maoists first floated the name of Madhav Nepal for president. But Prachanda changed that decision overnight, dumping Nepal as well, and put forward Ramraja Prasad Singh as his party's candidate for the top job.

Singh of Nepal Janawadi Morcha was a member of the National Panchayat and had owned up to perpetrating terrorist bomb attacks in Kathmandu in 1985. The proponents of the politics of violence favoured their own kind.

The Maoists had the UML's support, so Singh's victory was assured. The names of influential Congress leaders like Girija Prasad Koirala, Sher Bahadur Deuba, Ram Chandra Paudel and Ram Sharan Mahat were also floated as candidates for the presidency but none of them wanted to stand in an election they knew they were doomed to lose.

I was playing golf near the airport one morning when I got a call from Congress leader, Ram Baran Yadav.

"The party is putting me forward as a candidate for the presidency. I need your help, Chief," he said.

He had made a good impression on me as the only person trying to restore communal harmony during the Madhes uprising. Even when his home in Janakpur was burned to the ground, he didn't waver from his steadfast stance. I was ready to help him in whatever way possible and headed straight to my office to make some calls.

I talked to the leaders of several large and small parties, including Narayan Man Bijukchhe, President of the Nepal Workers and Peasants Party, and Chitra Bahadur KC, Chair of Rastriya Janamorcha.

"Yadav believes in democracy and is also from Madhes. We need to help him out," I told everyone.

Everything fell into place eventually and Ram Baran Yadav became President. It was matter of national pride to have a self-made farmer's son from Madhes as the first Head of State of the Republic of Nepal. The Army has a special relationship with the President who is its Supreme Commander and guardian.

"The Army will always have the President's back so long as you remain the guardian of the unity and integrity of Nepal and of the democratic process," I told him. "You must ensure the country is not divided along ethnic lines. You must play your part as the highest authority." The day before the President's oath-taking ceremony I called the PM, "Is the attire ready? He has to wear the *daurā suruwāl.*"

"Thanks for reminding me. I'll make the arrangements," he said.

The President took the oath wearing the formal *daurā suruwāl.*

I went to meet him three days after the ceremony. He spoke very respectfully. I asked his permission to say a few things. "Go right ahead," he said, smiling.

"You have to rise above ethnic lines as the representative of all Nepalis, keeping in mind the national interest. It's time for you to make history."

"How can the message of national unity be disseminated as a priority?" the President asked.

"You already made a start on that in the oath-taking ceremony," I said, "You just need to continue along the same lines."

"What do you mean?" he asked.

"You are from Madhes but your choice of clothes, including the *daurā suruwāl,* coat and *topi* represented the dress of the mountains. When we're not in uniform, we wear the same," I said, "Seeing the Supreme Commander wearing national dress will lift the morale of soldiers in all ranks of the Army."

"During the Army's national festivals, it's customary for the Head of State to wear *mayalpos* and *bhādgāunle topi*," I informed the President.

"I'm from the Tarai. What if I wear *kurtā suruwāl, gamchhā* and *dhākā topi* sometimes?" he asked.

"That would be great. The *kurtā* and *topi* will strike a balance betweenTarai and mountains," I said.

Another Madhesi candidate, Paramananda Jha of the Madhesi Janadhikar Forum, became Vice-President. He was a former Justice of the Supreme Court. For the oath-taking ceremony on 23 July 2008, he came wearing *kurtā* and *dhoti* without the *topi*. It was reported that he would be taking the oath in Hindi.

I felt this wasn't right and I met the President and Girija*babu* to discuss the issue

"This is just not done," I said directly, "Not even wearing national dress and opting for taking the oath in Hindi."

"So what?" Girija*babu* tried to calm me down.

"If the Vice-President takes the oath in Hindi, it will lead to street protests, burning tyres."

"So what can be done then?" he asked.

"He should wear *daurā suruwāl* and take the oath in Nepali," I said.

"Who says people from Madhes have to know Nepali?" Girija*babu* argued.

"He must have given thousands of verdicts wearing national dress," I said.

I felt that Girija*babu* or the President should have stopped the Vice-President from going ahead with his plans but they didn't think it was necessary.

Soon after the Vice-President took the oath the whole country was enraged by what he had done to the extent that the matter was taken to the courts. By then it was already time for the Army's Fulpati celebrations to which theVice-President was an invitee. We had mentioned that national dress was compulsory and he came dressed in *daurā suruwāl* and a grey coat.

The pending case over the matter of the oath rendered the VP's office inoperative. The Interim Constitution was amended to remove this deadlock. The seventh amendment to the interim statute paved the way for taking the oath in one'smother tongue. Vice-President Paramananda Jha took the oath again, this time in *daurā suruwāl* and *bhādgāunle topi* and his native language, Maithili.

The CA elections made history. In some constituencies where Maoist leaders won, the number of votes cast reportedly exceeded the total number of voters. No matter how the elections had gone, everyone accepted the results. They also got the thumbs up from the international community. Girija*babu* had to leave the government immediately but seemed reluctant to give up office. During our frequent meetings, I always told him to hand over quickly.

Prachanda and I still used to meet for dinners.

"What's happening, Chief? It seems Girija*babu* is in no mood to leave," Prachanda said. He was growing suspicious,

"There's a conspiracy by foreigners brewing against us."

"Both of you are schemers. It's up to you to find out who's behind all of this," I used to say.

"It's only a matter of few months. There's no alternative to the formation of a Maoist-led government," I assured Prachanda.

I used to meet PM Koirala almost every day.

"This delay in leaving office doesn't seem fitting, sir," I told him

"The Maoists are getting arrogant. We need to teach them a lesson," he said.

"First you give too much ground to the Maoists, go ahead with an election marred by fraud and after all that you want to teach them a lesson?" I scoffed.

Girijababu was like a wounded tiger, bitter about being dumped by the Maoists after their promise to make him president. But in the end he had no option but to leave.

Prachanda, the unopposed candidate for Prime Minister, came to dinner at Shashi Bhawan.

"Now that I am going to be the Prime Minister, what should I focus on, Chief?" he asked.

"There are just three things you need to do after which you won't have to worry," I said.

"What are they?" Prachanda asked.

I gave him the following three suggestions which I merely repeated from the past:

First, for the sake of communal harmony and for Nepal to remain unified in diversity, we needed the monarchy, even if it was just symbolic as it had been during Juddha Shumsher's time.

Second, the Maosists should hand over their arms to the state and have faith in the national army. It was governed by laws and had never overstepped the constitution. The elected Parliament could amend the laws governing the Army if and when they felt it was needed so the so-called democratisation of Army wouldn't be necessary.

Third, young former combatants should be given vocational training and education to help them integrate into society. It would allow them to start a new life either at home or abroad. Some of them might want to join the Army, while others might want to return to their home villages or go abroad. All of them could use some help. The ones who wanted to study should be assisted until they completed their degrees.

"If you can achieve these goals, then Maoists will be voted into power for the next 50 years," I said, "You've already been voted in as the number one party through a democratic process. Now is the right time to govern the country in the same spirit."

"We'll govern through democratic process, *dai*," Dahal assured me.

Prachanda became the PM a few days later.

We had a tense relationship throughout his time in office but we were still very cordial. He invited my whole family to dinner at Baluwatar several times, the only Prime Minister to do so.

Congress didn't join the government but the UML and Madhesi parties became coalition partners. The UML sent its team under Bamdev Gautam's leadership as Deputy Prime Minister and Home Minister.

I called and congratulated him the same evening he took office. "It seems like you've passed the civil service exams for the Deputy Prime Ministership and Home portfolio," I joked.

I invited him to dinner.

"I can't come for dinner but I'll drop by for a while," he said.

"It'll be best if you come alone with only one bodyguard, otherwise there'll be unnecessary rumours about you meeting the Army Chief right after taking office," I said.

But Bamdev came in with a noisy entourage around 8 pm. Unlike other communists, he didn't do things discretely. Uma and I congratulated him and also put a garland on him.

"We need your support, Chief, to move forward together," Bamdev began.

"Take a stand on Army integration and other national issues and we'll always be there to help," I said. I used to always tease him about his big build and commanding voice, saying he looked like Stalin.

He and I had met frequently even when I was the second man. During the King's direct rule, there were talks that the Palace was hoping to get his support. There were some people who criticised him for receiving *tikā* from King Gyanendra after 4 October.

"Why shouldn't I have the King's *tikā* on my forehead?" he had replied fearlessly.

The Maoists were holding their plenum in Kharipati. Rumours were rife about differences between Prachanda and Mohan Baidya's faction. Prachanda was accused of going soft and deviating from the revolutionary line.

His ADC, a colonel, called a day before the Kharipati

plenum. "The Baidya faction may cause trouble. We might need to be rescued," he said, quoting the PM.

It was the Army's duty to assure the PM of his safety.

"If there's any problem, bring the PM and Baburam out to the terrace," I said, "Have soldiers stationed all the way up to there and, if anything happens, inform us immediately and they'll get them out."

The ADC team already comprised about 30 people but the PM didn't want to take risks and asked for additional security.

"Assure the Prime Minister our airborne team is mobilised," I told the colonel.

I decided that it would be best to make our Kharipati Academy the base. I ordered that a helicopter be kept on standby for a possible emergency evacuation. The Special Forces' rescue team was also ready at Kharipati.

There was a lot of heated discussion at the plenum but luckily the PM didn't need to make a hasty getaway. It was ironic that Prachanda was so frightened of his own cadres that he nearly had to be airlifted out in an Army helicopter.

Eleven

The Army On Target

The Maoists were holding their first mass assembly led by Prachanda himself in Kathmandu and the proposed venue was to be the Army Pavilion at Tundikhel. Preparations were underway for their cadres to parade at the venue and there were plans to bring people in from all over the country so that Tundikhel would be entirely covered with Maoists.

Prime Minister and Defence Minister Girija Prasad Koirala had given them permission to hold the mass meeting there but even despite this the Army could not agree with the decision. No soldier could tolerate the Maoists stomping their boots on our historical parade ground. It would have been like allowing them to trample on our chests.

Even after the Comprehensive Peace Agreement, the Maoists had continued their hostile behaviour towards the Army. I understood very well their intention in parading at the Army Pavilion – it would be a victory parade, to show they had won the war. This would also be in keeping with their long-cherished dream of attacking the Army's morale.

Baluwatar is only 15 minutes away from HQ but I didn't have the patience to contain my outrage even that long. I called the PM immediately and told him that the Maoists would not be allowed into Tundikhel.

"Mr Prime Minister, have you ever heard of any party holding its mass meeting inside Delhi's Red Fort?" I began.

"I don't understand what you're saying, Chief," he said in a timid voice.

"Besides national programmes, has Tundikhel ever hosted any party-specific assemblies?" I asked.

The PM was getting my drift and admitted: "They've just entered the peace process. I didn't want to antagonise them so I said yes."

"Except for State-sponsored events, there is no way the Army will allow anyone holding party flags to enter the Army Pavilion," I said. I was not going to budge.

"It's about peace and the constitution," the PM tried to persuade me. "The Army shouldn't hold a grudge. It needs to soften its stance."

"Over my dead body," I replied.

"Okay then, do whatever your rules say," he said and hung up abruptly.

I told high-ranking Army officers about my conversation with the Prime Minister. "The Maoists should know about it. Leak the conversation," I told them.

Our conversation was splashed across the media and became the talk of the town. However, this didn't stop the Maoists from going ahead with their preparations for the parade. Pamphlets with pictures of the crumbling Palace were plastered across the city. They even spread rumours that they would enter the Army Pavilion and demolish the royal seat.

They started lobbying against our decision. "We're a democracy now, so why can't we have a programme at the Army Pavilion? The King's army can't prevent people from entering Tundikhel."

I made the Army's stand clear to journalists, advocates, political leaders and human rights activists at a gathering in Shashi Bhawan, "I'm ready to take any step required to keep the Maoists out of the Army Pavilion," I told them.

The Maoists had put their propaganda machine into high gear with posters, pamphlets and loud slogans all over the capital. They also sent emissaries to try to convince me to let them use the Pavilion. I sent them back with this terse answer: "The Army Pavilion is our property and I will personally shoot anyone who sets foot on it without our permission. Maoists can hold their programme there over my dead body."

Our sentries were on standby in and around the Pavilion as the day of the Maoist function approached. The night before, we surrounded the area with our soldiers, armed to the teeth. We dispatched soldiers in civvies onto the roofs of Mahankal's old hospital and the temple there. We set up CCTV cameras and walkie-talkies everywhere. If anything did happen, it was important to have footage to prove what actually did take place.

It worked. The Maoists pulled back from certain confrontation and bloodshed was avoided. Instead of the Army Pavilion, they moved their meeting to the nearby Open Theatre where Maoist Chairman Pushpa Kamal Dahal pointed at the Army Pavilion and roared, "Who is this Katawal guy?" However, the Maoists still hadn't got the message.

In March 2008, two years after the ceasefire, a lieutenant from Ramechhap was taken from his home by the Maoists. I immediately called the PM who also held the Defence portfolio. "The Maoists have captured one of our officers. You have to tell them to release him immediately," I said.

At this point, Girija*babu* didn't want to rock the boat and anger the Maoists in any way for fear of what it would do to the peace process. He tried to change the subject.

"The Maoists taking away an army officer is a serious matter," I insisted. "Tell them to release our officer immediately or I will tear down their headquarters."

Back then, the Maoists' main office was in Buddhanagar. I prepared the Ranger Battalion in Singha Darbar to be ready for action and instructed the Valley Division to start working on a rescue plan. Reports about the abduction spread across the world. There were phone calls from everywhere, including the UN headquarters in New York and from New Delhi. "No one can harm soldiers in the Nepalese Army as long as I'm alive. Release our lieutenant now or I will destroy the Maoists' central office," I told mediators who had come to negotiate on behalf of the Maoists. The Maoists were obviously terrified because the next thing we knew the officer had been released.

I recalled the troops, the rescue mission was called off and yet another bloody confrontation was avoided.

A most unexpected incident, in the form of mutiny, took place at the APF Battalion in Shamsherganj of Nepalganj. On 21 June 2008, around 200 APF personnel took as many as 17 senior officers hostage. They had put forth demands including sacking of the battalion commander and their own promotion.

It was a calculated move to destabilise security agencies. Instead of taking lawful action against them, the government formed a team under a joint secretary of the Home Ministry to hold talks with the mutineers and comply with their unlawful and unreasonable demands.

We were watchful of the developments. There was no doubt who the provocateurs and infiltrators were and what they really wanted to do. We had concluded that the Army was their ultimate target.

Three weeks later another misadventure took place in Nepalganj. Some Nepal Police personnel deputed to provide security in the jail rebelled on 8 July.

The government repeated the rituals of forming a committee to comply with the demands of mutineers. Notwithstanding the potential risks, the Army, on the other hand, decided to swing into action. The Mid-Western Division ordered the brigade commander to surround the jail with four army personnel carriers (APCs), while two choppers hovered over the jail compound.

This manoeuvre compelled the rebelling jail guards, led by a sub-inspector, to surrender.

I went to meet PM Koirala at his official residence in the evening to inform him about the incident. He expressed happiness over the Army's action. I briefed him about our findings and concluding decisions we made. We had once again thwarted the Maoist design to destabilise security agencies, particularly the Army, boldly and carefully. The PM asked me to remain vigilant.

The headquarters alerted all commanders down the chain of command to the possibilities of recurrence of similar incidents within the Army barracks and posts all over the country.

After the Maoists entered mainstream politics, there was a spike in opportunistic support. The same people who used to say "terrorists shouldn't be given water" became devotees of Prachanda overnight. They were mostly people from the civil service and civil society. Former generals, greedy police officers, zonal commissioners who had committed atrocities and former government secretaries changed their colours and became Maoists. People close to the Royal Palace and even those enjoying prestige and privilege in the security forces were catching up with this red shift in Nepali politics. High-level officials were competing to be closer to the Maoists and Prachanda's residence started getting a long queue of visitors out on "morning walks".

These born-again Maoists felt some of Prachanda's power and charisma would rub off on them. Some of them were out to destroy my reputation over Prachanda's oath-taking ceremony at Sheetal Niwas. There was a tradition for the seating arrangements on stage at such ceremonies: the President was usually flanked by the Vice-President on his right and the Prime Minister on his left. Other dignitaries like the Chief Justice and the Speaker of the House were seated on either side. The chief ADC sat right behind the Head of State and the Army Chief sat to the left of the ADC.

The seating for Prachanda's oath-taking was arranged in the same way. I had just returned to Shashi Bhawan when I received a call.

"*Namaste* Chief, I'm calling from the Cabinet Secretariat."

"What is it?" I asked.

"The Prime Minister-designate doesn't want to see a single soldier around, so could you take care of that?" the caller said.

"Don't worry. Everything will be in line with usual practice," I said.

My reply triggered an uproar. Home Secretary Umesh Mainali called.

"The higher-ups do not want you seated on stage," he gave it to me straight. I told him the same thing I had said earlier.

The Defence Secretary called soon after with the same request. If I didn't attend the programme that would create another controversy, I thought. Anyway, it's not Maoist Chairman Prachanda's programme. The President's hosting it and he's the Army's Supreme Commander. I was determined to attend and sit where Army Chiefs had always sat.

I reached Sheetal Niwas for the ceremony a bit early. If anything went wrong, the Army would be blamed, so I had to tread with care. I noticed that the Army Chief's seat was not in the designated place on stage. The guards told me they had been ordered not to put the chair on the stage. I didn't say anything rude and quietly sat beside the VIPs and senior officers. After the ceremony concluded, people stood in a long queue on stage to congratulate the Prime Minister but I didn't join them. What was the point of climbing onto a stage where I had been supposed to sit but was denied my place?

Since I didn't go up, neither did the other generals. And when they didn't go, the high-ranking police officials also stayed put. We headed directly towards the tea stall where I met Dr Prakash Chandra Lohani whom I had known since my Hong Kong days.

"Be careful of what you do, Chief," he warned me.

"What's wrong?" I asked.

"I was just talking to Mr Cloud (the soon-to-be Defence Minister Ram Bahadur Thapa "Badal") a while ago," he said. "He told me 'It's payback time for Katawal now. His hands will be tied behind his back soon'."

"No problem. I'll send him a thick knotted jute rope," I replied.

Tea wasn't over yet and the PM, already covered in garlands and *khadas,* was still receiving congratulations from well-wishers. Just then a Maoist Constituent Assembly member and a former minister from the Nepali Congress walked towards me.

"There's a huge uproar in our party because you didn't go up to congratulate the Prime Minister," the Maoist CA member who was a regular at my place said, "The soon-to-be Defence Minister is already warning he'll get back at you."

I pretended I didn't know who he was talking about.

"Badal," the comrade said.

"I don't know of any cloud," I said dismissively, "Go tell your Mr. Cloud that if anyone alive thinks they can tie me up, I'll send them the rope myself."

But it didn't matter what they were trying to do since Prachanda was already Prime Minister. The Army had to respect the people's vote and Rookmangud the Army Chief could not be as inflexible and stubborn as Rookmangud the private individual.

The next day I decided to go and congratulate the PM on behalf of the Army.

"Please come by at 3:45," an officer from the Secretariat told me.

I always arrive five or 10 minutes before any appointment, so I was standing outside the Prime Minister's chamber when he showed up.

"Congratulations," I said and saluted him.

He had a vice-like handshake.

"Please have a seat, Chief." He gestured towards a chair.

"I didn't see you at Sheetal Niwas," he said, looking away, "What happened?"

"There was barbed wire around you and they wouldn't let me in," I replied, "There were orders not to have the Army around, so I didn't want to embarrass all of you and simply followed orders."

"Who told you that?" the Prime Minister asked politely, "Why didn't you inform me? Anyway, let bygones be bygones. Let's forget about it. I'm in a tough spot now and need you to help me out."

"I'm always there for any constitutionally-valid support that the Nepalese Army can give," I said.

"I've been invited to China. I want to go but there's pressure against it from both internal and external elements and our own ministers. What should I do? I need frank advice," he told me.

I couldn't make out if this was a trick question to check what I really felt or if he genuinely wanted my advice.

"I'll do whatever you say," he added.

"Aren't you the elected Prime Minister of a sovereign country? Don't you have the freedom to make decisions as the executive head chosen by the people?" I asked.

"Of course, I have."

"So why give in to pressure from others? You can be fully confident and go."

"So will the Army support me regarding this visit?" He seemed to need reassurance.

"The Nepalese Army will back you fully on this matter."

"How will it look if I embark on my first official visit to China?" he said, slowly opening up.

"Everyone will understand you're going to China for the Olympics," I told him, "It's just that China's the first place you've been invited. I don't think anyone will take it differently."

"So I can go then, right Chief?" he repeated.

"Please do. The Army is fully behind the Prime Minister."

"Okay then, Chief. I'm heading off to China," he said.

"The Army has never compromised the country's unity, integrity and the democratic system and we will remain faithful to you during your tenure," I said and shook his hand before leaving.

He nodded with a smile and said, "Now we have to work together."

Two days after returning from China, he called me to Baluwatar. Defence Minister Ram Bahadur Thapa was there as well and we started talking over cups of tea.

"Call Sita," the PM instructed someone.

The PM's wife, Sita, came into the room and I got up to greet her.

"I went to China because of him," he told his wife gesturing towards me, "The visit went really well and the credit goes to him."

He was warming up to me and said: "We need to move ahead together and get rid of the distrust. You and I have great chemistry, *dai*."

I was taken aback by the sudden charm offensive and the change in Prachanda's tone. It wasn't consistent or smooth. There was something unnatural about it, especially when he'd slip and the officious sternness would return to his words. One moment he would be all milk and honey and the next moment there was a sharp edge to his voice. This wasn't a man I could trust.

One day a source in the Maoists informed me that Prachanda was planning to use a team of YCL instead of our soldiers to provide security at Baluwatar. I couldn't approve of that because the Army alone was responsible for the security of the PM and his residence and that wasn't going to change.

"Don't let anyone in with weapons except for the Army bodyguards," I ordered the commander at Baluwatar.

I went to meet the Prime Minister at Singha Darbar the next day. He said he was under pressure to bring in the YCL for Baluwatar's security.

"You're not just a party leader now. You're the country's Prime Minister. The Nepalese Army is responsible for your security and you don't need anyone else," I said, "Having your fighters and YCL in the residence will actually pose a danger to you."

The PM agreed.

During the last government led by Girija Prasad Koirala, Maoist Minister Matrika Yadav had also created a nuisance by saying he didn't need the Army as his bodyguards.

I had told Yadav that VIP security was the Army's responsibility and it wasn't up to him to decide. Still he continued to snub the soldiers, calling them names and humiliating them in public. They used to complain to me about how the minister belittled them.

"We aren't there for Matrika. We're there for the security of a minister so, if he doesn't want security, he can abandon the official minister's residence," I sent my final words.

Matrika Yadav wanted to publicise the fact that he didn't need military protection but we didn't give him that opportunity. Once, he padlocked the security room at the minister's residence. I ordered the commander there to break the lock and enter.

"Don't raise hand or voice first and just continue with your duties no matter what the minister says. If he hits you, however, then give him the appropriate response," I told them, "Just because he's a minister doesn't mean a soldier will stand for mistreatment with folded hands."

All through his tenure, Matrika Yadav's attitude didn't change. We once caught a poacher inside Bardiya National Park and the Army was conducting a court of inquiry when Yadav reached Bardiya overnight.

The colonel called me, "The Minister's here. What should I do?"

"No minister or Prime Minister can be part of a court of inquiry," I said, "Don't let the minister enter the barracks." Yadav slunk quietly away.

It looked like even the Communications Minister Krishna Bahadur Mahara wanted to lock horns with the Army.

Radio Nepal and Nepal Television wrote a letter to the Army's Directorate of Public Relations few days after Krishna Bahadur Mahara was sworn in as minister instructing us to pay them for broadcasting for our programmes. The Army programmes stressed national unity and Nepali nationalism and the Army's own activities. Mahara was trying to take us off the air after all those years.

I called Krishna Bahadur Mahara as soon as I heard about the letter. "What are you trying to do, Minister? You've just been appointed and you're trying to give us grief already? Is this how you repay friendship?"

"Please tell me what the matter is. What happened?"

I told him about the letter. "That is just not done," I told him.

"Don't worry, Chief, I'm here. I'll see to it," Mahara assured me.

It was clear that, after their surprising victory in the 2008 elections, the Maoists thought they were on top of the world. It was also clear that their strategy was to weaken the Army in every way so as to install an autocratic regime, which was why the Maoists wanted the Defence portfolio at any cost. Our view was that integrating the Maoist militants would be easier if the Maoists didn't have the Defence portfolio. We didn't think it right that a Maoist leader and guerrilla commander should be giving orders to the national army. In other countries post-conflict, the same person didn't hold power over both the national army and their former opponents. But since the distribution of ministerial portfolios was purely a political decision, we were in no position to do anything about it.

Soon enough, the Prime Minister and Defence Minister started treating the national army as if it were their stepson. Contrary to the peace agreement, they wanted collective integration into the Army. The Nepalese Army has always had established criteria for recruitment, transfer and promotion, as per the constitution, law and regulations. But the Maoists were looking for a chance to try to sabotage the Army's chain of command from the Defence Minister's chair.

Despite knowing the party's intentions, Defence Minister Ram Bahadur Thapa had to keep us in our rightful place. In our first formal meeting, I briefed him about the situation in the Army and our plans.

"Our party also has a small army. We need to take care of it as well," the Defence Minister said. He was trying to give more importance to his own fighting force than the national army, even though he was the country's Defence Minister. Thapa then started sending personal letters and calling everyone from officers to soldiers for meetings. I countered with the order that no Army personnel were to go anywhere without permission from superior officers.

The Defence Secretary called me one morning at around 6 am. "The Minister wants to visit the Chitwan barracks," he said, "And they want your HQ to give permission to the barracks."

HQ had an unwritten policy about not allowing Maoists in army barracks as long as the party still had armed combatants. Even PM Prachanda was put in a hotel in Mahendranagar and not in the brigade HQ and had to be turned back from the Amargadi Base in Dadeldhura. The Defence Minister knew this very well and was trying to manipulate the situation for propaganda purposes.

"In the present situation, even the Defence Minister cannot enter the barracks," I told the Defence Secretary, who was being hounded by the Maoists and kept calling me back.

"Just because the Defence Minister wants to enter through the backdoor doesn't mean the barracks will open its gates. Stop calling me about this," I said, and hung up.

I alerted the divisional commander, brigade commander and battalion commander. "Don't let the Maoist minister even peep in from the gate," I ordered.

Defence Minister Thapa was scheming to remove the Army's fangs while Baburam Bhattarai who was Finance Minister was cutting back its budget. He started tightening the career course, which could have led to immense frustration among the rank and file. The Maoists wanted to demoralise the Army from within and dismantle it from the outside.

We needed to take a lot of courses abroad to modernise the Army and bring it up to international standards. All this required a budget which the Maoists now controlled. We were like a vehicle without fuel.

On the other hand, Congress and the UML were pampering Maoist combatants in the name of the peace process. They looked the other way when the Maoists ransacked the treasury to dole out money to their fighters. It's clear now that the Maoists presided over the plunder of the exchequer, allocating Rs 10 billion for the 97,000-strong Nepalese Army and Rs 5 billion for their 19,000 dummy fighters.

Half of the soldiers in the Army didn't even have proper

barracks, while billions were spent on temporary camps that would have to be vacated in a few months. Despite knowing about these irregularities, no one in the government dared utter a word against them.

After some time, the daily travel allowance for military training also dried up. This was the last straw and I went to see the Finance Minister.

"The Army is our foundation," the Finance Minister said, trying to sweet-talk me, "We're ready to support the Army in every possible way."

His insincerity was disappointing.

People are suspicious of individuals and institutions which aren't very open about themselves. The Nepalese Army was in a similar predicament when I became Chief because it wasn't a tradition to be transparent. We were dedicated to democracy, the people and the law, but many people still saw us as the army of an autocratic monarchy.

The only way to shed this image was to become more transparent, which is why we increased our interactions with the political leaders, media, legal professionals and civil society.

I made arrangements to also interact with the general public once a week. Sometimes, when I was about to leave for the office, a large group of people would arrive at Shashi Bhawan. Sometimes these would be journalists and human rights activists but at other times they would be the families of Army and police personnel, officials and ordinary citizens who had been killed by the Maoists.

They expected the State to help them since they'd lost family members in the line of duty. They submitted affidavits and I would console them saying I would take their case to the government. I would go to the office, immediately write a covering letter and pass their requests on to the Defence Ministry.

But the Maoist ministers and officials were outraged that I was meeting their opponents and accepting their testimonies. They thought I was playing politics at Shashi Bhawan. The PM and Defence Minister were informed of what I was doing.

"If offering a cup of tea to conflict victims standing on my doorstep is a crime, then I'm ready to face the punishment," I replied when my actions were questioned.

"The security forces personnel who were killed were mobilised by the people's representatives. If meeting their families as well as the general public is a crime, then I will commit that crime many more times," I said.

The Maoist ministers were determined to drag the Army into every controversy, to weaken it and wear it down. I had countless altercations with the Maoists over dozens of issues. They wanted all their recruits to be inducted into the national army but as long as I was Chief I was going to allow no such thing, especially as it went against the peace process.

We weren't opposed to the entry of guerrillas into the Army *per se* but we wanted it to be done using established criteria and on a case-by-case basis. We had already informed the United Nations and other national and international bodies about this but the Maoists wanted all their fighters to be taken in all at once. For them, I was the obstacle to be removed.

Army recruitment row

The Comprehensive Peace Accord of 2006 stated that the Nepalese Army should "not recruit additional servicemen". But the Maoists tried to misinterpret this, influencing even civil society and the media that the Army's routine recruitment procedures violated the accord.

There were around 95,000 soldiers in the Army when the peace agreement was reached. Age, resignation, retirement or death left thousands of vacancies every year that needed to be filled and we recruited regularly to fill these vacancies. If we stopped recruitment completely, as the Maoists demanded, the Army would have ceased to exist in a few years. The provision regarding Army recruitment in the Peace Accord was meant to signify that the Nepalese Army should be limited to a troop strength of 95,000 and didn't mean all recruitment should be stopped.

PM Girija Prasad Koirala was convinced by our argument. The government permitted us to regularly fill vacant positions through both open and internal competition. On 23 May 2007, the Defence Ministry sent us a written directive stating that regular recruitment was allowed without increasing the size of the force, as per the Comprehensive Peace Accord.

But the Maoists protested just for the sake of it, so they could create a nuisance. UNMIN and other international agencies didn't speak out.

A government under the Maoist Chairman Prachanda had been formed just four months previously and I had raised the issue of army recruitment with him. "We will only be filling vacant posts in accordance with the peace agreement," I had told him. Prachanda had kept quiet.

The Army HQ decided to call for applications in accordance with the Public Service Commission's criteria. On 15 October 2008, HQ informed the Defence Ministry that it had advertised to fill the vacant positions. After completing all the procedures, the vacancy announcement appeared on 2nd and 3rd November that year in *Gorkhapatra*. There were around 52,000 applicants from whom the Army raised Rs 5.5 million in examination fees alone. There were thousands of young people at the examination centre, some of whom had sold their cattle and other possessions just to get there.

The selection process for the Army was lengthy because the applicants had to sit written as well as oral tests and go through a medical exam and physical tests. It had already been three months since the written test and the ones who had passed and were, therefore, one step closer to the job were filled with enthusiasm.

That was when the Maoists started raising objections to the recruitment because it ostensibly violated the Peace Accord. Soon, everyone from the ministers to the district level leaders started speaking out against the Army's recruitment.

We didn't react to any of this. We had already completed 75 per cent of the recruitment procedure and were certain that the protests wouldn't amount to much. It was only after the PM and the Defence Minister also ordered us to stop recruitment that we had to take the matter seriously. They hadn't uttered a word when we briefed them about the process before calling for applications but they were now suddenly objecting to it. On 24 December 2008, the Defence Minister sent a letter telling us to suspend the recruitment process.

We called a PSO meeting immediately. We concluded that

suspending recruitment near its final stage might enforce negative views about the Nepalese Army and the democratic process which could lead to anarchy. As per the PSOs' suggestion, we sent a letter to the Ministry on 31 December stating that we were unable to suspend the recruitment process. The Defence Ministry didn't seek any further explanation or discussion on the matter.

After a few days, I was called to Baluwatar. The Defence Minister was also there. The Prime Minister gave me a direct order: "Stop the recruitment." But I didn't agree. I had seen through this cunning move by the Maoists to discredit the Army. They knew the kind of anger that suspending recruitment at this late stage would generate and thought they could benefit from it.

But as the Army Chief I stood my ground and there was nothing the PM or his Defence Minister could do about it. I just ignored every order they gave to terminate the recruitment process and went right ahead with it. Around the same time, the Supreme Court validated the Army's recruitment process and ruled that it was in accordance with section 5.1.2 of the peace agreement. This put an end to this particular Maoist conspiracy to undermine the Nepalese Army.

What's more interesting is that, despite the Maoists threatening to stop the recruitment process, HQ continued receiving a recommendation list from the Defence Ministry's Secretariat with names to be shortlisted for selection. Minister Thapa's own son, Pratik, was apparently preparing the list.

While the recruitment row was at its peak, I had to attend the recruits' passing out ceremony at the training centre in Trishuli.

"The whole world is in the grip of terrorism, extremism and authoritarianism," I told the young graduates, "The world's fight is against these doctrines. The Nepalese Army will also not bow down to terrorism, extremism and authoritarianism and is always ready to fight them. Only then will the rights of Nepalis be safeguarded and democracy strengthened."

My speech to the young graduates added further fuel to the fire. The Defence Minister was enraged and began venting his ire through public speeches. "The Army Chief can't be involved in politics," he would shout into the microphone. However, he found that complaining publicly about his subordinate staff actually backfired against him and was unbecoming of a senior political figure.

A weapon to destroy the National Army

"The new Nepal should move forward in a new way. The Army should implement the 30-year service ceiling to have uniformity with the other security forces," the PM and Defence Minister told me one day.

Maybe to win my confidence, they casually mentioned that even the civil service was planning to implement the 30-year service ceiling, reassuring me personally that I would be able to serve my full term.

The PM and Defence Minister pretended to be naïve and asked me who would be affected by the 30-year rule in the Army. I, too, went through the motions by asking our legal department chief, BA Kumar Sharma.

Eventually, I told the PM and the Defence Minister that if

we implemented the 30 years of service rule, there wouldn't be anyone left beyond the rank of full colonel except for some technicians. They tried to dangle a lollipop in front of me by tempting me with all kinds of offers if I went ahead with implementing the 30-year cut-off.

"Both your sons were guerrillas. Why haven't you made them party chief and general secretary or even PM and minister?" I asked both of them.

"Don't they need knowledge and experience?" they echoed each other.

"Precisely," I replied, "You just explained why the 30-year ceiling won't work in the Army." They looked a bit dumbfounded after that.

I called for a PSO meeting the next day and informed them about the Maoists' plans to implement the 30-year rule. They were all worried about the repercussions for the Army's structure: the top generals would all have to go, leaving just the skeleton of the Army. Most of the subedar-majors from all formation HQs, who work closely with the commanders, would have to take early retirement.

I had nothing to lose personally since I had less than six months left in office but I couldn't let this decision by the Maoists suck the life out of an institution of which I was still the head. I decided to take a firm stand against the decision.

Everywhere around the world the army structure in democratic countries was more or less the same. None of them had a 30-year ceiling. Every promotion required certain training and qualifications, and Nepali generals who went on UN peacekeeping missions needed to be on par with their foreign counterparts. But the Maoists clearly wanted to bypass these established parameters and were bent on the 30-year ceiling so they could bring in their own fighters and take over the Army from within.

The Maoist leadership also had a strategy to appoint one of their own as Army Chief within a few months. This just wasn't going to happen.

About eight generals

The controversy about the extension of tenure of eight Army generals was another major reason the Maoists resented me.

The four-year tenure of eight Army Brigadier Generals – Nara Bahadur Kandel, Narendra Bahadur Rawal, Kumar Budhathoki, Pawan Bahadur Pandey, Pradip Bikram Rana, Shiva Kumar Paudel, Ramesh Bista and Raju Pratap KC – was ending on 16 March 2009.

There was a provision to extend this by another three years. After the Defence Minister approved the Army Chief's recommendation, the Cabinet had to endorse the decision.

Of the eight generals, six had received world class military training and were equally qualified. They were so capable that they could have joined any command in a UN peacekeeping force. A board led by Lt General Kul Bahadur Khadka assessed their qualifications, competence and how important they were to the organisation, and its report concluded that the tenure of all eights generals should be extended.

Based on this, I sent a recommendation to that effect to the Defence Ministry. We wanted to give the Ministry plenty of time to make the decision so HQ sent the files on 26 January.

It was understood and accepted that the Army Chief didn't promote incompetent individuals, so usually seeking the government's endorsement on such matters was just a formality. We had done our homework before deciding to keep the generals and were hoping for the Ministry's immediate endorsement.

Instead, almost a month went by without any word from the Ministry. Despite repeated calls from the Army Chief's Secretariat and the Army Secretariat we always got the same wishy-washy message: "a decision will be made soon".

Defence Secretary Baman Prasad Neupane had requested Minister Thapa to sign off on the recommendation several times. But Thapa sat on it and hid the files in his drawer. After three months, the documents were presented to the Cabinet, and since the proposal was in line with our recommendation, we presumed there would be no complications.

Instead, the PM called Defence Secretary Neupane and Cabinet Secretary Pratap Kumar Pathak and yelled at them for bringing the proposal to the Cabinet. Defence Minister Ram Bahadur Thapa was quietly seated in the same room.

They were playing games. The proposal was sent with the Defence Minister's consent but Minister Thapa pretended that he knew nothing about it. The Defence Secretary couldn't take in anymore and said, "This isn't my proposal, it was presented to the Cabinet as per the Minister's decision."

Prachanda who was already furious at the officials was now really angry. "Did you have to do it just because the Minister said so? Couldn't you take a cue from his body language and realise that the government doesn't want to extend the tenure?" he asked.

This was strange logic and the two secretaries had nothing to say to it. It was now certain that the tenure of the eight generals wouldn't be automatically extended. All of this was in fact unfolding as per the overall strategy of the Maoists to undermine and take over the Army without a single shot being fired. They had delayed the decision regarding the generals till the last moment so that the Army would have no time to go to the courts to challenge it.

On 16 March 2009, exactly 15 minutes before the eight generals' tenure was due to end, I called the Defence Secretary in a last-ditch attempt to save their jobs.

"I couldn't do anything, Chief," he told, "Their tenure won't be extended. Nothing worked."

I was worried that this would really hurt the morale of the Army. It would also give the message to the public that the Maoists could do what they wanted with the Army. I was still determined to prevent this from happening, ready to coax, entice or even threaten them.

I went to see Prachanda.

"Well, we couldn't get around to doing it in time," he hemmed and hawed. "We thought it wouldn't make much difference and decided not to extend their tenure. There'll be new generals to replace them, so just get started with the recommendations now."

I was enraged by this flippant attitude.

"The eight generals won't go home," I told the PM bluntly, "They'll continue working."

He looked surprised that I was challenging the decision. "You're trying to jeopardise the peace process, Chief," he said,

"Don't force us to come down hard on you."

"You know me very well. Do you think I can be intimidated so easily?" I snapped back.

When his threats didn't work, Prachanda tried to tempt me. "Help us out and we'll reward you generously," he said.

The eight generals were already aware of the government's decision not to extend their tenure. Two of them came to see me in my office.

They were crestfallen and asked: "We'll have to take off our badges and belts now, sir."

I told them not to and immediately ordered the Military Secretary to tell the eight generals to continue reporting for duty in their uniforms until my next order. I then informed the top political leadership about the incident, including the Maoists' coalition partner, UML Chairman Jhalanath Khanal, at his residence in Dallu. But after an hour-long discussion, he was still wavering.

"It would have been better if the matter was discussed earlier. Now, the government has already made its decision," he said meekly.

We decided to take the matter to court. I had already asked BA Kumar Sharma to seek expert opinion. The next day I called all the eight generals and took the risky step of telling them to continue working until the court made a decision.

Finally, on 24 March the Supreme Court issued an interim order not to retire the eight generals. The Maoist government appealed against the verdict, directly challenging its own Army, which rarely happens anywhere in the world.

Withdrawing from the National Games

The Army Sports Club had been participating in national and international games because we believed discipline to be of the essence both in the military and the sports. We had been preparing for the Fifth National Games which would start in March 2009. Teams from all over the country had arrived and the tie-sheet had already been published.

During this period, the Maoists had just registered their own club at the District Administration Office and they had somehow managed to request the organisers of the games to let them take part. The Prime Minister had given direct orders to the Sports Minister, Gopal Shakya, and the Sports Council's Member Secretary, Jeevan Ram Shrestha, to let the Maoist club take part in the competitions.

The government's decision came after the inauguration of the games by the President and in violation of the rules and norms. The Army Club protested the government's decision, citing the regulations of the Sports Council and the Olympics. Most members of the Sports Council could not defy the government, fearing a backlash from the Maoists.

I was informed about the matter through our Sports Board and Directorate of Military Training .

"What are the boys saying?" I asked.

"They don't want to participate in any games where the Maoists have been given last-minute entry," the Colonel in charge of sports said. He also listed the games that the Army Club had decided not to take part in.

As Army Chief, I supported their decision to withdraw from the games if the Maoist club participated and recalled them. This was yet another proof that the Maoists had an authoritarian streak.

At about that time, the Army Sports Club was playing in games at Tundikhel and I went there to boost their morale. I saw Minister Gopal Shakya dozing on a chair.

"*Namaste*, Minister," I greeted him cheerily and shook his hand.

There were a lot of officials and members of the Sports Council watching the game. I said to the Minister in front of everyone: "Aren't you ashamed of what you've done? You have the audacity to come here to face my boys?"

The Minister looked startled, his face went dark but I wasn't finished.

"How can a minister break universal rules governing sports?" I asked. "You should have at least thought about your position."

He looked washed out and started blurting out excuses.

"I had no option, Chief. It was the Prime Minister's orders," he said.

"If everything's decided by the Prime Minister, why do we need laws and rules? What's the point of appointing a minister who can't even use his own judgement?" I berated him, and left.

The peace agreement didn't allow Maoist combatants to leave the cantonments, which was why the Maoists had decided to enter their team only after the games had started.

My staff seemed concerned that I was being a bit too confrontational with the Prime Minister and other ministers. "You just yelled at another one," they said.

"This is a fight to protect democracy and the rule of law," I replied to remind them there was a larger fight going on.

The Nepal police and APF also had their clubs participating in the games and I heard their teams were also upset about the Maoists' arbitrariness and high-handedness. I called both the Inspectors General of Police and told them about their players' resentment. They agreed that the Maoists' behaviour was outrageous and praised the Army's decision to pull out. But they said the police couldn't challenge the government's decision.

During their time in power in 2008-2009, the Maoists used every opportunity to tarnish the Army's image and diminish us. But my bottom line was always to protect democracy and the Army's honour. As a soldier, I was not going to make any compromises regarding those values. If I had shown even the slightest hint of giving in, the Maoists would have run roughshod over the Nepalese Army to attain their self-avowed goal of setting up a one-party communist dictatorship in Nepal.

They had come to the conclusion that I was standing in their way and that they needed an Army Chief who would let them do as they pleased. So they started devising plans to make Kul Bahadur Khadka the Army Chief. His two-year tenure would end on 20 June 2009 after which he would retire. My tenure extended until 9 September 2009.

The Maoist strategy was to send me home before the end of my term by seeking clarification regarding my stand on recruitment in the Nepalese Army, the extension of the eight generals' tenure and the Army's withdrawal from the National Games.

After waging a decade-long armed conflict in the name of their so-called "People's War", the Maoists said they were now engaged in peaceful democratic politics. But they were still fighting state security forces with different tactics. The goal was still to take over the Nepalese Army.

I had two options, either to protect the country from becoming a communist dictatorship or give in to the Maoists' strategy. I chose the former. I was ready to fight the Maoists to the finish.

Made in the USA
Monee, IL
07 July 2026

56551577R00281